TODAY'S RAILWAYS
REVIEW
OF THE YEAR

VOLUME
4

PETER FOX
DAVID CARTER

From the Publisher

This fourth volume of Today's Railways Review of the Year covers the most important events of the 1990 for British Rail, London Underground, light rail transit, railway preservation, Channel Tunnel and European railways.

The volume is published later than last year because of pressure of work. By analysing a year's news in one book, all clearly-divided into topics, we hope that readers will be able to put the numerous developments in context. We hope you enjoy reading it!

We would like to thank all contributors and photographers and the following organisations:

British Rail (British Railways Board, BR Property Board, Network SouthEast, InterCity, Western Region); Department of Transport; NUR; ASLEF; Eurotunnel; London Underground Ltd.; Docklands Light Railway; Transport 2000; Railway Development Society; NS; SNCF; BAA plc; Centro; Metro; Merseytravel; Greater Manchester PTE; South Yorkshire PTE; Tyne & Wear PTE; Strathclyde PTE; London Regional Passengers Committee; The CTCC and various regional TUCCs.

PETER FOX (Publisher and Editor)

◄The West Coast Main Line became more of a 'unit train' operation during 1990 with push-pull trains being the norm. This excellent telephoto lens shot shows a typical Euston–Manchester service slowing for the pick-up only stop at Watford Junction with Class 90 No. 90015 hauling a rake of Mark 3 coaches with a DVT at the other end.   *Dr. M. Rhodes*

▼Work proceeded on the extension of the Docklands Light Railway to Bank. This photograph shows the formidable-looking gradient from the mouth of the DLR tunnel to Bank to the existing line outside Tower Gateway.   *Brian Morrison*

CONTENTS

Edited by Peter Fox & David Carter.

Written by David Brown, David Carter, Maxwell H. Fowler, Peter Fox, Brian Garvin, David Haydock, Paul Jackson, Kevin Lane, Les Nixon, Paul Shannon and Neil Webster.

Published by Platform 5 Publishing Ltd., Lydgate House, Lydgate Lane, Sheffield, S10 5FH.

Typesetting by Nicolette Williamson and Lynne Barrott.

Printed by Nuffield Press Ltd., Hollow Way, Cowley, Oxford, OX4 2PH.

ISBN 1 872524 29 X

Further copies of this book may be obtained from Platform 5 Publishing Ltd. at the address shown above. Please enclose 10% of purchase price (UK) or 20% (abroad) to cover postage and packing.

Volume 1–3 (1987, 1988 and 1989) are still available as follows:
Vol 1. Special offer price £5 plus £1.20 postage and packing. Vol 2 £11.95, Vol 3 £13.95 plus 10% postage and packing. Overseas customers should double the postage and packing cost.

▲A early casualty of the proposed conversion of Edinburgh/Glasgow–Inverness services to Class 158s was the overnight sleeping car service, the only such service to be run by Provincial. On 4th January, 47636 'Sir John de Graeme' sits with coaches 10501 and 10600 forming the 23.30 Glasgow–Aberdeen and Inverness. This was the night of the last Glasgow–Aberdeen sleeper, the last Inverness service being on the night of the 5th. *Maxwell Fowler*

Title page: Typical non-HST North-East–South-West services during 1990 were provided by Class 47/4 locos with twin fuel tanks hauling seven Mark 2 air-conditioned coaches, the short-formation trains which had been running to virtual HST timings having had to be increased in length due to there not being sufficient brake power. Here Class 47/4 No. 47827 is seen at Burton-on-Trent on 14th July with the 16.22 York–Birmingham. *A.O. Wynn*

▲BR standard Class 8P 4–6–2 No. 71000 'DUKE OF GLOUCESTER' returns to main-line running after the most remarkable locomotive preservation project ever undertaken. It is seen at Norton Hammer, between Sheffield and Millhouses on 14th March on its return test run to Derby. Behind the loco are the GWR dynamometer car and a red Mark 2 BFK, plus 13 BR coaches.

James Shuttleworth for 71000 Steam Locomotive Trust

▼The green A4 4–6–2 No. 60009 'UNION OF SOUTH AFRICA' was renamed 'OSPREY' during 1990, a name originally allocated to it but never previously carried. It is seen here at Newburgh on a crew-training special from Perth to Thornton on 13th April. *Les Nixon*

Britain's Railways in 1990

As with many businesses and organisations, 1990 was a tough year for British Rail. More above-inflation fare increases were made to offset falling government support and falling property income. Despite a modest increase in the planned Public Service Obligation payment (PSO) for 1991–94 to offset the effects of the recession, the long-term aim was clear. In its annual report, the Central Transport Consultative Committee said: "It would appear that passengers have become part of the experiment to see what extent BR can manage without some of the subsidy".

For, apart from this 'blip' as the government likes to call such events, the PSO had been falling every year since 1983. Ministers were clearly embarrassed by reports of falling quality and highlighted 'record' investment. Some rejected reports of rail expansion on the continent. In his last few months as transport secretary. Cecil Parkinson spent much time critising the SNCF's TGV as expensive and lavish in its use of energy. Despite hopes of a change, his successor Malcolm Rifkind also towed the line on BR finances, although to be fair, one cannot expect an overnight change.

Talk of the privatisation of BR waned somewhat. Perhaps surprisingly, the Liberal Democrat Party did consider privatisation as a long-term option.

On the passenger side, two events dominated the scene. The first was the introduction of electric services on the East Coast main-line between London King's Cross and Leeds. The second was more of a non-event than an event – the non-appearance of the Class 158. This was scheduled to be running on many provincial lines by the summer timetable, but production difficulties and the refusal of BR to accept the finished product meant that it was not until the onset of the winter timetable

▶The scene at London Charing Cross station on 5th April with the new roof under construction.   *Allan Mott*

▼The Channel Tunnel test train on its first trip out at Pirbright on 3rd May with 73205 leading taking current via the experimental bogies on 83301 (see page 79). 4 TC unit 8007 completes the train.*Chris*   *Wilson*

that any 158s were in service at all. The resultant effect on many provincial routes was disastrous, as many old DMUs had by then become very unreliable and had been withdrawn as BR did not want to go to the expense of shopping them. Thus cancellations and the use of unsuitable vehicles on some routes was the order of the day. To make matters worse, when the new 158s did appear, the displaced 156s were not used to augment the depleted fleet thus making cancellations unnecessary, but were used to replace loco-hauled services!

The main news on the freight side was the decision to close Speedlink because of heavy losses. This was criticised by many people, since a wagonload service will clearly be required when the Channel Tunnel opens.

BRITISH RAIL'S FINANCIAL CRISIS

The real extent of BR's financial problems did not become apparent until the latter half of the year. In July, BR was allowed an increased external financing limit of £700 million for 1990/91, a small increase on the previous year. This was

increased for 1991/2 in November's autumn statement to £1.12 billion.

The Chancellor's statement also increased BR's permitted investment programme to over £4 billion for the next three years. Of this £2.9 billion would come from the government through grants (1.65 billion) and loans from the National Loans Fund and repaid with interest (1.25 billion). The PSO for Network South East and Regional Railways would therfore by slightly increased, but later on available for Regional Railways only.

Both Cecil Parkinson and his successor Malcom Rifkind never stopped repeating the figures of '£3.7 billion' and 'over £4 billion' respectively that BR would be investing over the next three years. It became a kneejerk reaction when quizzed over the poor services.

The £2.9 billion compares to about £6 billion on trunk roads alone. Most of BR's investment is for replacement of old equipment not for new capacity. The government does not expect – or get – any financial return from new roads. However, roughly a half of BR investment (generally in the profit making areas like InterCity and Railfreight) must equal or exceed the 8% return rule; safety and replacement investment in Regional Railways and NSE is not required to always meet the 8% rule.

The rest of BR's investment programme would be financed from fares and from property rent, sales and development. Before the economic recession, revenues from property had been buoyant – BR even managed to reduce its debt as a result – to a minute fraction of those overseas railway administrations. The story in 1990 was different and a key cause of BR's problems.

The collapse in property income led to deferred and cancelled investment in all sectors. One casualty on Network South-East was the Class 471 programme to improve services between London and the Kent Coast. Delays also occured on Regional Railways, for example of the £12 milion 'Ivanhoe Line' in Leicestershire and Derbyshire. Another was the £15 million Nottingham–Mansfield–Worksop 'Robin Hood Line'. Railway finances were not helped by the £75–£83 million cost of 1989's strikes.

There was little money for the rail development without the relaxation of the 8% rule and the introduction of Cost-Benefit Analysis (CoBA). One precedent was set in 1990 though. The Department of Transport decided to appraoch the Treasury directly for money to build the London Crossrail on the grounds of reduced rail congestion.

BR ANNUAL REPORT 1989–90

The BR Group recorded a profit for the third year running after taking into account property sales and letting. A loss on ordinary activities of £26.4 million therefore became a surplus of £269.8 million after interest and extraordinary items. Investment of £175 million was the highest in real terms for 15 years. The rail strikes in 1989 had a cost of £83 million, causing an operation loss on railways for the first time since the pit strike in 1984.

The Board's principal financial objective, set in 1987, was to reduce the level of support to £665 million by 31st March 1990. Actual support required by that date was £574 million.
● **SAFETY.** No passenger was killed in a train accident in 1989/90 in contrast to the tragic three accidents of 1988/89. The number of staff killed whilst working on the railway rose from 14 to 15.

Mention is made of 'Operation Clean Sweep which was accelerated following the derailment of an Oxford–London Paddington train by vandals. The operation involved clearing linesides of materials (sleepers, rails, rubbish etc) that could be used by vandals.

Work was almost complete implementing the recommendations in the Fennell and Hidden Reports.
● **INTERCITY.** Income was £833 million and an operating surplus of £46.4 million was achieved. As one of the Board's non-supported businesses, InterCity exceeded the minimum requirement of achieving a 2.7% return on net assets employed. Punctuality and reliability deteriorated compared with 1988/89; enquiry bureaux became more efficient, however.
● **NETWORK SOUTHEAST.** Income support was £930 million resulting in an operating loss of £138.1 million before interest and government grant. the Public Service Obligation requirement was cut to £143 million. Punctuality and reliability worsened, carriage cleaning targets were not met (caused partly by water shortages in the South East), and maximum load factors were exceeded in peak periods.
● **PROVINCIAL.** Income of £276.4 million was greatly offset by costs resulting in an operating loss of £509.4 million before interest and grants. Within the sector, income on express services increased by 8%, from rural services by 1%, on urban services operated in conjunction with Passenger Transport Executives and an other urban services by 8%. In 1989/90 a Provincial train was slightly more likely to be on time but less likely to be actually running and less likely to be clean.
● **RAILFREIGHT.** This profitable sector produced an operating surplus of £59.4 million on an income of £693.9 million. Traffic carried totalled 143 million tonnes. Government targets on return on capital employed were not met.
● **PARCELS.** Gross income was £119.8 million and the operating loss was £15.9 million.
● **PROPERTY.** Sales of property topped £319 million and income from letting was almost £121 million. Gross contributions from the Property Board to BR amounted to £412.2 milion, up nearly 24% on the previous year.
● **INTERNATIONAL.** Gross sales of £90 million by British Rail international produced a net contribution to the Board of £28 million.
● **MAINTENANCE.** British Rail Maintenance Ltd produced a surplus of £14.4 million on income of £257.3 million.
● **PERSONNEL.** The number of employees in the Group fell by 882 to 134 361.
● **POLICE.** The number of crimes reported in 1989 was up almost five per cent at 878 905, although robberies fell by 17%.

The annual report ends with a five year summary of key rail statistics. The main trends are easier to distinguish when three years are chosen:

		Year to 31/03/88	Year to 31/03/89	Year to 31/03/90
PASSENGER				
Passenger Receipts	(£M)	1319.6	1780.0	1822.7
Passenger jouneys	(M)	685.9	763.7	746.5
Miles estimated	(M)	18780.0	21327	20706
FREIGHT				
Freight Income	(£M)	605.8	655.0	671.9
Net tonne miles	(M)	9971	11249	10403
OPERATIONS				
Passenger train miles	(£M)	200.9	222.2	225.3
Freight train miles	(£M)	32.0	32.2	30.7
ASSETS				
Diesel locomotives	(No.)	2338	1920	1835
Electric locomotives	(No.)	243	260	260
HST Power cars	(No.)	197	197	197
Coaching vehicles	(No.)	16164	14258	13833
Freight vehicles	(No.)	39007	24922	21970
Stations	(No.)	2526	2596	2970
Route open for traffic	(miles)	10395	10314	10307
STAFF				
Group total	(No.)	173760	135243	134361

BR STAFF

The year was not affected by industrial action to the same degree as 1989 although there were serious localised disputes, particulary in the North West.

BR decided to update uniforms for staff and produce a glossy 'Next'-style catalogue from which staff have a choice of outfit. Staff did appear smarter, helped in part by the fact that the uniforms were offered in many sizes to ensure a comfortable fit for all shapes. Excessive overtime was still the norm on BR, encouraged by low basic wages.

Signal & Telecommunications Staff

BR conducted a major review of conditions for 6900 key S & T staff following the Clapham crash. Plans unveiled in 1990 include: a limit on hours worked; a new grading structure and more performance-related pay; recruitment of 700 more staff; quality initiatives on design, installation, testing, training, documentation procedures and communications.

THE GOVERNMENT'S ENVIRONMENT WHITE PAPER

In September, Chris Patten, environment secretary unveiled his white paper, 'This Common Inheritance'. Amongst the 350 commitments and re-statements of policy were measures to increase energy efficiency, tougher speeding penalties and expanding MOT tests to cover fuel efficiency and noise. The government did not mention evaluating new road schemes against public transport options on the same basis.

Commentators suggested that Mr Patten's enthusiasm for change had been dampened by Cecil Parkinson and John Wakeham at the departments of transport and energy respectively. Also, John Major and Norman Lamont were said to have insisted that tax reforms on private and company cars be delayed for fear of upsetting motorists.

THE 158s ARRIVE AT LAST

▶ Class 158 construction at BREL Ltd's Derby Carriage Works.

▼ The interior of the new Class 158 DMU taken on a press run.
Peter Fox (2)

ELECTRIFICATION PROJECTS COMPLETED (C) UNDER CONSTRUCTION (U) OR ANNOUNCED (A)

Date	Type	Route
12/03	750 V dc	Farlington Jn/Portcreek Jn–Fareham (C)
12/03	750 V dc	Fareham–Eastleigh/St. Denys (C)
30/04	25 kV ac	Leeds–Leeds Neville Hill Depot (C)
25/06	25 kV ac	Hitchin–Northallerton/Leeds (C)
12/09	25 kV ac	Belford–Edinburgh (C)
/10	25 kV ac	Stansted South Jn–Stansted (C)
	25 kV ac	Drem–North Brewick (U)
	25 kV ac	Hitchin–Edinburgh (U)
	25 kV ac	Edinburgh–Carstairs (U)
	25 kV ac	Redditch–Lichfield Trent Valley (U)
	25 kV ac	Heald Green–Manchester Airport (U)
	750 V dc	Tonbridge–Redhill (U)
	25 kV ac	Cambridge–King's Lynn (U)
	750 V dc	Clapham Junction–North Pole depot (U)
	25 kV ac	North Pole depot–Willesden (U)
	750 V dc	Hooton–Chester/Ellesmere Port (A)

SEMAPHORES, MARK 1s AND VACUUM BRAKES

In the North West of England, semaphore signals, Mark 1 coaching stock and vacuum-braked wagons were still in evidence in 1990.

▲Class 31/4 No. 31426 is seen at Arnside with the 13.18 Barrow–Manchester Victoria on 24th July. The loco-haulage of these services was due to shortage of DMUs (see 'Provincial' section). Many of the coaches used on these services were in Network SouthEast livery, having been displaced from Paddington commuter workings. *Paul Shannon*

▼The last vacuum-braked freight workings in the North-west are the block limestone trains from Tunstead to Oakleigh and Lostock. These trains started in the steam era and used to be worked by Class 9F 2–10–0s and later by Class 25 diesels. The 15.29 ex-Tunstead is seen at Mobberley with revised blue-liveried 47532 in charge *Paul Shannon*

▲A vintage scene at Cockwood Harbour between Exeter and Newton Abbot as Class 47/4 No. 47834 'FIRE FLY' hauls a charter special on 15th September formed of the Venice-Simplon-Orient Express Pullman car set.
P. Underhay

▼A modern scene at the new Hedge End station on 9th May as Class 442 unit No. 2402 'County of Hampshire' works the re-openeing special for the 'Solent Link' electrification scheme.
Chris Wilson

"ADVERSE WEATHER CONDITIONS"

▲On 22nd November the wires came down on the ECML between Hitchin and Stevenage. This was the result.   *Allan Mott*

▼The day Britain stood still. On 8th December blizzards brought chaos to BR as well as other transport. At Birmingham New Street, the RTC's 31970 was stranded for 24 hours along with 156 414 and many other trains.   *Philip Crumpton*

TICKETS

Important alterations were made to tickets from 13th May as follows:
● STANDARD RETURNS became OPEN RETURNS with reducing validity from three months to one month, on any train, on any day.
● WHITE SAVERS became SAVERS (one month validity) allowing travel on most outward trains on any day, with no restrictions on return travel. This was a very important change, as previously savers on many InterCity routes.
● BLUE SAVERS became SUPERSAVERS (one month), valid on most off-peak trains except on Fridays and other busy times.
● The old colours of red, white and blue respectively were still used in promotional literature.
● APEX fares were offered on more routes as was the successful 'London Daybreak' fare, offered on Saturdays and Sundays. Holidaymaker APEX fares were attractive and afternoon/overnight HST services to Torbay and Newquay (plus loco-hauled services to Bournemouth) loaded well.
● AWAYBREAK tickets on Network SouthEast had their validity reduced from one month to five days. Nearly all NSE first class and standard class single or return tickets became valid for one day only. For passengers travelling to destinations near the boundary of the NSE area, it was often cheaper to buy a saver return to the next station outside NSE than to buy two NSE singles.

BR SPEAK

A number of choice examples of BR newspeak appeared during the year. These are listed below, together with their English translation (in italics):

Aircraft-style seating. *Seating with no leg space nor window.*
Changing market requirements. *No money (for new trains).*
Cheap Day Return. *Expensive Day Return.*
Customer. *Passenger.*
Heritage DMU. *Clapped-out first generation DMU.*
Improvements in reliability. *Service cuts.*
Life-expired coaches. *Recently refurbished Mark 2s.*
Unreliable units (Network SouthEast). *Class 307.*
More reliable units (West Yorks PTE). *Class 307.*
On time. *Nine minutes late.*

InterCity

The sector managed to weather the storm best, compared with the other sectors faced with economic recession and cuts in government support. The trend towards earlier departures and earlier returns continued (e.g. a new 06.20 Edinburgh–London King's Cross). More regular interval departures, and a better Sunday afternoon/evening service on several routes were introduced.

InterCity's main problem was reliabilty, or a lack of it. Punctuality worsened, cancellations increased. Passengers or customers regard reliability as more important than anything else according to successive surveys and was therefore urgently in need of attention.

INTERCITY CHANGES IN 1990

East Coast Main Line

From 14th May, Leeds enjoyed a practically all-electric service to London Kings Cross. Highlight of this was a new 1 hour 59 minute Leeds–London timing (2 hours 9 minutes northbound) for the 'Yorkshire Pullman'.

Despite continued criticism of the new Mark 4's ride characteristics and relatively poor reliability, InterCity 225 services proved a success. Loadings also improved on the Leeds–London service due to prolonged major roadworks on the M1 in south Leeds!

The £420 million ECML electrification project continued apace, together with associated signalling improvements. Over the Easter weekend, signalling formerly carried out in the well-known Northallerton signalbox was transferred to the new control centre at York; this controls 100 route miles, mainly on the ECML. Tweedmouth signalling centre was completed in July and work on others at Tyneside, Morpeth and Alnmouth continued. Track and signalling work intensified at Newcastle.

More services were offered on the ECML from May with 18 services each way between Edinburgh and London on weekdays. However, October saw the end of the 'Cleveland Executive' HST service which had, since a year earlier, been operating only the up direction anyway. this decision was heavily-criticised and resulted in the Eaglescliffe–Northallerton line having no booked passenger trains using it. BR replied that passengers prefer to drive to Darlington to pick up the London trains. This is not surprising if the alternative is a service of only one train! Certainly Durham, Darlington and Northallerton maintained their growth as park-and-ride railheads. Silver standard accommodation was also offered on selected North East–London services for the first time in 1990.

'The Humber-Lincs' Cleethorpes–London HST service was accelerated by omitting stops at Grantham and Huntingdon. This meant that Huntingdon was vitually eliminated from the InterCity network. Further south, Stevenage's status was assured as an M25 railhead.

On 1st October the 'Hull Executive' was upgraded to the 'Hull Pullman'. Silver standard was extended to this key business train too.

In November approval was given for electrification between Leeds and Bradford Forster Square. This could enable InterCity trains to run electrically-hauled throughout between King's Cross and Bradford.

Class 91 locomotives operating York/Leeds–London services had their No. 1 end below-buffer fairings removed in February for safety reasons. Modification were planned.

At the south end of the ECML two new 'high-density' commuter sets were introduced in May. Mark 2F FOs were converted at BREL Derby and RFS Engineering in Doncaster to TSOs with 75 seats, mostly unidirectional. Air-conditioning was upgraded. Services were hauled by Class 47 or 91 locomotives or, occasionally, by 89001 'Avocet'. The 06.35 Grantham and 07.15 Peterborough to London King's Cross (18.03 & 17.36

return respectively) were formed of 10 coaches each (8 TSO, FK, BFK) with 592 standard class and 66 first class seats.

West Coast Main Line

The Glasgow–London Euston service was expanded to seven services each way on weekdays. Line speed improvements and the removal of stops at Stafford and Crewe meant that the 'Royal Scot' could travel from London to Glasgow in 4 hours 47 minutes.

Standard regular hourly departures were re-introduced for services between Liverpool Lime Street and London Euston. More Manchester Piccadilly–London services were sent via Stoke-on-Trent and Macclesfield and the route offered no less than seven northbound and five southbound Pullman services. Silver standard was extended to some Carlisle/Preston/Blackpool–London services.

Wolverhampton/Birmingham–London trains were increased in length as the year progressed in response to rapid growth on the route.

InterCity sleeper services to and from Barrow-in-Furness and to and from Stranraer ran for the last time in 1990. InterCity Motorail operated a new service between London Euston and Fort William.

InterCity announced plans for the £750 million modernisation of the WCML from the mid-1990s. Most of the expenditure involves essential renewal of assets, but plans included a fleet of new trains each with a top speed of 155 mph. The remainder will be spent on track improvements and the installation of ATP.

Many more services were operated push-pull due to the delivery of further Mark 3 driving van trailers (DVTs).

Midland Main Line

More track was approved for 110 mph-running with faster services the result. Hendon–Sharnbrook (excepting Luton Station) and Leicester–Trent Junction were upgraded. The Sheffield–London St. Pancras 'Master Cutler' was able to run to a 2 hour 8 minute timing at an average speed of 77.3 mph.

A new Pullman service ran from Nottingham to London and was titled 'The Robin Hood Pullman'. Appropriately, this service actually starts from Sheffield, home-town of the folk hero.*

More HST services on the Midland Main Line were extended beyond Sheffield to Leeds.

Refurbished 'high density' stock was introduced on the 06.18 and 06.35 Derby to London St. Pancras services (17.30 and 18.04 return). Six-coach formations (4TSO, FK, BSO) offered 321 standard class seats and 42 first class seats. Class 47 locomotives provided power.

Great Western Main Line

HST formations were increased to 2+8 for all services, the extra coaches having been cascaded from the ECML. Only four loco-hauled sets remained for regular services. Swindon benefitted from an even more intensive service.

InterCity Cross-Country

Amongst the reshuffling of services were some noteworthy accelerations. For example, 'The Cornish Scot' Glasgow Queen Street–Penzance was speeded up to cut the journey by a full hour. The existing Newcastle–Poole service was also changed from May by becoming the Edinburgh–Poole 'Dorset Scot'. This supplemented the other service from Edinburgh, 'The Cornishman'.

---

* Robin Hood's real name was reputed to be 'Robin of Loxley'. Loxley was a village (now a suburb) to the north of Sheffield.

◄47837 hauls the first 'electric' train into Edinburgh prior to the official energisation ceremony. The special train consists of 91019, a rake of Mark 4s and 82215. The event took place on 12th September.
Douglas Young

► The Class 50s' only regular InterCity duty in 1990: 50036 nears Pangbourne with the 11.18 York–London Paddington on 3rd May.
John Chalcraft

►▼Following its transfer from ScotRail and its major refurbishment, DBSO 9702 is seen leaving Ipswich at the rear of the 13.00 Norwich–London Liverpool Street on 28 September.
John Augustson

►▼▼A number of Mark 2F FOs were converted into TSOs for InterCity commuter services into St. Pancras and King's Cross. 74 2+2-style seats were provided. The seats were close together and there was little luggage space, thus rendering them most unsuitable for the Summer Saturday holiday services that they were also used on. 6810 is seen at Sheffield on the 09.20 Bristol–York on 2nd June.
M.A. King

▼Some Class 91s operating London King's Cross–Leeds services suffered from cracking of their front fairings. As a safety precaution these were removed for a while for modifications to be made. 91006 is seen, minus fairings, on the 07.50 King's Cross–Leeds 'Yorkshire Pullman' on 25th May.
David Percival

A new Swansea–York loco-hauled service was introduced, replacing a service from Cardiff (Tenby on Summer Saturdays). The short-formation loco-hauled services had trouble due to them occasionally failing to stop in time at a red signal. This is because the brake power of a locomotive as a function of its weight (the "brake percentage") is much less than the brake percentage of a coach. Thus the smaller the number of coaches in a train, the lower the brake percentage of the train. It was therefore found necessary to increase the minimum train length before a speed restriction had to be imposed to seven coaches.

Timekeeping on cross-country services improved during the year, in contrast to the general trend. The relatively slow section of line between Doncaster and Sheffield was improved with the opening of the Swinton Curve, mentioned in more detail in the Provincial section. InterCity did contribute to the curve's re-instatement and the investment paid off: Doncaster–Sheffield was achieved in 3½ minutes less.

1990 also saw the end of portion working at Carstairs. BR believes that customers do not like portion-working. This development was ahead of the route's electrification which will result in greater operating flexibility, reduced costs and faster journeys.

With the imminent opening of the M40 through Oxfordshire, InterCity made great efforts to improve services south of Birmingham to the Thames Valley and beyond. There was a general improvement in services to and from Bournemouth and Poole, with more change promised for 1991.

InterCity Anglia (Norwich–London Liverpool Street)

Services suffered from unreliability on what is regarded as a 'Cinderella' route, an outpost of the InterCity empire. Problems usually occured south of Colchester.

From 14th May push-pull operation was phased in. Mark 2F DBSOs from ScotRail had been refurbished at BREL Derby and Devonport Dockyard at a total cost of £682,000. At the other end of the typical 13-coach train was a Class 86/2 locomotive. Each train included a refurbished Mark 1 buffet car. The £400,000 scheme to modernise these 11 vehicles involved the installation of new cushioned seats, new tables, full carpeting, phonecard telephones and new catering equipment.

InterCity Catering

The InterCity sandwich reached new high standards, and new prices, in 1990. Sir Clement Freud was brought in to 'design' (in BR parlance) two new sandwiches: poached salmon with dill and mustard mayonnaise selling at £1.85 and corned beef with red tomato chutney at £1.65 – bringing the choice of fillings to 11. InterCity decided to retain Sir Clement as a consultant on catering matters. Eight million sandwiches were sold by BR in 1990.

Also to be found in the buffet were more beers and lagers, including 'Sapporo' a Japanese lager beer at £2.10 per can. A new range of hot meals (priced at £2.95 to £3.95) including lasagne, curry and rice, cottage pie, and a new range of cakes were introduced on certain trains.

▲▶ The focus of attention for the electrification of the East Coast Main Line moved northwards to Tyneside and Northumberland. 47624 heads a catenary gauging train at Alnmouth on 20th May. *Stephen Miller*

The famous diamond crossing just east of Newcastle station was removed during 1990.

◀ 37184 stands on new trackwork on 30th March. Track has also been lifted from platforms 4, 5 and 6. *Robin Trinder*

▶ The entire layout at Newcastle was modernised. By 15th August the scene looked like this. 43074 heads a service for Edinburgh and 43051 propels and southbound service into the station. *David Carter*

▲Hot summer weather caused several operational problems for BR during July and August. In some cases speed restrictions were applied whilst on 28th July services were delayed on the Bournemouth line by a series of health fires. Class 47 No. 47452 slows to walking pace near Beaulieu Road with the 15.40 Poole–York on that day. *L.A. Nixon*

▲On 29th July 1990, 47802 is seen at the head of the 09.00 Brighton–Glasgow Central ('The Sussex Scot') at Redhill, being diverted over the Redhill–Reading line.
Duncan Street

▶With HST power car, 43038 leading, the inaugural down 'Robin Hood Pullman' passes Wellingborough on 14th May. This new Pullman service leaves London St. Pancras at 17.25 and runs to Nottingham and then on to Sheffield. It is only advertised as a Pullman to Nottingham. *Chris Milner*

▶Class 47 No. 47851 heads the 09.00 Poole–Edinburgh 'Dorset Scot' past Alnmouth on 19th May. *Stephen Miller*

◀47211 approaching Curriehill with the down 'Night Scotsman' running over five hours late after blockage of the West Coast Main Line at Beattock caused it to be diverted via Dumfries. *Douglas Young*

▶▼The 09.58 Glasgow Central–London King's Cross arrives at Motherwell on 1st October, the first day of the new weekday service. 43096 is at the rear of the HST set led by 43102. The train travels via Carstairs to Edinburgh and is formed off the 06.35 ex-Newcastle. *Michael McGowan*

▼Class 90s found their way onto occasional passenger workings in East Anglia during 1990. 90014 "The Liverpool Phil" passes New Hall with the 10.30 London Liverpool Street–Norwich on 11th August.
Dr. Iain C. Scotchman

►By the end of 1990 the short reign of the class 81s on London Euston e.c.s. workings was over. On one of its last duties 81017 stands at Wembley with InterCity e.c.s. for Euston during October. *Michael J. Collins*

◄During the summer timetable of 1990, all Sunday trains between Birmingham and the West were diverted via Kidderminster and Worcester Shrub Hill instead of via the Lickey incline. 43191 'Seahawk' heads the 08.05 York–Plymouth near Worcester Tunnel on 8th July. *Stephen Widdowson*

►▼On 14th May all internal Scottish services between Inverness/Perth and Edinburgh were changed to run via Fife, i.e. using the single line from Hilton Junction to Ladybank. the exceptions were InterCity services such as 'The Clansman' seen speeding through Greenloaning (near Gleneagles) behind 47636 'Sir John de Graeme' with the 10.10 Inverness–London Euston on that day. *Max Fowler*

▼◄HST power car 43010 'TSW Today' heads the 08.15 special service from Birmingham New Street to Weymouth at Southampton. This was a press run in advance of new HST workings to the south coast from 1991. 158 740 can also be seen on a driver training run in advance of the introduction of the Class 158s on Portsmouth–Cardiff Services. The date is 17th November. *Alex Dasi-Sutton*

▼Despite the delivery of the Class 90s, the Class 85s saw some top-link work during the summer. Here, 85011 arrives at Carlisle with the 11.33 Glasgow Central–Brighton (The Sussex Scot) on 23rd August. In the centre road is 90011 which had arrived with a service from Birmingham International. *Michael J. Collins*

BR Network

INTRODUCTION.

The Kettering–Corby passenger service ended in June. It had started in 1987 under the 'Speller Amendment'and Corby council had put in a total of £220,000. The service proved unreliable resulting in poor patronage. Another problem was that no attempt was made to provide a train service to Glasgow. Many of the population of Corby are of Scottish origin, moved in when Stewart's and Lloyds opened up their steelworks in the town. There is thus a large demand for travel to Scotland, hence the Kettering stop in the former "Thames-Clyde Express". To reach Glasgow, it was necessary to change at least three times and connections were poor.

Gainsborough–Barnetby was reprieved earlier in the year. This had been intended to be bus substitution testbed, but the proposed replacement bus services had ridiculously long journey times as compared with the train service.

More good news came in the form of the experimental passenger train operation over the Blackburn–Clitheroe–Hellifield line.

The reopening of the Paisley Canal line resulted in five new stations being added to the network on 30th July. Major stations opened at Meadowhall Interchange and Swinton in South Yorkshire. There were station resitings at Bradford Forster Square and Sudbury. Major stations rebuilt or refurbished included Oxford, Eastleigh and East Croydon, the latter only half-finished by the end of the year.

The most significant line to be reopened was that over the River Ness at Inverness with the rebuilding of the collapsed Ness Bridge, once again linking the Far North and Kyle of Lochalsh lines with the main BR network.

"Total route modernisation" of the Chiltern lines progressed in preparation for the proposed future transformation of services.

One of the annoying speed restrictions on the West Coast main line was addressed with a major track upgrading project.

An important 'missing link' in Network SouthEast third-rail territory was bridged with the electrification of Solent-area lines between Fareham and Eastleigh/St. Denys.

LINES CLOSED TO PASSENGERS (P) AND (PF) OR FREIGHT (F)

DATE	LINE	LOCATION
/03	Rosyth Dockyard–Inverkeithing S. Jn. (PF)	(Fife)
17/03	Aldwarke Jn. (MR)–Mexborough E. Jn. (PF)	(S. Yorkshire)
13/05	Northallerton High Jn.–Eaglescliffe S. Jn. (P)	(N. Yorkshire/Cleveland)
28/05	Kettering North Jn–Corby (P)	(Northamptonshire)
15/07	Princes Risborough–Chinnor (PF)	(Bucks/Oxon)

LINES REPRIEVED

Gainsborough (Trent East Jn)–Barnetby (Wrawby Jn).

LINES OPENED OR RE-OPENED TO PASSENGER/OR FREIGHT

DATE	LINE	NOTES
19/02	Thorney Mill–Colnbrook (f)	(Buckinghamshire)
17/03	Swinton North Jn–Mexborough East Jn (PF)	(S. Yorkshire)
19/03	Mexborough East Jn–Swinton South Jn (PF)	(S. Yorkshire)
14/05	Inverness–Muir of Ord (PF)	(Highland)
30/07	Paisley Hawkhead–Shields Jn (PF)	(Strathclyde)
20/10	West London Jn–Acton Wells Jn (PF)	(Greater London)

STATIONS CLOSED

DATE	NAME	LOCATION	NOTES
22/01	Cargo Fleet	(Middlesbrough, Cleveland)	
29/01	Holborn Viaduct	(Greater London)	Replaced by St. Pauls Thameslink
14/05	Altofts	(Nr. Normanton, W. Yorkshire)	
04/06	Corby	(Northamptonshire)	'Speller amendment' trial service
09/06	(Bradford Forster Square)	(W. Yorkshire)	Station re-sited close by
28/10	(Sudbury)	(Suffolk)	Station re-sited close by

SEASONAL USE OF STATIONS AND LINES

DATES	STATION	LINE	LOCATION
25/03–07/10	Stanhope	Bishop Auckland–Stanhope	(County Durham)
19/05–01/10	Clitheroe	Blackburn–Hellifield	(Lancashire/N. Yorkshire)
15/07–09/09	Trawsfynydd	Blaenau Ffestiniog–Trawsfynydd	(Gwynedd)
29/07–09/09	Ironbridge Gorge	Telford	(Shropshire)

STATIONS REPRIEVED

Gainsborough Central, Kirton Lindsey, Brigg (Lincolnshire/Humberside).

TEMPORARY STATION

08/02–21/02   Over (Gloucester). Opened as response to flooding in the area.

▶ 156 458 crosses the new Ness Bridge after the official opening ceremony at Inverness Station on 9th May. The train carried invited guests both ways over the River Ness after Malcolm Rifkind, Secretary of State for Scotland, reopened the link to the North of Scotland. *Michael McGowan*

▶ 156 514 prepares to leave Paisley Canal station with a re-openeing special for the route. The headboard reads "THE PAISLEY CANAL LINE REOPENS – Strathclyde Transport – WHAT A SENSIBLE IDEA". One wonders why the same PTE allowed this line to close only eight years previously to be replaced by a bus service. What a stupid idea! *Tom Noble*

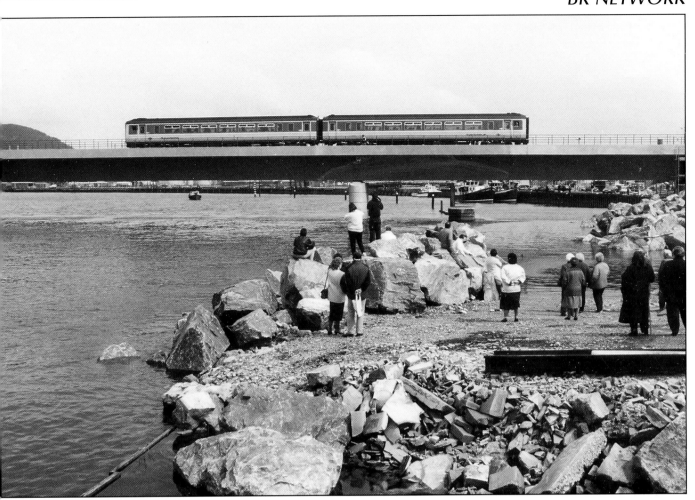

STATIONS OPENED OR RE-OPENED

DATE	NAME	LOCATION	COST
20/01	Rams Line Halt	(Derby–Peartree)	
23/04	Priesthill & Darnley	(Nitshill–Kennishead)	
14/05	Hedge End	(Eastleigh–Botley)	£350,000
14/05	Swinton	(Mexborough–Rotherham)	£650,000
14/05	Shieldmuir	(Motherwell–Wishaw)	
14/05	Whinhill	(Port Glasgow–Branchton)	
29/05	St. Paul's Thameslink	(Blackfriars–Farringdon)	
04/06	Tame Bridge	(Hamstead–Bescot)	£600,000
09/06	(Bradford Forster Square)	(Shipley–Bradford Forster Square)	
30/07	Corkerhill	(Paisley Hawkhead–Shields Jn)	
30/07	Cookston	(Paisley Hawkhead–Shields Jn)	
30/07	Dumbreck	(Paisley Hawhkead–Shields Jn)	
30/07	Mosspark	(Paisley Hawkhead–Shields Jn)	
30/07	Paisley Canal	(Paisley Hawkhead–Shields Jn)	
05/09	Meadowhall Interchange	(Rotherham–Brightside)	
10/09	Walsden	(Todmorden–Littleborough)	£240,000
24/09	Worle	(Yatton–West Milton)	
01/10	Whiston	(Rainhill–Huyton)	
02/10	Bloxwich North	(Walsall–Hednesford)	£280,000
28/10	(Sudbury)	(Marks Tey–Sudbury)	
03/11	Woodsmoor	(Davenport–Hazel Grove)	£300,000

STATIONS RENAMED

DATE	FROM	TO	LOCATION
14/05	Haringay Stadium	Haringay East	(Greater London)
29/09	Stansted	Stansted Mountfitchet	(Essex)

MAJOR TRACK AND/OR SIGNALLING WORK UNDER WAY OR COMPLETED

LOCATION	NOTES
Aldwarke–Thrybergh (S. Yorkshire)	Major rationalisation
Barnsley–Meadowhall (S. Yorkshire)	Signalling work
Barnstaple (Devon)	New run round loop
Blackfriars–Farringdon (Greater London)	New alignment
Bradford Forster Square (W. Yorkshire)	Station re-sited
Cardiff Queen Street (S. Glamorgan)	
Dewsbury (W. Yorkshire)	Centre road re-instated
Eastbourne–Hampden Park (E. Sussex)	
Hanwell (Greater London)	
Huddersfield (W. Yorkshire)	
Holyhead (Gwynedd)	
Heald Green–Manchester Airport (Greater Manchester)	
Ilford (Greater London)	Increased capacity at depot
Knighton (Shropshire)	New passing loop
Landore (W. Glamorgan)	Increased capacity at depot
London Marylebone–Aylesbury	Total route modernisation
Manors (Tyne & Wear)	
Newcastle (Tyne & Wear)	Preparation for ECML electrification
North Pole (Greater London)	Channel Tunnel train maintenance depot
Reading (Berkshire)	Trackwork for new 'Networker Turbo' depot
Slade Green (Greater London)	Trackwork for new 'Networker' depot
Sudbury (Suffolk)	Station re-sited
St. Phillips Marsh (Avon)	Increased capacity at depot
Sheepcote Lane (Greater London)	New chord for Channel Tunnel trains to North Pole depot
Weedon (Northamptonshire)	Curves eased
York–Scarborough (N. Yorkshire)	Track upgrading
London Liverpool Street (Greater London)	Modernised track layout
Hull–Bridlington	Level crossing/signalling modernisation
London Waterloo–Stewarts Lane Chord (Greater London)	Upgrading for Channel Tunnel passenger service
Redhill–Tonbridge (Surrey/Kent)	Upgrading mainly for Channel Tunnel freight services
Stewarts Lane–Cheriton, via Brixton	Upgrading mainly for Channel Tunnel passenger service
Beckenham Jn Orpington, Sevenoaks	
Tonbridge and Ashford ('BTR 1') (Greater London/Kent)	
Stewarts Lane–Ashford via Catford, Bickley,	Upgrading mainly for Channel Tunnel passenger service.
Swanley and Maidstone East ('BTR 2') (Greater London/Kent)	

▶The temporary halt at Over (Gloucester) built of scaffolding, plywood and roofing felt due to the closure of the bridge over the River Severn nearby. Cardiff Valleys Class 116 power twin set C 392 waits for the minibus connection from Gloucester before forming the continuation of the 12.02 Birmingham–Cardiff. *Tom Clift*

▶The Kettering–Corby passenger service ceased on 2nd June. Class 108 DMU 51916/ 54194 is seen after arrival at Corby on the last day. *Kevin Lane*

▼A section of the Inverness–Kyle of Lochalsh line was temporarily converted to double as a road in the autumn of 1990 to allow Highland Regional Council to tackle potentially dangerous rock above the road alongside Loch Carron. Part of the safety devices included semaphore signals at each end of the shared stretch. This was the scene on 7th November. One wonders why a similar solution in reverse has not been considered for the new Dornoch road bridge. Surely the few trains a day on the far North main line could be accommodated on a single track tramway over the bridge? *Tom Noble*

REFURBISHED STATIONS

NAME	LOCATION	COST		NAME	LOCATION	COST	
Alresford	(Essex)	£ 100 000		Kirkcaldy	(Fife)		
Aldershot	(Hampshire)	£ 900 000		Kettering	(Northamptonshire)		
Bristol Temple Meads	(Avon)	£2 000 000		Keighley	(W. Yorkshire)	£ 102 000	
Bromsgrove	(Hereford & Worcs.)		a	Largs	(Strathclyde)	£ 160 000	
Burnside	(Strathclyde)	£ 300 000		Leatherhead	(Surrey)	£ 150 000	
Barnsley	(S. Yorkshire)			Leicester	(Leicestershire)	£ 400 000	
Bicester North	(Oxfordshire)	£ 500 000		Leighton Buzzard	(Bedfordshire)	£1 800 000	
Bodmin Parkway	(Cornwall)	£ 120 000		London Cannon Street	(Greater London)	£ 700 000	
Bradford Forster Square	(W. Yorkshire)		b	London King's Cross	(Greater London)	£ 500 000	
Battle	(E. Sussex)	£ 63 000		London Paddington	(Greater London)		f
Berkhamsted	(Hertfordshire)	£ 500 000		London Marylebone	(Greater London)		
Beverley	(Humberside)			Malton	(N. Yorkshire)		
Clapham Junction	(Greater London)	£1 490 000		Moorthorpe	(W. Yorkshire)	£ 30 000	
Chester	(Cheshire)	£ 750 000		Mytholmroyd	(W. Yorkshire)		
Cholsey	(Oxfordshire)			Mirfield	(W. Yorkshire)		
Clacton	(Essex)	£ 300 000		Mexborough	(S. Yorkshire)		
Cardiff Queen Street	(S. Glamorgan)			Maryport	(Cumbria)	£ 51 000	
Clapham High Street	(London)			Middlesbrough	(Cleveland)		h
Cross Gates	(W. Yorkshire)		c	Machynlleth	(Powys)	£ 136 000	
Caerphilly	(Mid-Glamorgan)	£ 200 000		Newbury	(Newbury)	£ 400 000	
Chester-le-Street	(Essex)			Normanton	(W. Yorkshire)		
Downham Market	(Norfolk)			Norwich	(Norfolk)	£ 111 000	
Doncaster	(S. Yorkshire)	£ 120 000		Oldham Mumps	(Greater Manchester)	£ 200 000	
Dorchester West	(Dorset)			Outwood	(W. Yorkshire)		i
Darlingon	(County Durham)		h	Oxted	(Surrey)	£ 130 000	
Dewsbury	(W. Yorkshire)			Oxford	(Oxfordshire)	£3 500 000	
Durham	(County Durham)		h	Penzance	(Cornwall)		
Eastbourne	(E. Sussex)	£ 250 000		Plymouth	(Devon)	£ 625 000	
Erdington	(W. Midlands)	£ 320 000		Penistone	(S. Yorkshire)		
Earlsfield	(Greater London)			Pokesdown	(Dorset)	£ 65 000	
East Croydon	(Greater London)	£3 900 000		Rainham	(Essex)	£ 672 000	
Eastleigh	(Hampshire)	£1 300 000		Ramsgate	(Kent)		
Elgin	(Grampian)	£ 400 000		Sheffield	(S. Yorkshire)		
Ely	(Cambridgeshire)			Swansea	(W. Glamorgan)		
Filey	(N. Yorkshire)	£ 454 000	e	Stoke Mandeville	(Buckinghamshire)		c
Fratton	(Hampshire)	£ 460 000		Shepley	(W. Yorkshire)		d
Great Missenden	(Buckinghamshire)			Shipley	(W. Yorkshire)		
Grange Park	(Greater London)	£ 80 000		Thorpe-le-Soken	(Essex)	£ 190 000	
Great Bentley	(Essex)	£ 100 000		Twickenham	(Greater London)	£ 270 000	
Guildford	(Surrey)			Twyford	(Berkshire)	£ 520 000	
Guiseley	(W. Yorkshire)	£ 30 000	g	Telford	(Shropshire)	£ 250 000	
Halifax	(W. Yorkshire)			Wilmslow	(Cheshire)	£ 500 000	
Hebden Bridge	(W. Yorkshire)	£ 950 000		Wivenhoe	(Essex)	£ 100 000	
Holyhead	(Gwynedd)			Wigan Wallgate	(Greater Manchester)	£ 165 000	
Hinckley	(Leicester)	£ 235 000		Weeley	(Essex)	£ 100 000	
Horsham	(W. Sussex)	£ 30 000	i	Worthing	(W. Sussex)		
Hertford North	(Hertfordshire)	£ 563 000		Weybridge	(Surrey)	£ 300 000	
Huddersfield	(West Yorkshire)			Windsor & Eton Riverside	(Berkshire)		
Hunstcross	(Merseyside)			Walmer	(Kent)	£ 86 000	
Ingatestone	(Essex)			Wendover	(Buckinghamshire)		
Knebworth	(Hertfordshire)	£ 270 000		Woodlesford	(West Yorkshire)	£ 30 000	i

Notes:

a New platform.
b Station resited.
c Platform raised.
d Platforms enlarged.
e New roof.
f Roof and concourse improvements.
g New car park.
h Enlarged car park.
i Improved car park.

▲▶ Class 47 No. 47425 'Holbeck' passes Prestatyn with the 09.30 London Euston–Holyhead on 7th April. Resignalling work was due to commence at this location a few weeks later.   A.J. Woof

▶ The "new" Bradford Forster Square (right) with the old platforms in the background. Class 142 No. 142 082 with a service for Skipton.
Les Nixon

Network SouthEast

1990 was an eventful year for Network SouthEast with several new projects completed and brought into service. May saw the completion of the "Solent Link" electrification scheme. This £16.4 million project connected two seperate electrified routes, London–Southampton and London–Portsmouth. An imaginative new timetable provided through electric trains from Victoria to Southampton via Hove and Havant, and between Waterloo and Portsmouth via Eastleigh. Resulting from this, main line and outer-suburban services from Waterloo were re-branded as "Solent and Wessex".

NSE was, however, hit hard by the effects of the recession. The increase in peak hour traffic levelled off and off-peak travel, most of it optional, fell considerably. The result was withdrawn trains, shortened trains, travel centre closures and the prostponement of investment projects. Reduced ticket office opening hours and cuts in staffing were also part of the cost-cutting programme. On electrification, projects for the Ashford–Hashings, Uckfield–Hurst Green and Reading–Tonbridge lines were delayed.

Holborn Viaduct station closed on 26th January and was replaced by a new station nearby, St. Paul's Thameslink. The station, between Blackfriars and Farringdon is situated near the re-aligned Snow Hill tunnel. A new half hourly Luton–Sevenoaks/Orpington service replaced Thameslink services to Purley. A new regular Luton–Guildford Thameslink service was also introduced. To help cater for increasing demand on these services, the first of 26 new dual-voltage class 319/1 EMUs with first class accommodation were delivered, although these spent the remainder of 1990 working peak-hour services north of the Thames.

Another new route area, known as "West Anglia", was introduced at the start of the year, encompassing the Cambridge line out of Liverpool Street and branches. On this route, through trains between London and Kings Lynn ended in May, to be replaced by a DMU shuttle from Cambridge until electrification work is completed. In the same area, the new line into Stansted Airport was completed and wired, and the first of the new class 322 "Stansted Express" EMUs were delivered. These spent the last months of 1990 providing a welcome improvement in accommodation on certain Liverpool Street–Cambridge trains.

On the Chiltern lines, the off-peak service was doubled from the start of the May timetable to a half-hourly operation. This weekday was reduced again from the start of the October timetable. This was mainly due to crewing problems. The new service was heralded as 'a more reliable service'.

Driver only operation spread on NSE, although its introduction was delayed on South Western surburban lines and on the London Euston–Northampton line.

On the locomotive side, the ranks of the increasingly unreliable Class 50 fleet were significantly reduced during 1990, being withdrawn from Paddington duties from July and concentrated on the Waterloo–Exeter "West of England" line. Their replacements on Paddington–Oxford/Newbury services included Class 47s displaced from the Kings Lynn line and from Scotland. On the Exeter line, however, the class 50 situation became critical towards the end of the year, and substitutions by Class 33 and 47 became commonplace. It was eventually announced that locomotive haulage on the route would end in 1992, new class 159 "Western Turbo" diesel units being introduced as replacements. Class 73 haulage on NSE services ended in October, despite 73109 having been painted in Network colours the month before.

An important stage towards completing the Network image occurred in 1990, when the last "modern" sliding door EMU was repainted from blue and grey to Network livery. This was class 455 No. 5839, and Sector Director Chris Green helped apply the final coat in Selhurst Paint Shop on 11 June!

▼ Sadly, 1990 saw the first of the lines reopened under the "Speller Amendment" legislation to be closed to passenger traffic, that from Kettering to Corby, when Bedfordshire County Council felt itself no longer able to subsidise the route. Originally reopened in 1986, NSE passenger trains ceased on 2nd June. On the last day, a Class 108 twin unit formed of vehicles 51916 and 54194 waits to depart from Corby with the 09.00 to Kettering. Even on this last day, few passengers were in evidence. *Martin Loader*

Work forged ahead with station and other infrastructure improvements, despite the decrease in revenue caused by the downturn in the economy. Possibly the most important station construction completed during the year was at Oxford, completed in July. The new building replaced the "temporary" structure provided by British Railways, and is an appropriately impressive edifice for the University City. The street frontage is shown above, and the glazed footbridge below. *Colin Marsden (2)*

▶Another new station building, in the now-typical Network style, was built at Rainham (between Chatham and Sittingbourne), one of the most important stations on the busy North Kent commuter route into Victoria. The red, white and blue bunting was up for the opening celebrations on 3rd May. *Colin Marsden*

◀The Waterloo Area Resignalling scheme was virtually completed during 1990, apart from the Waterloo station area itself where a new building was erected to house the temporary panel formerly in the 1936 SR concrete signal box, demolished during November. Control of all other parts of the area was transferred to the new Signalling Centre situated in the former Wimbledon West yard. Among the boxes abolished was the distinctive overhead structure at Epsom, seen here on 12th May; it came out of use on 29th July. *David Brown*

ANGLIA REGION CHANGES

▲ WEST ANGLIA

This new route branding was introduced at the start of 1990, incorporating the Liverpool Street–Cambridge–Kings Lynn line and associated branches to Enfield, Chingford, Hertford East etc. The new badge is seen here on 317 367, and was also carried by certain members of classes 305/1, 312, 315 and 321. *David Brown*

▲ ◄Class 317/2 units, formerly on "Great Northern Line" outer suburban services from Kings Cross, took over duties on the Liverpool Street–Cambridge line from March, although continuing to be based at Hornsey EMU depot. Carrying "West Anglia" route branding and internal maps, but apparently still without the necessary destination blinds, 317 367 pulls out of Broxbourne with the 09.22 Cambridge–Liverpool Street on 12th May. At this time, it was possible to see Classes 312, 317/2 AND 321 working these trains. *David Brown*

◄The remaining through Liverpool Street–Kings Lynn trains were withdrawn in May, bringing to an end regular Class 47 locomotive haulage on the line. Specially prepared for the occasion and carrying a headboard provided by the Cambridge University Railway Circle, 47581 "Great Eastern" prepares to depart from Kings Lynn with the final working, the 10.00 to Liverpool Street, on Saturday 12th May. *Jonathan Cordle*

◄For the remainder of the year, the service to Kings Lynn was operated as a shuttle from Cambridge, except when completely closed at weekends for electrification work to proceed. Virtually all services were worked by venerable class 101 DMUs, something of a change from the refurbished Mark 2 loco-hauled coaches with APT-style seating previously used. A pair of twin-units, formed 54402/51208 + 54220/51222, passes Harbour Junction on 13th July forming the 17 28 Kings Lynn– Cambridge. *Steve Turner*

► A new weekdays-only service from Stratford to Broxbourne via Tottenham Hale commenced in May, necessitating the reopening of the long-disused platforms 11 and 12 at Stratford. They are seen here on 21th November, having been refurbished with typical NSE waiting shelters.
Dr Iain C Scotchman

▼The last of the 1956-built Class 307 Southend line EMUs was withdrawn from Network SouthEast service in June, all services on the line from Liverpool Street now being in the hands of new Class 321 units. A special farewell run took place on 30th June, composed of units 307 129 and 307 108; it is seen here at Southend Victoria, with one of its replacements in the sidings in the background. Some units of this class were eventually sent to West Yorkshire PTE, however, for Doncaster–Leeds. *P.J. Rayner*

► 1990 also saw the demise of the last unrefurbished examples of Class 302 on the London Tilbury and Southend line and on rush hour services out of Liverpool Street. On the former route, 302 267 departs from Leigh on Sea in unseasonably dull weather on 6th June, forming the 13.18 Fenchurch Street–Shoeburyness via Tilbury service. Rebuilt examples of Class 302 will continue in service for some time to come however, as the delivery dates of the proposed replacement Class 331 "Networker" units slip further and further into the future... *Chris Wilson*

▼ Many services on the LT&S were taken over by Class 310 units, which were introduced on this route in some numbers during 1990. 310 088 and 081 approach Purfleet on 9th August with the 17.41 Fenchurch Street–Pitsea. The weather appears to be appreciably better than in the previous photograph! *Paul D. Shannon*

◄"OPERATION CRABSTICK"

On the weekend of 17/18th February, the Bournemouth main line between Eastleigh and Southampton was closed to all traffic while some unexploded bombs at Eastleigh Airport were disposed of in an exercise codenamed "Operation Crabstick". To plug the gap, shuttle services between Eastleigh and Southampton via Fareham and via Romsey were run, worked exclusively by diesel electric multiple units of Classes 205 (3 H) and 207 (3 D). This provided something of a "last fling" for these units in the Hampshire area prior to the completion of the "Solent Link" electrification, and several units were borrowed from Selhurst for the weekend to supplement Eastleigh's own allocation. Thus at Woolston on 17th February, Selhurst-based 207 002 speeds through with the 15.00 Southampton–Fareham–Eastleigh shuttle, while 205 029 rumbles away with the "normal" Southampton-bound stopping service.

Chris Wilson

◄Loco-hauled peak hour services between Euston and Northampton ended with the May timetable changes, being replaced by Class 321 EMUs. The final up "Northampton Cobbler", the 07.37 ex-Northampton, was appropriately hauled by the one and only NSE liveried a.c. electric locomotive, 86401 "Northampton Town"; it is seen here after arrival at Euston.   *Fastline Promotions*

▼A strange sight in Southern suburbia. On Saturday 14th April, a VSOE special was run from Dorking to Bristol Temple Meads and return. Departing at 08.29, the Pullmans are seen here approaching the pick-up stop at Epsom in charge of a very clean 47582 "County of Norfolk", the only example of its class in "old" NSE livery with a black ex-headcode panel. Tickets were advertised on Capital Radio!   *David Brown*

CLASS 73s NAMED

▲ 73112 was named "University of Kent at Canterbury" on 3rd April, having been immaculately repainted into old-style InterCity livery for the occasion. This was somewhat anachronistic, as it was an NSE-allocated locomotive. A normal duty was towing a pair of class 438 4 TCs on the 07.38 Southampton–Waterloo stopping service, as seen here on 17th April, approaching Wimbledon. New for 1990, this new high-level vantage point resulted from the completion of a multi-story car park. The 73 + TC formation was replaced by a single 4 Vep on this service from October, in a somewhat misguided attempt to dispense with the useful TC trailer units.   *David Brown*

▼ However, a Class 73 in full Network SouthEast livery had to come, and 73109 was so adorned for its naming as "Battle of Britain 50th Anniversary" at Folkestone Central on 8th September. At the same time, newly restored Bulleid Pacific 34072 "215 Squadron" was rededicated, following which the two locomotives worked a special along the sea-wall to Dover. In this view of the train leaving the distinctive portal of Shakespeare Cliff tunnel, the swirling steam makes it obvious which engine is doing most of the work! Sadly, 73109 was plagued with technical problems following its release to traffic, and was little seen for the remainder of the year.   *David Brown*

CLASS 50 IN DECLINE

1990 saw a large reduction in the fleet of class 50 locomotives, and the concentration of the remainder on the Waterloo–Salisbury–Exeter route. They were replaced at Old Oak Common for services from Paddington by more Class 47s, transferred partly from Stratford following the cessation of loco-hauled trains to Kings Lynn, and partly from Haymarket following the introduction of class 156 and (eventually) 158 diesel units to "Scotrail Express" services.

At the start of the year, NSE operated 28 class 50s. 50023/24/26/31–36 were based at Old Oak Common, and 50001–3/5/7/9/16–18/27–30/43–45/48–50 at Laira. By the end of the year only 17 were left, of which 50050 had been stopped since the late summer undergoing repainting in original blue livery as D 400 following a successful appeal to raise money by readers of "Rail" magazine. These were 50001–3/7/17/18/24/27–30/33/37/43/48–50, all at Laira. This list includes 50037 "Illustrious" which was returned to the NSE fleet from the departmental

pool in 1990, taking up duties on the Waterloo–Exeter line on 27th May.

The logic of concentrating the Waterloo–Exeter fleet at Laira, 50 miles from the western end of the line, seems questionable. By the autumn, the depot was often struggling to have 50% of its fleet in traffic, and further withdrawals merely made the situation worse. Old Oak Common continued to receive two examples each night for light servicing, and the depot's expertise was increasingly being called upon to attend to cripples sent over from the London end of the route. Expensive failures involving main generator and traction motor flashovers became more common, and this as much as anything led NSE to urgently assess the replacement situation (see below). In the meantime, by the end of the year, Old Oak Common Class 47s and SR Class 33s were shouldering much of the load to keep the Salisbury line running.

▲ During the latter part of 1990 the reliability of the Class 50 fleet on the "West of England" line caused serious cause for concern among NSE engineers, and there were frequent substitutions of Class 47 or even Class 33. One of the latter, 33025 "Sultan" speeds through Farnborough (Main) on 7th August, with a late-running Salisbury–Waterloo service. *David Brown*

◀ The exodus of the class away from Old Oak Common began on 28th May and was completed by the middle of July, after which the class was rarely seen on "Thames" routes. Two examples of OC locomotives withdrawn in 1990 were 50031 "Hood" and 50023 "Howe" – in the twilight of their days they are seen double-heading the 09.35 Oxford–Paddington service through West Drayton on Saturday 28th April. "Hood" was one of the first of its class to leave the London depot, being transferred to the Laira DCWA departmental pool on 28th May; while "Howe" hauled the last booked Class 50 working out of Paddington on 12th July before going to Laira for Exeter line duties, on which it lasted only a few days before further transfer to the DCWA fleet to eke out its last days. *David Brown*

▼ Now in Network SouthEast livery, but retaining its Scottish "Holyrood" nameplate, 47707 speeds through Harbury in charge of the 11.18 Woverhampton–Paddington via Leamington Spa on 21st July. *Bryan Hicks*

◀ NSE announced in November that it was buying the last of the Regional Railways class 158 production (and three additional vehicles) to form 23 Class 159 3-car units for the Exeter line. Dubbed "Western Express", these would be based at a new depot at Salisbury and the first would be in service by March 1992. Although very similar to the 158s, the NSE units would have a much improved first class section with 2+1 seating and tables. To give the Press and local dignitaries along the route a taste of the future, NSE borrowed new 158 732/7 for a run from Waterloo to Exeter and back on 15th October. The special is seen here waiting to depart from Waterloo.
Chris Wilson

STOCK REPLACEMENT ON THE ISLE OF WIGHT

◀ The last five 2-car units of class 483 stock, refurbished from LT 1938 tube stock at BRML Eastleigh, were delivered to the Isle of Wight during 1990, and for much of the year the old (Class 486) and new trains could be seen working together on the Island. On Saturday 1st September the final units of Class 483, numbers 008 and 007, grind to a halt at Ryde Esplanade with the 13 51 Shanklin–Ryde Pier Head, about to pick up holidaymakers returning to the mainland via the ferry to Portsmouth. On the left "old" 486 031, with unique control trailer No. 28 leading, waits to depart with the pier shuttle. *David Brown*

◀ In a somewhat surprise move, five vehicles of the "old" Isle of Wight stock were donated to London Transport by NSE. While still on the Island two vehicles were repainted into historic liveries; trailer 44 into 1930s maroon and cream, and Control Trailer 27 into the slightly more elaborate 1920s style with black lining and lighter red doors. Following transport via the Fishbourne ferry and low-loader to Fratton, the unit ran under its own power up the Portsmouth "direct" line on 18th October, for handover to LT. Standing in one of the District Line bay platforms at Wimbledon, it met up again with the forth rail for the first time in 25 years! Displayed at Morden Depot Open Day on 24th November and subsequently in storage there, it is hoped that commercial sponsorship will eventually enable this unique working example of the once commonplace "standard" tube stock to be restored to original condition for use as a "heritage" train. *Chris Wilson*

THAMESLINK DEVELOPMENTS

HOLBORN VIADUCT CLOSURE

The two remaining platforms of the redundant SR City terminus at Holborn Viaduct finally closed on 26th January, to make way for the realignment of "Thameslink" tracks (see below) and the new Ludgate office development. On 24 January, "Kent Link" EPB units 6405 and 5404 wait to depart with evening peak services. Following closure, such services were altered to start and terminate at Blackfriars. *Rodney Lissenden (2)*

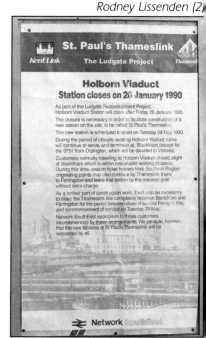

St. Paul's Thameslink

Kent Link   The Ludgate Project

Holborn Viaduct
Station closes on 26 January 1990

As part of the Ludgate Redevelopment Project, Holborn Viaduct Station will close after Friday 26 January 1990.

The closure is necessary in order to facilitate construction of a new station on the site, to be called St Paul's Thameslink.

The new station is scheduled to open on Tuesday 29 May 1990.

During the period of closure, existing Holborn Viaduct trains will continue to serve, and terminate at, Blackfriars (except for the 0751 from Orpington, which will be diverted to Victoria).

Customers normally travelling to Holborn Viaduct should alight at Blackfriars which is within reasonable walking distance. During this time, season ticket holders from Southern Region originating points may also continue by Thameslink trains to Farringdon and leave that station by the manned gate without extra charge.

As a further part of construction work, it will also be necessary to close the Thameslink line completely between Blackfriars and Farringdon for the period between close of service Friday 11 May and commencement of service on Tuesday 29 May.

Network SouthEast apologises to those customers inconvenienced by these arrangements. We are sure, however, that the new facilities at St Paul's Thameslink will be welcomed by all.

Network SouthEast

▶ On the last day, the final service to depart from Holborn Viaduct was a special organised jointly by NSE and Hertfordshire Railtours. Formed of Class 411 '4 Cep' EMUs 1605 and 1513, both immaculate in Network stripes, the tour was allegedly oversubscribed by a factor of three! The stock is seen here standing in platform 2 at Victoria, waiting to run ECS to Holborn for the start of the tour. Impressive (and different) headboards were carried at both ends of the train.   *Rodney Lissenden*

REALIGNMENT OF "THAMESLINK" ROUTE THROUGH THE CITY

▶For the last two weeks of May, through "Thameslink" services did not operate, while the massive reconstruction of the route between Blackfriars and Farringdon took place. The track alignment was altered to dip sharply out of Blackfriars, enabling the line to run under rather than over Ludgate Hill. The removal of the cast iron bridge enabled a clearer view of St. Pauls Cathedral, as seen on 17th May.   *Alan Mott*

▼The sharp dip north of the platforms at Blackfriars on the realigned route may be appreciated from this view of 319 047, which was just reaching the top of the slope with the 14.00 Luton–Guildford service when photographed on 19 July.

Chris Wilson

ST. PAULS THAMESLINK

◀St. Pauls Thameslink is the City station on the realigned Thameslink route between Blackfriars and Farringdon. Opened two weeks after the start of the May 1990 timetable revision in an incomplete state, it is part of the Ludgate office development. When opened, parts of the 12-car length platforms were in open air, although when the station is fully complete in 1991 daylight will be excluded. Train services through the station are formed exclusively of Class 319 units and in this view 319 052 approaches from Farringdon with the 11.30 Guildford–Luton service on 7th June, one week after opening. *Dr. P.K. Chown*

THAMESLINK DEVELOPMENTS

▲Thameslink services from Luton to Guildford commenced with the May timetable, although for the first two weeks services south started and terminated at Blackfriars due to the realignment work at St. Pauls. The new service was tortuously routed via Herne Hill, Tulse Hill, Crystal Palace, West Croydon, Sutton, Epsom and Effingham Junction. On 19th May, 319 019 approaches Effingham Junction off the Bookham line with a down service. At this stage, the Class 319 units operating the service had not been fitted with new blinds to display "Guildford". *David Brown*

▶The first of the 26 additional Class 319 units was delivered in 1990. The day after arriving at Selhurst Depot, 319 162 stands inside the inspection shed, still waiting for shoegear to be fitted. Apart from a small amount of first class accommodation, Class 319/1 differ from the earlier series in having a "spoiler" below the cab front, and light grey NSE livery. The destination blinds show several exotic terminating points not yet on the Network, such as "Milton Ernest" shown here! *David Brown*

CLASS 322 ENTERS SERVICE

New from the workshops of BREL Ltd. York during 1990 were the Class 322 EMUs for "Stansted Express" duties. They are based closely on the Class 321 but with an improved interior, 2+2 standard class seating and distinctive grey, green and white livery. 322 481 made a special high-speed demonstration run from York to Kings Cross on 20th July; it is seen here near Peterborough, sporting an appropriate headboard.   *Alan Mott*

SOLENT LINK ELECTRIFICATION

▶ For the "Solent Link" electrification between Eastleigh and Portsmouth, a brand new station was opened at Hedge End, between Eastleigh and Botley. Served by the new hourly Waterloo–Eastleigh–Portsmouth Harbour service, it serves an attractive new suburb of Eastleigh where several house-building companies are erecting estates. As at Oxford and Rainham, the attractive NSE house style has been adopted.
        Mervyn Turvey

▼▶To provide enough stock for the new "Solent Link" electric services in the rush hours, the two remaining Class 431 4 Rep units were reformed with various class 438 4 TC vehicles to make up four new 6 Rep units, still classified 431 but numbered 1903–1906. They each used one high-powered Rep driving motor coach, and were formed up at Eastleigh in time for the May timetable changes. However, 1903 only lasted in this state until October, being reformed yet again (see page 38). The Reps were booked to cover two peak workings in each direction on Mondays to Fridays, although they occasionally turned up on weekend reliefs. The second of the morning workings was the 07.04 from Portsmouth Harbour to Waterloo via Eastleigh. 1904 approaches Port Creek Junction with this working on 20th July. Another Rep would have been attached at Eastleigh for the journey to London.
        Chris Wilson

Solent & Wessex

▲The new "Solent and Wessex" line badge, depicting (presumably) yachts on the Solent! This has replaced the former "South Western Lines (outer suburban)", "Wessex Express" and "Portsmouth Express" brandings, and is applied to all SW main line electric stock and the remaining Eastleigh-allocated DEMUs. *David Brown*

◀To inaugurate the "Solent Link" electrification and to officially open the new Hedge End station (see page 33), a special was run from Waterloo to Portsmouth and Southsea via Eastleigh on 9th May. Appropriately formed of 2402 "County of Hampshire" and conveying (then) Transport Minister Cecil Parkinson, the special is seen here passing Cosham on one of the newly electrified sections. Sadly, the 442 disgraced itself by developing a fault which prevented it attaining full power, no doubt adding fuel to Mr Parkinson's prejudices against rail transport 2409 was sent as a replacement for the return trip to London. *Chris Wilson*

◀One result of electrification from Havant to Southampton was that it became possible to work Bournemouth line trains diverted onto the Portsmouth "direct" line due to engineering works electrically throughout. This occurred on various weekends towards the end of 1990, and on 25th November Class 442 2420 was photographed on the approach to Guildford forming the diverted 12.30 Waterloo–Weymouth service, non-stop from Guildford to Fareham. *David Brown*

▲It was intended that the four 6 Reps (see page 37) should be further reformed to move the power car into the centre of the unit, but only one was completed during 1990. Utilising spare power car 61253 and vehicles of disbanded 1903 the 'new' 1902 entered service in October, although it was quickly withdrawn when it developed a fault and it was discovered that fitters had not been trained to work on it! It re-entered service in December. Modifications to 62153 involved removal of cab fittings and rebuilding of the cab end to eliminate windows and reorganise the cabling – it is seen here in Clapham Yard after working the 06.00 Poole–Waterloo. *David Brown*

►Four more class 421 4 Cig EMUs were given the "Greyhound" treatment for use on the newly-electrified services, and the whole sub-class was renumbered into the 13xx series during May and June, the "new" conversions being numbered 1314–1317 from the start. 1315 was uniquely outshopped with headlamp and marker-light arrangements similar to those on TC 8028, and is seen here ex-works departing from Woking on 12 May with the 09.05 Basingstoke–Waterloo service.

A.C. Smallbone

THE LAST "HASTINGS" DEMU BOWS OUT

▲The last of the narrow-bodied "Hastings" DEMUs to remain in revenue-earning service, green-liveried 203 001, was finally withdrawn in May. Mainly used in its final years on the Ashford–Hastings "Marsh Link" line, it was photographed on just such a duty on 5th May, standing at Rye with the 11.13 ex-Hastings.   *Philip Barnes*

▼ The somewhat incongruous collection of literature carried on the side of power car 60014 just prior to withdrawal!   *Philip Barnes*

▼Following withdrawal, 203 001 was sent on an abortive trip to Cardiff Cathays for conversion into a "Sandite" unit. As Cathays were unable to do the work, the unit had to be sent to Ilford to be modified. Three coaches became a sister unit for 066, unsurprisingly being numbered "067". Speeding through the pouring rain at South Croydon, 067 returns to Selhurst following a "Sandite" spreading sortie down the Uckfield line on 24th October. The remaining trailer was converted into another "Sandite" coach, working between the driving coaches of withdrawn 207 011.   *David Brown*

◄The first of the Southern's fleet of de-icing and "Sandite" units were repainted into NSE livery during 1990, replacing the drab blue formerly carried. On 15th October, East Wimbledon-based unit 005 approaches Clapham Junction, returning from a Sandite-spraying sortie down the Guildford "new" line.   *Chris Wilson*

▼◄Network SouthEast sponsored the first International Flower Festival in the grounds of Hampton Court Palace on 11–15th July. As well as an augmented service of "normal" trains from Waterloo to Hampton Court, a number of specials were run on which guests paid for the privilege of being served canapes and drinks and having a gardening personality aboard for the 20 minute run to/from Waterloo! These specials, normally formed of just-facelifted Class 421 4 Cig units 1832 and 1833, were named "The Tudor Rose" and carried an appropriate headboard. The ECS of one such working is seen here passing Thames Ditton on 14 May.   *Dr P K Chown*

▼Work continued during 1990 on the modernisation of the Chiltern lines, ready to receive the new Class 165 "Network Turbo" units in 1991. Apart from station refurbishment and the construction of a new depot at Aylesbury, the lines out of Marylebone are being completely resignalled. Resignalling was well in progress at Princes Risborough on 18th April, when a typical piebald Class 115 DMMU, formed of vehicles 51660 + 59660 + 59675 + 51666, was photographed approaching with the 15.45 Marylebone–Aylesbury service.
                    Paul D. Shannon

Provincial

INTRODUCTION

1990 was the year of the stringent cuts in response to the falling public service obligation payments (PSO). Some BR management even made public statements about the link between PSO cuts and a worsening service on many lines. BR tried to minimise rolling stock requirements to meet financial targets. Off-peak cuts were worst. On the Esk Valley line. for example, services were reduced to four each way between Middlesbrough and Whitby reducing stock requirements to one Class 143 Pacer.

BR threatened councils with withdrawals of services at off-peak times. Several responded by offering revenue support (especially for late-night services) and/or capital support (e.g. investment in stations, level crossings, etc.), but others refused to be held to ransom in this way.

THE CLASS 158s

1990 should have been the year to see widespread introduction of new Class 158 units on many express routes, with consequent cascade of Sprinters to other services. Despite the first 158s being despatched to Haymarket for crew training, production difficulties – delaying the whole programme by up to 18 months – meant that hopes were not fulfilled. In March BR criticised BREL's quality control accusing it of 'garden shed engineering' The government had removed BREL's liability for delays in 158 production prior to the company's privatisation. Unfortunately Provincial decided to save costs by withdrawing many first generation DMUs, despite not having anything to replace them with. This resulted in cancellations and short formations in many areas, plus the occasional loco-hauled substitution.

At the end of the year, because of 'changing market requirements*' Regional Railways agreed to letting Network South-East have part of its new build of Class 158s, to be redesigned Class 159 and for use on London Waterloo–Exeter services (to replace ageing Class 50-hauled sets).

It is unclear whether this means lack of capital, the decision to push for Trans-Pennine electrification or both.

▶Due to late deliveries of Class 158s and also due to problems with Pacers, most Manchester–Barrow services were loco-hauled during the latter half of 1990. 31530 is seen near Hest Bank with the 11.17 Barrow–Manchester Victoria service on 23rd July.   *Paul Shannon*

▼Eventually the 158s went into service. 158 716 stands in Glasgow Queen Street on 3rd November, its next tour of duty being the 11.25 to Aberdeen.   *Mervyn Turvey*

PROVINCIAL CHANGES ITS NAME

The sector wanted both a new name and a new image and came up with "Regional Railways" in 1990. The new organisation is decentralised, with five regional business units and offices in each area (in brackets). They are ScotRail (Glasgow), Network NorthWest (Manchester), North East (York), Central (Birmingham) and South Wales and West (Swindon). The headquarters is in Birmingham. In charge was Gordon Pettit who replaced Sidney Newey during the year.

SERVICE CHANGES IN 1990

The delays with the Class 158 introduction resulted in Pacers operating some long-distance workings, much to the chagrin of passengers. Locomotive-haulage was particularly common around Manchester. Services which saw locomotives included: Manchester Victoria–Blackpool North/Barrow/Southport, Preston–Barrow and Blackpool North–Liverpool.

Other older stock failed to see the year out, however, with the last 'Calder Valley' Class 110 DMU being withdrawn in April. Norwich Crown Point did re-trim most of its Class 101 DMUs for longer service, with some appearing in Network SouthEast livery on the Cambridge–Kings Lynn shuttle.

On the Express network, most East Anglia–North West Services were routed via Loughborough instead of via Grantham resulting in longer journey times. This alteration was a classic case of sectorisation gone mad, being made so that Provincial did not have to pay for slow lines on the ECML. Belper, north of Derby, joined the Express network thanks to groundwork carried out by the local Transport 2000 group, but Beeston was removed from it. The latter was served by an improved local service.

Birmingham–Cardiff Express services were routed via Bromsgrove instead of via Kidderminster.

Highlight of the new Network NorthWest timetable in May was the 20-minute frequency along the Leeds–Manchester core of the North Trans–Pennine service together with faster journeys on the route. Hull–Manchester Piccadilly, Scarborough–Manchester Piccadilly and Newcastle–Liverpool trains were supplemented by an hourly Wakefield–Huddersfield–Staly-bridge–Manchester Victoria–Chester/North Wales service to achieve this end. Huddersfield gained new importance as an interchange station. Elsewhere, the off-peak Southport–Manchester Victoria service was diverted and extended via Manchester Piccadilly to Stockport.

In the East Midlands, a new half-hourly Nottingham–Derby service was achieved by dovetailing the Nottingham–Crewe and Lincoln–Derby services.

Sunday services returned on many lines including Plymouth–Gunnislake and Cardiff–Penarth.

SETTLE-CARLISLE DEVELOPMENTS

On 17th April a 'prospectus' for the line was unveiled. The 24-page document was drawn up by a number of local authorities and various other bodies including BR. The aim of the prospectus was to lure developers to the Settle–Carlisle corridor. Ideas were suggested: for example, Ribblehead station could become a navvy museum; the crumbling Hellifield station a restaurant or a shopping complex. Unfortunately, the most obvious development was not suggested, namely the return of InterCity services from the East Midlands and South & West Yorkshire to the route.

On 1st October, three-car Neville Hill-based Class 156s took over services, replacing locomotive-hauled trains, but unfortunately two-car units were also used on some occasions when 3 cars were needed. Track improvements and repairs to the line's spectacular structures continued. Because of the substitution of Sprinters for loco-hauled services, the piloting of certain trains with unusual locomotives on off-peak saturdays to attract railway enthusiasts came to an end.

▼The piloting of service trains with unusual locomotives continued to attract railway enthusiasts in 1990. Here, reinstated Class 25 No. D 7672 pilots 47422 leaving Appleby with the 12.42 Carlisle–Leeds on 25th February. *A.J. Woof*

THE PTEs IN 1990

The seven PTEs (Strathclyde, Tyne & Wear, Merseyside, Greater Manchester, West Yorkshire, South Yorkshire, and West Midlands) supported Provincial services to the tune of £100 million during the year. None were happy with BR's performance leading to increased contractual tension between the parties. Passenger Transport Authorities, through the PTEs, also pay BR about £265 million in capital investment a year. The stakes were high.

Greater Manchester PTE

Greater Manchester PTE's main problem during 1990 was unreliability of services caused by the poor performance of the pacer fleet which resulted old 2-car DMUs with one power car being substituted on many services. In addition, the non-delivery of 158s to other areas caused a delay in the cascade of Sprinters, with Class 31 loco-hauled trains in evidence out of Manchester Victoria. The Piccadilly–Deansgate section also suffered from congestion with delayed trains causing "ripple" effects.

Strathclyde PTE

Twenty two new Class 320 EMUs entered service on North Clyde services in Glasgow following resolution of a dispute over manning and safety. Introduction of the £29 million fleet allowed the withdrawal of the last unrefurbished Class 303 and all remaining Class 311s. Investment in station security seemed to pay off, with crime falling. The progressive PTE also announced a £17 million plan in November for line and station re-openings and service improvements. Eight new stations opened in 1990 alone (see BR Network section).

▶The last Class 311 set in service was 311 104 which worked its last service on 9th November. It is seen on 8th September at Bellgrove on a Milngavie–Springburn working, passing next to the remains of a station building destroyed by fire the previous July.
Tom Noble

▼Class 320s took over from the Class 311s and unrefurbished Class 303s. Two Class 320 sets, with 320 319 leading, are pictured east of Craigendoran with a Helensburgh–Airdrie service on 25th October. *Tom Noble*

Tyne & Wear PTE

Reliability of services was poor, paricularly on the Newcastle–Sunderland line. The PTE witheld £50,000 of BR's Section 20 grant in response (from an anual grant of £700,000). Councillor Ned Murray on the Tyne and Wear PTA said: "If we withold their subsidy we are guilty of criminal offence, but if we pay it, BR are guilty of not providing a service, which in my opinion is also a criminal offence".

West Midlands PTE (Centro)

The PTE expressed disquiet over the nature of the relationship between itself and BR. It wanted section 20 grants to bear a closer link to service quality. Centro did manage to make BR freeze its fares following poor reliability. More positively, approval was granted for Redditch–Lichfield Trent Valley cross-city electrification. October saw the delivery of the first Centro-financed refurbished Class 150 Sprinter, No. 150 116.

West Yorkshire PTE (Metro)

Reliability targets agreed with BR Provincial in the first months of 1990 were not achieved and the PTE witheld £180,000 from the £10 million Section 20 grant it pays for local services each year. BR threatened legal action and service cuts as a result.

Class 307 EMUs in MetroTrain livery were introduced on Leeds–Doncaster services. These units had been displaced from Network SouthEast's London Tilbury and Southend line.

Further rapid expansion of services on existing and new routes was outlined in Metro's RailPlan 2. Forty three new station sites are suggested.

PROVINCIAL

►With the adoption of the brandname 'Centro' for the West Midlands Passenger Transport Executive came a new livery for trains on sponsored services. 150 116 depots Leamington Spa with the 12.02 to Birmingham Snow Hill on 3rd November. *Brian Hicks*

▲New Class 320 3-car units Nos 320 312 and 320 315 stand in the sidings at Glasgow Central waiting to enter service. The date is 2nd August. *John Augustson*

▼West Yorkshire Passenger Transport Executive brought several Class 307s from Network SouthEast to operate the Leeds–Doncaster local service. Sporting the WYPTE livery, Class 307 No. 307 120 is seen at Leeds on 19 July. *John Augustson*

►A Class 156 leaves the Meadowhall Interchange station on 27th September with the 16.35 Sheffield–Hull. The Tinsley Viaduct of the M1 is in the background. *Tom Clift*

South Yorkshire PTE

Swinton station opened on 14th May together with the £3.4 million Swinton Curve. This curve links the Midland main line with the former GCR Sheffield–Doncaster line. Previously InterCity trains crossed over at the scissors junction at Aldwarke whereas since the building of the Holmes Chord and the reopening of Rotherham Central station, PTE trains to Doncaster had run straight down the GCR alignment. They now cross from the MR to the GCR route at Holmes, back to the MR at Aldwarke and back to the GCR at Swinton. The new double-track 40 mph curve eliminates the 15 mph speed restriction at Mexborough and is laid on the route of a previous single-line connection which was closed in the 60s. The connection at Aldwarke is now from the GCR to MR northbound and reverse only, the connection from MR to GCR northbound and reverse having been lifted. The new Swinton station has three platforms and is served by the half-hourly Sheffield–Doncaster services, the hourly Sheffield–Leeds via Moorthorpe as well as Sheffield–Pontefract–York services.

Meadowhall Interchange station also opened to serve the £400 million shopping complex. It has four platforms, two on the main line and two on the Barnsley line. It was an immediate success, with overcrowded trains being the norm in the period before Christmas. Amazingly, no booking facilities have been provided, with the result that at busy times up to four BR staff (ticket inspectors and railmen) could be seen working, generally on the footbridge, carrying out such duties as issuing tickets from Portis machines, often in the pouring rain. Information on trains was difficult to come by at first, especially for passengers heading in the Sheffield direction, who had no way of finding out whether their next service would leave from Platform 1, 3 or 4. This was to be rectified later.

Another problem was that the station was not finished in time for the opening of the shopping centre, passengers having to be bussed from Brightside on the first day, 4th September.

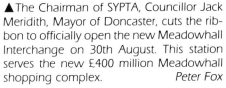

▲The Chairman of SYPTA, Councillor Jack Meridith, Mayor of Doncaster, cuts the ribbon to officially open the new Meadowhall Interchange on 30th August. This station serves the new £400 million Meadowhall shopping complex. *Peter Fox*

◄▲Pacer unit 142 033 has just set down 116 passengers from the 10.15 Huddersfield–Sheffield at Meadowhall Interchange on 8th September. The train is standing in Platform 4, which is bi-directionally signalled. Because there is no signal at the south end of the up Barnsley line platform (No. 3), it is not possible to admit a train to No. 3 platform if a train is signalled on either of the main lines. Thus many up trains were using Platform 4 instead of Platform 3 to add to the confusion of Sheffield-bound passengers. Note that the steps down to the platform had not been finished and therefore passengers had to use the ramps. *Peter Fox*

◄▲Rationalisation of the complex track layout between Aldwarke and Mexborough was completed in the spring. The new layout at Aldwarke is in evidence is this view, taken on 10th October, of 150 132 forming a Sheffield–Cleethorpes service. Only the remains of the troublesome switch-diamond crossing can be seen. *Dr. Les Nixon*

◄The re-instated Swinton curve was opened to traffic on 12th March. This benefits Regional Railways, InterCity and Railfreight. Class 101 DMU (51495 + 51174) leaves the new curve behind at Mexborough East Junction whilst working a crew-training run on 16th March. *M.A. King*

WESTERN REGION MISCELLANY

►Following the completion of the Southampton–Portsmouth 'Solent Link' electrification project in May, the former Salisbury–Portsmouth DMU stopping service was discontinued and replaced in part by a new Bristol Temple Meads–Southampton all-stations diagram. This brought SR DEMUs to Bristol on a daily basis for the first time since 1977. On 26th September one of the eight surviving Class 207 units, No. 207 013, arrives at Westbury with the 11.48 Bristol–Southampton. The new '44' headcode replaces the '85' previously allocated to this route.   *Geoff Gillham*

▼►Following problems with the non-operation of track circuits, all Class 155 'Sprinters' were withdrawn from the Westbury–Weymouth route in May. A basic service was introduced using DMUs borrowed mainly from Plymouth Laira. Class 101/108 power twin set No. 879 arrives at Maiden Newton with the 15.05 Weymouth–Westbury on 3rd August. 'Sprinters' returned to the route two weeks later following the introduction of axle-counters at strategic points.   *Geoff Gillham*

▼Summer 1990 saw the return of the daily Class 37-hauled Cardiff–Weymouth working, this year using the rake of NSE-Livered stock displaced from Old Oak Common. Normally, the locomotive and coaches would spend all day in sidings at Weymouth. However, during the period up to 20th August, when 'Sprinters' were banned south of Castle Cary, they were used to form the 11.55 stopping service to Westbury. Locomotive and stock then returned as the 14.50 Westbury–Weymouth e.c.s., seen here nearing Cattistock on 3rd August with 37428 'David Lloyd George' leading.   *Geoff Gillham*

▲37428 is seen working the 08.03 Cardiff–Weymouth on the approach to Bradford-on-Avon on 22nd May.   *Mike Goodfield*

▼The Summer timetable saw many non-ETH Class 37s pressed into service by Cardiff Canton for services to Weymouth, due to a shortage of Class 37/4s. On 13th September, Departmental sector 37158 in pristine ex-works condition on its first run since returning to Canton after overhaul at Doncaster Works (the first of the class to be painted in the new 'Civil link' livery) approaches Clink Road Jn., Frome with the 08.03 Cardiff Central–Weymouth.   *Steve McMullin*

▲Taking the place of the usual convential DMU, Class 50 No. 50008 'Thunderer' calls at Yelford with the 12.57 Exeter St. Davids–Barnstaple on 28th June.   *Don Gatehouse*

▶Covering a 'Sprinter' diagram, Class 47 No. 47634 approaches Cwmbran with the 16.10 Cardiff–Manchester Piccadilly on 12th May.   *Steve Turner*

▼Class 20s were used 'top and tail' on the Matlock line for the part of the summer. 20070 leads the strange formation through Ambergate with a service to Derby on 14th August.   *L.A. Nixon*

▲Class 47 No. 47503 'The Geordie' passes Diggle with the 08.04 Newcastle–Liverpool on 18th March in the last full year of locomotive-haulage of Trans-Pennine services. The distant signal has since been removed. *A.J. Wook*

◄31400 is seen south of Shaw with the 09.40 Manchester Victoria–Rochdale–Oldham–Mancester Victoria–Blackpool North working on 9th June. *Paul Shannon*

▼Summer 1990 saw a further reduction in the number of loco-hauled services on the North Wales coast line. Apart from London Euston/Crewe–Holyhead workings, only the 09.44 Manchester–Llandudno and 17.04 return were booked for the loco-haulage on weekdays. Mainline-liveried 31423 'Jerome K. Jerome' waits at Llandudno with the 17.04 to Manchester on 13th July. *Geoff Gillham*

It had been hoped by BR that the start of the summer timetable would see these Class 158 DMUs on Glasgow–Edinburgh/Aberdeen routes. ScotRail was forced to use Class 156s instead, as the Class 47/7s and Mark 3 coaches had already been transferred to InterCity. These were obtained from Neville Hill, Leeds and Norwich. Other 156s were re-deployed from Aberdeen–Inverness services. As a result the Glasgow–Aberdeen service became hourly and was operated by two-car Class 156 units whilst four-or six-car sets became the norm for Glasgow–Edinburgh services.

This situation prevailed until 17th September when the first six-car Class 158 took over on the 07.00 Edinburgh–Glasgow Queen Street. On 1st October, the start of the winter timetable, all Glasgow–Aberdeen services were changed to Class 158 operation with their use on Glasgow–Edinburgh services following as units became available.

Delivery of the last ScotRail Class 158 by November permitted all remaining diesel locomotive-hauled services such as Edinburgh–Aberdeen and Glasgow/Edinburgh–Inverness to be converted to Class 158 operation. However, snowfalls at the end of December saw the 158s in trouble as they had no snowploughs or means of fitting them. Class 156s were therefore used as pilots on Glasgow/Edinburgh–Inverness services!

The transfer of Class 156s from Aberdeen–Inverness services to lowland services meant that loco-hauled services were re-introduced. Class 37/47 hauled trains, usually with three or four coaches, were often seen in the summer. In early May a Network SouthEast coach managed to find itself in one of the rakes.

Peak-hour services between Perth, Dundee and Montrose, plus summer dated extras between Ayr and Carlisle, and Glasgow and Ayr were also diesel-hauled. Sometimes a Class 26 would appear as motive power, sometimes even a pair of Class 20s.

Re-opening of the Ness Bridge on 9th May assured the future of the Far North lines. The new bridge was built of steel with two centre piers. The temporary Muir of Ord maintenance depot set up in 1989 closed as a result.

Route and service changes included the use of the Ladybank–Perth line for Inverness/Perth–Edinburgh trains. Girvan to Ayr local services were extended through to Kilmarnock. The introduction of a new Edinburgh–Stranraer service gave a connection for Stranraer at Glasgow off the London sleeper following the withdrawal of all Stranraer Sleeping car services.

▲Before the introduction of Class 156s in May and Class 158s in September and October, Class 47 locomtives soldiered on operating Glasgow Queen Street Edinburgh push-pull services. In this view, 47715 is seen approaching Polmont with the 11.30 from Glasgow to Edinburgh. Note that the train does not consist of a full rake of Mark 3 coaches. The date is 13th January.

▶With the end of push-pull working on the Glasgow–Edinburgh/Inverness routes came the end for the need of DBSOs on ScotRail. These vehicles were transferred to InterCity for use on Norwich–London Liverpool Street services. On 3rd May, a DBSO brings up the rear of the 13.30 Glasgow Quesn Street–Edinburgh at Falkirk High.

Max Fowler (2)

▲Class 47/7 No. 47701 heads the 07.25 Glasgow Queen Street–Aberdeen through Arbroath on 11th April.　　　*L.A. Nixon*

▼After having being worked by Class 156 "Super Sprinter' units since May 1989, the Aberdeen–Inverness route reverted to locomotive-haulage from May 1990, the Class 156s on the route being required on Glasgow–Edinburgh services. 47509 'Albion' pulls the 11.26 Aberdeen–Inverness away from Nairn on 15th June.　　　*Geoff Gillam*

▲Class 156 units 156 50   0 and 156 455 near Lenzie with the 10.00 Glasgow Queen Street–Edinburgh on 2nd May.   *Tom Noble*

▼A new hourly service linking Glasgow Queen Street, Stirling, Perth and Aberdeen was introduced with the May timetable. Borrowed Class 156s, rather than new Class 158s being used for the first six months. On 13th June, Ex-Norwich 156 468 climbs away from Perth forming the 13.32 Aberdeen–Glasgow.   *Geoff Gillham*

▶156 432 leaves Maybole station with the 12.18 Girvan–Kilmarnock on the first day of the new service which connects the Ayrshire coast and the Glasgow–Carlisle service at Kilmarnock. The date is 14th May.
Michael McGowan

▲ Class 158 DMUs made their long-delayed debut on Glasgow–Edinburgh services on 17th September slipping quietly into use without ceremony. On 21st September, three sets, led by 158 717, form the 10.00 Glasgow Queen Street–Edinburgh and is pictured passing Cadder Signalbox.
Tom Noble

◄158 712 is seen on the outskirts of Dundee with the 12.25 Glasgow–Aberdeen on 3 October during the first week of Class 158 operation on this route. *Tom Noble*

Near white-out conditions prevail at Dalwhinnie as Class 47 No. 47640 heads north with the 11.42 Edinburgh–Inverness on 1st March. *A.O. Wynn*

Railfreight

The division of Railfreight into two distinct business units – Trainload Freight and Railfreight Distribution – became firmly established in April 1990. Trainload Freight comprised the bulk sub-sectors Coal, Construction, Metals and Petroleum, whilst Railfreight Distribution continued to look after Freightliner and Speedlink networks as well as certain bulk flows such as chemicals and industrial minerals. Within Trainload Freight seven senior managers were appointed to report directly to the Managing Director, Leslie Smith. These seven comprised a national business manager for each of the four sub-sectors plus a business policy manager, a trainload services manager and a finance manager. The national business managers had their net revenue accountability sharpened by assuming sponsorship of the contracts with area operations managers and traction & rolling stock managers. This role had previously been co-ordinated by regional freight managers, whose posts were withdrawn.

SUCCESS AND DEFEAT

Railfreight's annual results published in Spring 1990 showed a large discrepancy between its two divisions. Trainload Freight acheived an operating profit of £132.8 million on a turnover of £516.7 million, lending credibility to its continuing re-investment in locomotives, rolling stock and infrastructure. Railfreight Distribution (RfD), on the other hand recorded an operating loss of £73.4 million on a turnover of £176.6 million. This poor performance was due to the worsening financial position of Speedlink which was found to be losing £30 million on a turnover of £45 million. An exhaustive review of Speedlink was commissioned, in which RfD exmained the viability of each fleight flow and considered ways in which costs might be reduced. The review makes depressing reading. No exisiting flow came anywhere near to covering its costs, and even if savings of 40% were to be achieved on running the present network, only 15% of flows became viable. RfD approached several thousand companies to see whether substantial new business could be acquired for Speedlink, but the response was pitiful. Rumours that Speedlink was to be abolished turned out to be well founded – the decision to abandon the wagonload freight network was taken in early December, for implementation in July 1991.

TRAINLOAD COAL

The pattern of coal supply to power stations underwent little change in 1990, thanks to the agreement which British Coal reached with National Power and PowerGen in November 1989. This agreement specified that only a limited increase in the use of imported coal would take place over the next two years. Of the trial ports used in 1989 the only one to become established as a major rail terminal in 1990 was Liverpool's Gladstone Dock. About half the coal burned at Fiddlers Ferry during 1990 came from this source.

Most of the coal supplied to power stations in the Aire and Trent valleys comes from Nottinghamshire, Yorkshire and the North East. From summer 1990, however, these traditional sources were supplemented by new long-distance flows of opencast coal from Scotland. Up to two trains daily were scheduled to run from each of two loading points – Blindwells near Edinburgh and Westfield in Fife – to York. Because of weight restrictions over the Forth Bridge, the coal from Westfield was conveyed in trainloads of 24 wagons as far as Millerhill, before being remarshalled into standard rakes of 36 wagons. From York the coal from both sources was distributed to power stations as required. The traffic from Blindwells alone was expected to amount to half a million tonnes in the first year of operation.

On 11th September the first trainload of colliery spoil arrived at British Coal's new multi-million pound terminal at Welbeck, near Wakefield. The Welbeck site was once used for coal mining and gravel extraction, and the material now being dumped here will help to restore the area to something akin to a natural landscape over the next thirty years. Between two and five trains a day have been programmed to run to Welbeck from Gascoigne Wood, the main railhead for the Selby mine complex. Each train consists of 47 HAA Hopper wagons, hauled by a single Class 56 locomotive.

Network Coal continued to contract in 1990. By the end of the year all household coal depots on the Southern Region had been closed – the last survivors were at Totton, Purley and Hove – and closures elsewhere in the country included Neasden, Cambridge, Oxford and Newport. Didcot yard, once the centre of Network Coal operations in the South East, was left with trip workings to only two depots, at West Drayton and Aldermaston.

TRAINLOAD CONSTRUCTION

Three-quarters of the business handled by Trainload Construction is aggregates for the construction industry in South East England. After several years of expansion this industry fell into sharp decline in 1990, and Trainload Construction was faced with a reduced traffic requirement on many of its routes.

The first half of 1990 was, however, marked by several successes. The firm Steetley, which had long eschewed rail transport, produced a new flow of roadstone from Whitwell, in north Derbyshire, to Witton, near Birmingham. The flow used exisiting sidings at both ends of the route and could thus be set up relatively cheaply. Three trains a week were incorporated into the timetable in May, and these were supplemented by a further one or two trains as required.

In London a new aggregates terminal was opened at Angerstein Wharf, operated by Bardon (London) Ltd and funded partly by a Section 8 Grant. Angerstein Wharf is situated on the eastern side of the capital and complements Bardon's other receiving terminal at Thorney Mill, near West Drayton. Traffic is received at Angerstein Wharf from Merehead and from Bardon Hill.

Other new roadstone flows in 1990 were Whatley–Slough, Mountsorrel–Cricklewood, Mountsorrel–Hythe, Marks Tey–Luton and Cliffe Hill–Luton. On the debit side, terminals at Aylesbury, Widnes and Pendleton were closed down during the year.

Following the successful short-term contracts to remove waste from Barking and Willesden to the Shanks & McEwan landfill site at Stewartby, a new flow was acquired from Chatham Dockyard in October 1990. This flow is expected to continue for twelve months, and requires a service of up to three trains daily from Hoo Junction.

TRAINLOAD METALS

A new block train service was introduced in early 1990 to convey imported steel from Boston docks to Round Oak and Brierley Hill steel terminals in the West Midlands. The traffic had previously been carried by Speedlink services, but Boston was deleted from the Speedlink network in January 1990 as part of Railfreight Distribution's rationalisation programme. The new Trainload Metals service gives a 24 hr turnaround of wagons and has attracted an almost fourfold increase in traffic.

The British Steel plant at Ravenscraig was much in the news in 1990, with the decision to cease production of steel coil early in 1991 and the possibility of total closure of the plant looming on the horizon. Coil traffic from Ravenscraig started to decline during the summer, but in its place came a new flow of slab steel from Ravenscraig to South Wales. The Metals timetable on the West Coast main line was recast in October, with all

the services between Scotland and South Wales running via Shotton (Dee Marsh Junction). Electric haulage was relinquished in favour of single or double-headed Class 37 traction, with the Mossend–Dee Marsh junction leg resourced from Motherwell and the Dee Marsh Junction–Llanwern/Margam leg resourced from Cardiff Canton.

British Rail's last operational hump marshalling yard, Scunthorpe West Yard, closed during the year. The yard was used almost exclusively for Metals traffic and it was found that the traffic could be handled more conveniently at Anchor exchange sidings, adjacent to the main 'C' entrance to Scunthorpe steel works. Another yard whose future came under discussion was Tinsley. This former hump yard had been removed from the Speedlink map in October 1989 and it survived in 1990 to cater for limited quantities of Metals traffic. With effect from January 1991, however, it was decided to shift the majority of Metals services from Tinsley to Aldwarke, and retain only a small group of sidings at Tinsley for trains to adjacent terminals.

Some rationalisation of terminals handling finished steel traffic was carried out during the year. Closures included Southampton Bevois Park, which was replaced by a more compact facility on the other side of the line, and Leeds Whitehall Road, which was uncomfortably close to similar terminals at Hunslet and Wakefield.

TRAINLOAD PETROLEUM

Two new petroleum flows were acquired in 1990. The first involved reopening part of the disused Staines West branch to serve an aviation fuel depot at Colnbrook. The purpose of the reopening was to give the smaller oil companies an independent means of access to Heathrow airport. The larger companies either have direct pipelines from refineries or else they use the Total rail terminal at Langley on the Western Region main line. The first train to Colnbrook ran on 1st March, and a weekly service was then operated from West Thurrock on North Thameside. This was later replaced by up to four weekly trainloads of fuel from Waterston.

The second new flow was liquid petroleum gas (LPG) from the expanding Wytch Farm oilfield in Dorset to a distribution terminal at Avonmouth. The new traffic was brought about because of the need for BP to market it increasing output of LPG over a wider area. The exisiting crude oil terminal at

Furzebrook was converted to become the LPG loading point whilst at Avonmouth BP invested £17 million in new discharge facilities. Up to two trains a day were scheduled to run from November 1990 onwards.

At the start of 1990 Trainload Petroleum still made extensive use of the Speedlink network to distribute petroleum products to BR fuelling points and certain other terminals. Where possible these flows were transferred to Trainload Petroleum services during the year. New trains were introduced in January between Fawley and South West England, between Ripple Lane and Canterbury. Further additions to the Petroleum network were a daily service from Ripple Lane to Stratford, Ferme Park and Old Oak Common, and a daily service from Immingham (Lindsey refinery) to Doncaster, Knottingley and Leeds.

CONTAINERS, CHEMICALS AND INTERNATIONAL

The Freightliner network saw only minor changes in 1990. One area of disappointment was the introduction of SNCF Multifret wagons on services from Parkeston (Harwich) Freightliner terminal. The intention was to run the wagons at 90 mph and carry inter-modal traffic from Parkeston to North West England and Glasgow. In the event the wagons were only authorised to run at 75mph, the service operated only as far as Garston, and on most occasions only a handful of conventional containers were carried.

New trainload flows from mainland Europe via the Dunkerque–Dover train ferry brought petfood to the Pedigree works at Melton Mowbray and bottled Evian water to a terminal at Neasden. Special trains also ran from Scunthorpe to Dover carrying steel for export.

In its Chemicals & Industrial Minerals section Railfreight Distribution introduced new trains from Immingham to Stalybridge, from Immingham to Stanlow, from Wilton to Langley Green, from Haverton Hill to Barry and from Saltend to Mostyn.

▼ Class 56 No. 56078 heads north on the West Coast main line near Leighton Buzzard with 6M66, the 06.30 Hoo Junction–Forders Sidings spoil train on 22nd December. The spoil comes from Chatham Dockyard which is being cleared for redevelopment.
Paul Shannon

NEW SERVICES

▲Between 11th and 15th June Seaham harbour received its first ever railborne consignment of steel pipes from Hartlepool. The pipes were tripped up the coastline from Hartlepool to Seabanks exchange sidings by a Thornaby Metals sub-sector locomotive. At Seabanks the wagons were handed over to Port of Seaham locomotive No 4, which propelled its load down into the harbour yard. This manoeuvre is illustrated on 14th June. A total of 80 BQW wagons were delivered to Seaham in this way, adding to the already buoyant steel section traffic which uses the port. *Michael Rhodes*

▼During the summer Ravenscraig steel works began to send steel slabs to South Wales in place of the traditional diet of hot-rolled steel coil. A special consignment of slabs approaches Oxenholme on Saturday 21st July, with traction provided by Class 90 No 90034. The same BAA wagons are being used that normally carry coil, and the train is running in the path of 6M24, the 05.25 Mossend–Dee Marsh Junction coil train. *Paul Shannon*

▲The rail connection to Whitwell quarry saw regular use in 1990, thanks to a new flow of limestone to Witton, near Birmingham. Initially the trains ran as specials, but in July a service of three trains per week was incorporated into the timetable. Class 56 No 56058 arrives at Whitwell on 17th August with 6D08, the 11.55 Witton–Whitwell empties. The wagons used for this traffic are four-wheeled PNAs owned by Tiger Rail. They are loaded and discharged by mechanical grab.   *Paul Shannon*

◀ Class 56 locomotives took their first ever regular duties in Scotland during the summer, hauling coal trains from Westfield and Blindwells disposal points to power stations in Yorkshire and Nottinghamshire. No 56106 arrives at Thornton Yard on 28th August with 36 empty HAAs, forming the 6Z74 special from Millerhill. The wagons will be taken up the branch to Westfield by a locally-based Class 37 locomotive.
Paul Shannon

◀The long-standing flow of lime from Tunstead to Margam for use in Port Talbot steelworks was replaced by a new flow from Hardendale (Shap) in 1990. A service of two trains a week was provided, routed via the North and West line through Shrewsbury. Class 37 no 37235 – officially a Network Coal locomotive – passes Sutton Bridge Junction on 3rd July with the 6Z35 special from Hardendale to Margam.
Don Gatehouse

▲ Class 47 no 47373 passes Southall on 19th April with 6Z74, the 11.00 Colnbrook–Ripple Lane special, conveying empty tank wagons from the recently opened aviation at fuel terminal at Colnbrook. The fuel had been loaded at the GATX storage terminal at Grays, and the empty wagons pictured here would be tripped back to Grays shortly after arrival at Ripple Lane Yard. This flow ceased during the summer, but was replaced by a more frequent and longer-distance flow from Waterston in West Wales, bringing pairs of Class 37s to the Colnbrook branch on a regular basis. *Paul Shannon*

▶ The Redland self-discharge train (SDT) continued to widen its sphere of operation in 1990. One unlikely destination was Hythe coal depot, on the Clacton branch. Class 56 No 56060 stands at Hythe on 24th February with the first ever SDT working to this location. Forty new SDT wagons were constructed during the year, bringing the total fleet size up to 160. An order was also placed with Powell Duffryn Standard for a rake SDT vehicles for use in France.
Michael J. Collins

▶ The Castle cement terminal at Curzon Street in central Birmingham, was reopened to rail traffic in 1990. This was a welcome move in an area of Railfreight which has seen a general decline over the last few years, with many terminals closing down or receiving reduced levels of traffic. The new service to Curzon Street comprised a weekly trainload from Padeswood, or Penyffordd in railway terms, hauled by a Trainload Construction Class 37/5 locomotive. On 30th July No 37682 passes Bescot with 6R63, the 12.35 Curzon Street–Penyffordd empties.
Paul Shannon

SERVICES WITHDRAWN

◄Network Coal services on the Southern Region at the Start of 1990 comprised three trains a week from Didcot to Purley and Hove, plus two trains a week to Eastleigh yard for Totton. Traffic levels declined during the year and Network Coal had little choice but to abandon its service in this part of the country. On Saturday 16th June Class 37 No 37274 passes Guildford with 6V04, the 10.10 Hove–Didcot, converying 14 empty HEA hoppers en route to the Midlands and South Wales. The train had been diverted via Dorking (Deepdene) and North Camp on this occasion due to the engineering work.   *David Brown*

▼Class 37 No 37896 stands next to Cwmbach ground frame at the northern entrance to Abercwmboi phurnacite plant on 6th August, whilst running round a special train of Cawoods containers from Ellesmere Port. The phurnacite plant had closed in March and the stockpile of processed fuel had diminished to only 5000 tonnes by the date of this photograph. *Michael Rhodes*

►In January 1990 all Speedlink services serving Westbury were withdrawn. The petroleum traffic which used to be carried by Speedlink was transferred to new Trainload Petroleum services. One of these runs from Ripple Lane to Frome and back and the other runs between Fawley and Plymouth (Tavistock Junction). Westbury yard is used as an interchange point for traffic from Fawley to Old Oak Common. Class 47 No. 47381 is pictured at Norton Bavant in the Wylye Valley with 6V62, the 10.56 Fawley–Tavistock Junction service. In the middle of the train are TSAs with bitumen from Fawley to Cattewater, whilst the TTAs at the front and rear are carrying fuel oil for BR depots at Old Oak Common and in the West Country.
                                    Steve McMullin

▲ Class 37 No. 37146 awaits departure from Radyr yard with the 7Z84 service to Alexandra Dock Junction on 28th March. A few weeks later Radyr lost most of its traffic when departmental and Network Coal services were transferred to East Usk Junction.
Michael Rhodes

► Class 08 No. 08942 shunts ballast wagons from Machen at East Usk Junction yard on 8th August. After closure of the Tidenham branch in March, Machen quarry became the only rail-served quarry in South Wales, and a new timetable was drawn up using East Usk Junction as a staging point. East Usk Junction also took over Radyr's Network Coal traffic in 1990, but at the same time lost its Speedlink services in favour of Cardiff Tidal.
Michael Rhodes

► Scunthorpe West yard was the last yard in the country to retain hump shunting. It was built in 1971 and had 19 sorting sidings which were used to handle the heavy steel traffic from Scunthorpe steel works. The yard had become an unnecessary liability in an age when most steel travels by the train-load, and it closed in May 1990. Its remaining duties were transferred to the more conveniently situated Anchor exchange sidings.
Michael Rhodes

WAGONS

One of the highlights of the year was the commissioning of twelve prototype steel-carrying wagons for Trainload Metals services. The order comprised four vehicles each of three different designs, with lengths of 19 m, 16 m and 13 m respectively. All three designs have a welded steel underframe and can be fitted with a flexible weatherproof cover if required. Two of the designs also feature a deep well with removable bolsters across it. This means that they can carry coil as well as plate steel. The new wagons were tried out on key metals flows around the country, and a full-scale order for one or more of the designs was expected to be placed early in 1991.

Other new railway-owned wagons were 45 small-wheel container flats for Freightliner services to and from Grain, and a batch of MEA open wagons for coal traffic in South Wales.

New privately-owned wagons to appear in 1990 included further Redland self-discharge hoppers, bogie hoppers for ARC, Tiger Rail (for hire to ECC), Bardon Hill Quarries, RMC and Marcon, and bogie tank wagons for Tiphook.

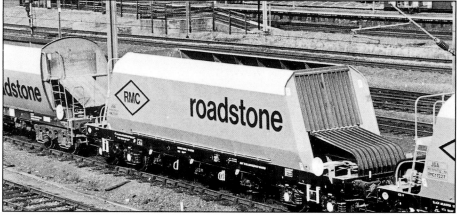

◄SNCF Mulfret wagon No 87 4572 236 stands at Harwich Parkeston Quay on 1st December. A fleet of 25 of these wagons found employment of Railfreight Distribution services between Harwich and Garston, but swapbody loads were rarely if ever to be seen. *Michael J. Collins*

▼Vacuum-braked MDV wagons survived in South Wales on local workings throughout 1990. Class 37 No 37695 waits at Maesteg on 11th September whilst its train is loaded with stockpiled coal for Newport docks. *Don Gatehouse*

◀Brand new BHA steel carrier No 962000 is pictured at Doncaster on 28th February. This is the medium-length variant of the three prototype designs; the shorter design is coded BGA and the longer one BJA.

anon

▶Following the successful operation of prototype vehicles, a production batch of 46 MEA open wagons were in fact conversions from redundant HEA hoppers, and their function was to replace MDV wagons on coal flows to terminals without hopper discharge facilities in South Wales. Class 37/5 No. 37699 winds its way up the valley from Ocean with a rake of MEAs forming the 10.18 Alexandra Dock Junction–Taff Merthyr service on 17th April. Deep Navigation Colliery is visible in the background.

John Chalcraft

◀JGA bogie hopper No RMC17226 stands at Peterborough on 31st October. This one of an order for 25 vehicles built by RFS Industries of Doncaster for use on limestone trains from Dove Holes quarry (Peak Forest). On the left-hand edge of the picture is an RMC hopper of earlier vintage – note the more rounded sides.

Allan Mott

▼Vintage wagons could still be found on some long-distance Trainload Metals services in summer 1990. Class 37/9 No 37901 crosses Poole harbour with 6V99, the 14.53 Hamworthy–Cardiff Tidal service on 14th August. The first and third wagons are BNXs whose design goes back to pre-Nationalisation days; the remainder of the train consists of BDA bogie bolster wagons which were originally built in the 1960s but fitted with strengthened frames and new air-braked bogies in 1978–81.

Paul Shannon

1990 was a year of disappointment for the Class 60. Whilst Brush fell only slightly behind its construction schedule at Loughborough, there were many problems to sort out before the locomotives could enter revenue-earning service. The first two Class 60s to be accepted into traffic were Nos 60017 and 60018 on 30th October – sixteen months after the first member of the class left the works site at Loughborough. The rate of acceptance improved during November, however, and by the end of the year BR owned a total of thirteen Class 60s, including ten based at Thornaby for Trainload Metals duties. Other highlights for RailFreight traction were the delivery of ARC's four Class 59 locomotives in October, and the acceptance of the last Class 90 locomotive, No. 90050, in August.

◀Class 59/1 No. 59102 is gently lowered on to its bogies to complete unloading at Newport docks on 20th October. All four locomotives were taken from here to Derby for testing before entering revenue-earning service in November. *Colin J. Marsden*

▲Class 59/1 No. 59102 passes Woodborough on its second day of working, 6th November 1990, with the 07.45 Whatley–Theale service. At the head of the train are some of ARC's recently delivered low track force wagons, designed to minimise the track damage on heavily used routes. With the introduction of the Class 59/1s increased loadings were possible on trains to Theale, Allington (combined with Chislehurst or Tolworth) and Dagenham (combined with Ardingly). *Mike Goodfield*

◄Almost the return of the freight to the Settle & Carlisle! During August Class 60 No. 60006 'Great Gable' made a number of training runs over S&C metals. Here it is seen approaching Garsdale with a rake of redundant coal hoppers on 30th August. *A.J. Woof*

▼Class 60 No. 60008 'Moel Fammau' is seen near Hatton with a Bescot–Banbury crew training run on 26 Spetember. *Bryan Hicks*

◀Blue Circle Cement took delivery of a new shunting locomotive for their works at Hope (Earles Sidings) in April 1990. Appropriately named 'Blue John', the locomotive was constructed by Hunslet-Barclay and carries works number Barclay 773/90. It is pictured hauling empty tanks from Earles Sidings to the cement works on 23rd May. Block train destinations served from Earles Sidings in 1990 were Northenden, Widnes, Dewsbury, Handsworth and Kirton Lindsey.

Les Nixon

TRACTION CHANGES

▲The winter timetable saw Class 90s employed on a number of Freightliner workings on the Anglia Region. A Mainline-liveried example heads a Parkeston–Ipswich working at Bradfield on the morning of 24th October. *Ian Cowley*

▼The replacement of loco-hauled trains by Sprinters led to many ETH-fitted locomotives being used on freight duties in 1990. Between 1989 and September 1990 Class 37/4 No. 37430 'Cŵmbran' was allocated to the Stanlow petroleum fleet, based for maintenance purposes at Immingham. This locomotive is pictured at Kirkham Abbey on 16th July with 7Z59, the 16.10 Scarborough–Stanlow empties.

Paul Shannon

▲Class 33 No. 33111 sets back into the oil siding at High Brooms after working the 10.30 feeder service from Tonbridge yard on 20th April. The traffic had been detached at Tonbridge from 6Y55, the Redhill–Canterbury West service, which had in turn fed out of an overnight service from Ripple Lane. From July the Canterbury and High Brooms tanks were worked direct from Ripple Lane, using Trainload Petroleum traction throughout and bringing to an end the regular use of Classes 33 and 73 on Southern Region oil trains.
Paul Shannon

Class 31 locomotives Nos. 31164 and 31293 prepare to leave Alexandra Palace sand terminal on 13th September with one empty JHA wagon for return to Fen Drayton via Kings Cross. From the October timetable change Class 56 traction was rostered on the Fen Drayton sand train, in common with many other Trainload Construction services in the London area. *Brian Denton*

▼Starting in April 1990 coal trains from Liverpool Gladstone Dock to Edge Hill were scheduled for haulage by four Class 20s, in order to enable a full load of 45 HAAs to be carried. On 26th May Nos. 20168, 20128, 20187 and 20052 run alongside Regent Road shortly before entering the docks with the early morning empties from Edge Hill. By the autumn the quadruple-headers had given way to pairs of Class 56s – still quite an impressive sight! *Paul Shannon*

▲Railfreight Distribution-liveried Class 90 No. 90042 approaches Warrington on 8th September with 6M24, the 05.25 Mossend–Dee Marsh Junction coil train. This was the final month of electric haulage for Metals trains on the West Coast main line. *Paul Shannon*

▼In November 1989 Railfreight Distribution's six Class 26 locomotives were transferred to Trainload ownership, and the members of the class could be seen on oil workings from Grangemouth throughout 1990. No. 26040 passes Greenhill Junction with empty tanks from Hawkhead on 14th May. *M.H. Fowler*

THE SPEEDLINK SCENE

▲A number of Speedlink services in the Central Belt of Scotland were regularly hauled by pairs of Class 20s in summer 1990. Eastfield's allocation was boosted in May by the transfer of eight such locomotives from Thornaby. Nos. 20137 and 20198 pass Lochgelly on 30th May with the 07.40 Mossend–Thornton Speedlink feeder service.
John Chalcraft

▲The Kronospan works at Chirk continued to receive timber from Brandon, Norwich and Ipswich in 1990. Chirk was initially served by a dedicated Speedlink trip from Warrington, but this train was withdrawn in July and replaced by a new trip working from Coton Hill yard, Shrewsbury. On the first day of the new arrangements, Monday 9th July, Class 47 No. 47238 Bescot Yard stands at Coton Hill with vans for Alscott and Donnington and 12 OTA wagons carrying timber for Chirk.
Paul Shannon

In January 1990 the final stage of 'Network 90' was implemented. this meant a modest reduction in Speedlink trip workings, with one or two areas such as Westbury and West London losing their Speedlink connections altogether. Of course the cutbacks of 'Network 90' paled into insignificance when the decision was taken at the end of the year to axe the Speedlink network completely in July 1991.

The volume of traffic handled by Speedlink declined in 1990 for a number of reasons. Firstly the bulk sub-sectors continued to transfer their wagonload traffic to their own dedicated services, such as Fawley–Plymouth petroleum. Secondly a number of customers abandoned using rail transport when it became clear that Speedlink had a limited future. Redland Rooftiles, for example, closed down their railheads at Acton, Brandon, Totton, Tiverton Junction, Cardiff, Rugby,

Gateshead and Plean. Thirdly the onset of recession began to take its toll on traffic levels in general during the latter half of the year.

Railfreight Distribution wishes to retain a high proportion of its international flows after the abolition of Speedlink, and is looking to create a dedicated network of services to and from Dover. Two depots for handling wagonload traffic between mainland Europe and North West England were opened during the year, at Warrington Dallam and at Bamber Bridge.

The Ministry of Defence uses the Speedlink network to transport stores between its depots. In autumn 1990 the conflict in the Gulf led to an increase in military traffic. This not only swelled Speedlink loadings in certain parts of the country but also led to the operation of a number of special trains, notably to the military ports of Marchwood and Ridham.

▲ Speedlink traffic to and from Aberdeen continued to justify the operation of two services in each direction each weekday. The daytime northbound service, 6A19 07.50 Mossend–Aberdeen is seen approaching Dunning on 30th August behind blue-liveried Class 47 No. 47003. This was one of approximately thirty Railfreight Distribution Class 47s to be placed in pool FDBT, indicating that its 'F' examination was overdue. *Paul Shannon*

▲ Class 47 No. 47283 passes Singleton, between Poulton and Kirkham, with the 6T64 Speedlink trip working to Blackburn on 3th September. The train is conveying two acid tanks from Salwick and one ferry van from Bamber Bridge, and its appearance at this unlikely location is due to the fact that trains may only depart from Salwick in a westerly direction. *Paul Shannon*

▼ Healthy Speedlink loadings between North West England and Scotland meant that the 20.15 Warrington–Mossend departmental service was often used to convey surplus revenue-earning traffic. On 18th July no less than eighteen revenue-earning wagons were included in the consist, which is pictured near Golborne behind grey-liveried Class 47 No. 47353. *Paul Shannon*

▲At Elgin East Yard on 26th September, Class 37 No. 37113 'Radio Highland' shunts a mixture of Railfreight vans carrying millitary traffic from RAF Lossiemouth. These will later form a special train to the south. Meanwhile No. 37209 arrives on the scheduled afternoon trip working from Aberdeen, comprising one timber wagon from Keith. *A.O. Wynn*

▼Speedlink withdrew from most terminals on the western side of London during 1990. Six traditional ferry vans form the consist of an Acton–Hayes & Harlington trip working on 4th June, most unusually hauled by Trainload Construction Class 56 locomotive No. 56040 'Oystermouth'. *David Brown*

TRAFFIC GAINED...

▲A new flow of propylene from Humber oil refinery to Stanlow was introduced during the year. Despite being sponsored by RfD (Chemicals & Industrial Minerals), the train was often hauled by a Trainload Petroleum Class 47 locomotive. On 30th May No. 47299 approaches Winwick Junction with 6E05, the Stanlow–Humber empties. *Paul Shannon*

▼ With the new trackwork leading to W.H. Bowker's terminal visible clearly in the foreground, Class 31 No. 31132 slows to a halt at Bamber Bridge with the morning delivery of one ferry van on 12th April. RfD's pool of Class 31 locomotives was disbanded in July and trip workings such as this were handled over to Class 47 haulage. *Paul Shannon*

▶The flyash traffic from Ratcliffe and West Burton to Fletton and Little Barford was under threat in 1990 and was expected to cease early in 1991, following the decision to use disposal points nearer to the two power stations concerned. Class 56 No. 56016 passes Frisby with empty CSA wagons for Ratcliffe on Tuesday 24th April. *Paul Shannon*

... AND LOST

▶Cement traffic from Tring ceased in May 1990. Laterly all that remained was a once-weekly train from Tring to King's Cross. The empties from King's Cross are pictured approaching Linslade tunnel behind Class 31 locomotives Nos. 31234 and 31134.

▼Class 37 No. 37214 leaves Cambridge Yard on 7th August with 6M03, the 03.40 Temple Mills–Toton Network Coal service. Cambridge coal depot closed in 1990 but Network Coal services continued to pass through the city on their way to and from Temple Mills and Letchworth.

Paul Shannon (2)

Parcels

The Parcels sector suffered a setback in May when the Royal Mail transferred its weekend traffic to road transport. At the same time all remaining Royal Mail services form London Bridge and Waterloo were withdrawn. The main reason given for the withdrawal of weekend trains was the prohibitively high cost of providing Post Office staff at stations. The Royal Mail's decision was bad news for BR because it meant that many expensive assets would now work only five days a week instead of seven.

Happier news came in July when the Parcel sector launched "Track 29"*, an overnight service for parcels and packages weighing more than 50 kg. Track 29 uses BR's existing network of 200 mail and postal trains to convey parcels between 29 key collection and delivery points. A fleet of 80 lorries provides connections to and from individual customers' premises.

The launch of the Parcels sector's new initiative was marked by the naming of Class 47 No. 47479 as 'Track 29'.

The most notable change to the Parcels sector's rolling stock fleet was the withdrawal of all Class 114 and Class 128 Diesel Parcel Units (DPUs) in October. Some of the Class 114 vehicles had only recently been converted for parcels use and fitted with Leyland engines, whereas the Class 128s were built as dedicated parcels units as long ago as 1959. Following the withdrawal of the DPUs all diesel-operated parcels trains reverted to locomotive-hauled operation.

This derives from the words of a Glen Miller hit of the war years:
"Pardon me boy, is that the Chatanooga choo-choo?,
Track 29. Boy you can give me a shine."

▲ Just a fortnight before parcels trains were withdrawn from London Bridge and Waterloo, Class 47 No. 47528 awaits the 'all clear' at London Bridge with the 15.58 empty van train to Tonbridge on 1st May.
Rodney Lissenden

◄ At 01.00 on 12th May, Class 31 No. 31421 stands at Ipswich after reversing back into the station with the 1E98, the 23.02 Liverpool Street–Peterborough/Norwich mail train. The train will be split here, with the front four coaches continuing to Peterborough behind the Class 31 and the rear two coaches being hauled by a Class 86 to Norwich. This was the last occasion that 1E98 ran. Postal traffic between Ipswich and Peterborough now goes by road.
Jonathan Cordle

▶Many locomtives and vans operated by the Parcels sector received a coat of red paint in 1990. TPO vehicle No. 80387 displays the latest variation of Parcels sector livery with yellow bodyside stripes and Royal Mail Travelling Post Office legend at Kidderminster on 1st May.

Fastline Promotions Limited

▼A mixed formation of parcels rolling stock, powered by Class 128 car No. 55992 and Class 114 unit Nos. 54902 and 55932, enters Stockport station on 17th July with 1G69, the 19.30 Manchester Piccadilly–Birmingham New Street mail train. All Class 114 and Class 128 vehicles were withdrawn in October.   *J.C. Hillmer*

▲In order to relieve platform congestion at Manchester Piccadilly, a number of parcels trains were amended in the May timetable changes to start back at Bolton. Scheduled departure times from Bolton were: 14.23 to Cardiff, 16.25 to London St. Pancras (via Crewe and Derby), 18.31 to Cardiff and 20.05 to Preston. Bolton only has one platform face available for the loading of parcels, so a fair amount of shunting takes place between each of the scheduled departures. Class 31 No. 31530 'Sister Dora' is pictured leaving Bolton with failed Class 47 No. 47543 and the 18.31 service to Cardiff on 19th July.   *Paul Shannon*

▲The 12.57 DPU train from Crewe South Yard to Cardiff seen at Marshbrook on 14th July with a train of Class 128 and 114 DPUs. All DPUs were withdrawn in October. *Geoff Bannister*

▼Fresh out of works after receiving a new cab and after being repainted from LNER apple green to Parcels red livery, 47522 'Doncaster Enterprise' passes Aristotle Lane, Oxford with the Gillingham–Preston parcels service. *Martin Loader*

Channel Tunnel Progress

◄On 1st December 1990, Britain was linked by land to the continent of Europe for the first time since the ice-age. Graham Fagg (left) and Philippe Cozette can be seen shaking hands following the breakthrough of the British and French service tunnels.

Eurotunnel

▼The two seen together after the hole had been enlarged so that Graham Fagg could join his colleague in the French tunnel.

Eurotunnel

The amount of space devoted in newspapers to the Channel Tunnel project fell as the year progressed. On the basis that 'no news is good news' this was a good thing and reflected the project's rapid progress. The emphasis gradually changed from tunnelling and its costs to layout, equipment and projected revenues. The latter seamed healthy for, despite the current recession, cross-channel traffic has continued its rapid growth.

Government inaction over a high-speed line to the Tunnel contrasted with Labour's plans for new line from Scotland all the way to Folkestone. Critics described this as typical over-commitment. The government hoped that BR, together with private companies, would effectively make a decision for them. Whilst stipulating strict environmental conditions on the construction of any new line, it stuck to the Section 42 ruling that no government assistance was available. Two companies realised that the 15% + return on capital needed to make a partnership with BR viable was unattainable and pulled out.

In contrast, money for road improvements in Kent was not a problem The government is spendind £800 million in the county, mainly on the M20/A20 and including the 23 km Ashford–Hollingbourne M20 'missing link'. BR was also unable to qualify for European Regional Development Fund or Transport Infrastructure Grants from the EEC. Government policy is to take into account any such grants when setting public expenditure levels and reduce support to the railways accordingly. BR is also still expected to achieve the same 8% rate of return on these grants. Apart from possible grants for Channel Tunnel project-related improvements, BR has come up against this 'additionality' barrier when hoping to electrify the North Wales Coast line to compete with the upgraded A55 Expressway.

▲In September, Transmanche Link staff celebrated the break-through of the north landward running tunnel at Holywell Combe. The tunnel boring machine can be seen in the background after having bored a distance of 8.1 km from Shakespeare Cliff.

Eurotunnel

CHANNEL TUNNEL PROGRESS

BUILDING OF THE CHANNEL TUNNEL

With continued round-the-clock operation and the benefit of more workers (bringing the total to about 9,000), better ground conditions, better tunnel boring machine reliability and accumulated experience, tunnel boring progress improved as the year went on. On average about 1.5 km (or 1% of the total distance) was bored each week. At the start of 1990, under one-third of tunnelling was complete, half being bored by May. The French had fewer problems meeting their boring targets in the early months of the year but the British later caught up. Talk began to change from distance bored to the rate of closure.

The service tunnel forged ahead and by August was 90% bored and lined. Billboard posters and newspaper advertisements started to appear all over Britain, in a campaign designed to increase public awareness of progress being made and showing the number of metres to be bored before the two service tunnels met – and before Britain ceased to become an island.

6th August saw the completion of 100 km of tunnelling, just under two-thirds of the total. Most of the remainder was undersea tunnelling which accounts for 77% of all boring.

September saw two milestones achieved: the breakthrough of the UK land running tunnel north to Holywell Coombe and the entry of the second UK marine running tunnel into the undersea crossover cavern 7.8 km out to sea.

CHERITON TERMINAL TAKES SHAPE.

As the terminal site needed to be level, over two million cubic metres of sand were used – transported from the expansive and infamous Goodwin Sands by an ingenious pumping technique. The excellent drainage characteristics of sand ensured that work progressed well on the terminal's foundations, even during the winter months. Earth noise bunds protect Newington and Peene villages from most noise and visual intrusion of the central terminal area and part of the Continental Main Line. Peene was probably noisier when trains used to travel along the embankment, still in situ, that once carried the Folkestone–Elham–Barham–Canterbury line!

As the year went on, the main thrust of activity gradually changed from earthworks to work on the structures such as the shuttle loading/ unloading ramps, overbridges and platforms – representing part of the 'lump sum works'. This was mirrored on the French side at Coquelles, a site three times larger than Cheriton due to the more accommodating local geography there.

By September, the short cut-and-cover section of tunnel at Holywell (between Castle and Sugarloaf Hills) was fully submerged before final landscaping and the start of work on the new A20 road extension to a point between Capel-le-Ferne and Dover where the existing A20 will be rejoined. The trunk road will be built above the cut and cover section, rising on a viaduct before disappearing in a tunnel under Round Hill.

The writer was lucky enough to be shown around the 600-metre Castle Hill tunnel sections, bored months previously by roadheader machines using the 'new Austrian tunnelling method'. Short lengths of tunnel had been excavated and sprayed with quick-drying concrete. Work was almost complete on constructing a final concrete lining. It is difficult to comprehend the scale of the project, the scene reminiscent of the grand underground sets in the science fiction film 'Total Recall'!

LOWER SHAKESPEARE CLIFF GROWS

During the year more tunnel spoil was deposited in the specially-constructed lagoons. A new strip of land 1.5 km long and 125 metres out to sea is nearing completion. By 1993, only a few ventilation and maintenance buildings will be sited on this new piece of land formed from 3.75 million cubic metres of (mainly chalk marl) spoil; a nature reserve may also be established.

At the end of October, an exploratory probe from the British to the French boring machine made contact, heralded by Eurotunnel as the first land connection since the Ice Age. Just over one decade after Norman Fowler – then transport secretary – invited fresh proposals for a Channel Tunnel project (and 188 years after Napoleon approved the first plans for a wood-lined tunnel) the dream became reality.

November saw the completion of all underland tunnelling, with the historic breakthrough in the service tunnels taking place on 1st December; this was achieved two weeks ahead of schedule, earning TML another bonus.

By the end of December, track had advanced from Dollands Moor into the terminal itself. Around 46 km of track will be required for the 420-acre site, including an eight-track platform area, a two-track shuttle loop and three of four on the Continental Main Line.

CHANNEL TUNNEL SAFETY

In March the five British companies in Transmanche-Link (Costain, Balfour Beatty, Tarmac, Wimpey and Taylor Woodrow) were fined £10,000 for failing to take reasonable steps to ensure safety following the death of a fourth worker on the British side of the tunnel. By May, the British operation had claimed six lives; the French Transmanche consortium's safety record was not as bad – two deaths since the start of tunnelling.

In July, The Health and Safety Executive (HSE) decided to prosecute TML for the fourth time over the death of a worker in October 1989. More recent accidents were still under investigation. The HSE also highlighted "the risk of catastrophic loss" after an inquiry into TML's safety precautions. There was criticism of poor safety procedure, safety training and management practice.

The death toll of eight by the autumn compared with 33 deaths on the 17-year Seikan tunnel project in north Japan, finished in 1987.

In October, ferry passengers at South Coast ports were handed leaflets warning them of the potential fire risk of using the Channel Tunnel, when opened. The 150,000 leaflets were distributed as part of a Fire Brigade Union campaign against plans to allow travellers to stay with their cars during the journey. The union claimed that a fire could occur if people ignored no-smoking signs in confined areas. Eurotunnel responded by reminding the union that the intergovernmental commission overseeing safety had given permission for their plan. The commission, incidentally, includes representatives from such bodies as the HSE and the Railway Inspectorate.

CHANNEL TUNNEL FINANCE

Arguments over finance continued. The relationship between Eurotunnel and contractors Transmanche-Link remained strained.

Eurotunnel's estimate of the Tunnel's completion cost was increased to £7.66 billion. In accordance, the company arranged a new ceiling of £8.5 billion in loans and equity for the project.

By the end of the year, tunnelling was over four-fifths finished and 70% paid for; 60% of the work on the terminals had been done and was within budget; 38 out of the 42 packages for fixed equipment had been placed and half the trains had been ordered. The scope for further cost escalations was more limited.

BR PREPARES FOR CHANNEL TUNNEL SERVICES

Passenger Services

Most of Kent's railways were originally built on the cheap. This fact, combined with years of neglect means that much work is required to bring track and signalling up to a reasonable standard.

Track work started at London Waterloo on the site of the former Windsor line suburban platforms on the northern side of the station. £98 million is being spent on the new terminal

ere. The new Stewarts Lane Chord began to take shape, to link South Western tracks with the classic route from London Victoria to Folkestone and Dover. Work also started on the e-design of certain important juctions and track layouts, for nstance between Chiselhurst/Bickley and Petts Wood in outh-east London. Further from London, work was underway o increase the maximum speed between Tonbridge and Dolands Moor from 90 mph to 100 mph.

Signalling contracts were issued as part of the £80million Kent Coast resignalling protect which covers the line between Chislehurst and Dover. This incorporates a new IECC signalling centre at Ashford, replacing seven existing signal boxes.

North Pole Maintenance Depot

Land was cleared in advance of construction of the £75 million depot. Class 373 'Three Capitals' trains will reach this site via another new link line, the Sheepcote Chord.

FREIGHT

New freight loops were started at Borough Green, Otford and Headcorn, as was work on the Tonbridge–Redhill Line. On a more general note, approval was given for the fleet of 30 dual-voltage Class 92 freight locomotives.

In December, Railfreight Distribution announced the site for its first international freight terminal for Channel Tunnel traffic. 'Port Wakefield' is a 200-acre site which includes the former Normanton locomotive shed. RfD has entred a three-way partnership with AMEC Regeneration and Wakefield City Council in an initial £22 million investment. Up to £175 million could eventually be invested.

One of the experimental Alsthom-designed bogie fitted with Brecknell-Willis third-rail shoegear under Trans-Manche Super Train bogie test vehicle 83301, converted from former Class 33/1 locomotive 33115.

David Brown

▼The site of North Pole depot on 22nd September with the North Pole Jn.–Old Oak East Jn. curve, which is to be taken out, in the foreground. In the background can be seen an HST on the 09.30 London Paddington–Pembroke Dock 'Pembroke Coast Express'.

Brian Morrison

▲Work proceeding on the new Waterloo International Terminal. The roof covering five of the old platforms is going and the arches on which Waterloo has stood for over 100 years have been exposed as foundation work pushes ahead. *B*

◄An aeriel view of Holywell Coombe and the Folkestone Terminal site, looking eastwards towards the tunnel portal.
Eurotunnel

The Shakespeare Cliff site on 8th October.

Rodney Lissenden

The Cheriton terminal of the Channel Tunnel takes shape with the running track bed and platforms now apparent. The photograph was taken from the tunnel portal on 8th October.

Rodney Lissenden

CHANNEL TUNNEL PROGRESS

CHANNEL TUNNEL RAIL LINK

On 14th June the government announced that it was unwilling to offer financial support towards construction of the European Rail Link (BR/Eurorail) high speed line between Folkestone and London. The two members of Eurorail, Trafalgar House and BICC immediately announced their withdrawal from the joint venture to revert to consultant and contractor status. The development of the £2.6 billion 68-mile high speed line therefore reverted to a purely public sector project. London–Paris projected journey times were back to three hours.

The future of the link had been complicated by the continuing dispute between European Rail Link and the SNCF over the sharing of revenues from international rail services. Under an agreement signed in 1987, the SNCF would take up to 80% of passenger revenues and BR 20%; on the planned opening of the high-speed line in 1998, Eurorail had wanted those percentages reversed.

The Folkestone–North Downs section of route would be 'safeguarded' and BR would continue to provide compensation for homeowners affected by planning blight along the whole of the route. A heated debate followed the announcement in the Commons. The Opposition pointed out that government thinking was at odds with that of industrialists and even the editors of the quality newspapers. It was also mentioned that the SNCF had just announced a £19.5 billion plan to build an extra 2000 miles of high speed railways over the next 20 years, including one from Paris to Strasbourg.

In its defence the government tried to highlight spending – almost £2 billion – on upgrading road and rail links in readiness for the Tunnel's opening in June 1993, mostly on rail. Eurorail, it said, had been asking for: £900 million in government grant and extra BR investment (to operate high-speed commuter services over the line); and a £1 billion 'soft loan' (on which interest payments would not start until 2010). The cost to the taxpayer was both too high and too risky. If the government reduced BR's required rate of return and provided the public funding being demanded there would be allegations of indirectly subsidising the private sector consortium. In response to Labour's criticism, the government accused the Opposition of irresponsible spending pledges.

Government critics insisted that the Eurorail consortium had only wanted £400–£700 million. John Prescott, opposition transport spokesman accused the prime minister of promising strict environmental modifications to the proposed line in the run-up to the 1989 Kent County Council elections so turning a profitable project into an unprofitable one. He wanted to see the abolition of Section 42 of the Channel Tunnel Act (1987) which prohibits public investment in international rail service-related infrastructure. Ironically, Labour MPs, backed by the National union of Seamen had originally insisted on the Section 42 rule! He also wanted to see a quick decision on the high speed line's alignment and the construction put out to competitive tender, both of which should have been done months ago he reminded the government. He urged Cecil Parkinson to accept European Infrastructure Fund support for the project. (Continued planning blight in Kent was also mentioned in the ensuing debate.)

The announcement came as no surprise. The government had seemingly been trying to prepare the public for the decision, there being 'leaks' to the newspapers and statements belittling the importance of the Tunnel for international trade. The government had said that only 6% by weight of Britain's trade will pass through the Tunnel(including bulk oil). Trade by value was not chosen. For instance, the Port of Dover currently handles almost 3% of trade by weight but 18% by value. The government went on to dismiss the Channel Tunnel as effectively only being the twelfth largest 'port' in the UK. The Tunnel would, Alastair Morton insisted, be important for non-bulk trade with considerable 'added value'. It has been estimated that up to 30% of unitised (i.e. containerised) trade could end up passing through the Tunnel.

Some aspects of the link were clearer: the ultimate destination was King's Cross making the station an important junction rather than a terminus; the Folkestone–'North Downs' (more specifically, Upper Halling near Rochester) section was practically certain; at some point, a high-speed line would be needed to prevent passenger growth from causing sclerosis on existing routes.

The BR review of the Upper Halling–King's Cross section would take some six to nine months to complete and would concentrate on maximising benefits to Kent commuters (therefore not ruling out government subsidy). Sir Robert Reid still hoped the high-speed line would be completed in 1998.

On 13th September, initial planning directions safeguarding BR's proposed route between Folkestone and Upper Halling were announced. BR would therefore have to be consulted on all applications for planning permission and new proposals which fall within, or affect, the 240-metre wide rail corridor. Safeguarding would not prejudice the review of the two alternative routes proposed by Ove Arup and Rail Europe.

BR also disclosed plans to meet environment objections to the proposed route. The main changes to plans drawn up in 1989 were in the Boxley valley, 2 km north of Maidstone. Instead of tracks at ground level, a large viaduct would be built. Generally, there would be more landscaping around the whole line and less agricultural land taken in its construction.

Meanwhile, in France work on the £2 billion 324 km TGV Nord line progressed, the route following that of most of the A1 autoroute between Lille and Paris. Planning has been relatively easy with the line crossing the deserted plains of Picardy and parts of the Ile de France. The extension from Lille into Belgium, incidentally, received a £290 million boost from the EC steel loan fund, European steel to be used in its construction.

By the end of the year it was apparent that BR's plans for a limited passenger service from Scotland and the North around London to Paris and Brussels were in disarray. BR said that work solving 'technical problems' on the more complex trainsets (numbering seven) would result in a delay in their introduction. Plans for a token ECML/WCML–London Waterloo (via the West London Line and the Sheepcot Chord) HST service as an interim measure therefore emerged. Scottish and Northern passengers would still have no option but to change trains at London Waterloo before their onward journey to the Continent. BR was, once again, underestimating the attractions of through services.

DEVELOPMENTS AT KING'S CROSS

Even though no firm decision had been made on a high-speed line from the Channel Tunnel to King's Cross, planning negotiations for what will be the biggest inner-city redevelopment in Europe continued. BR faced a setback when Barts Hospital trustees defended their ancient rights to the part of the 54 acres of land sold to the Great Northern Railway between 1846 and 1852. Barts could claim the part of the site that would not continue in railway use i.e. those areas destined for office, shopping and leisure development. The judgement undermined the value of the land to BR and the London Regeneration Consortium, so jeopardising the financing of the new £500 million station. Negotiations would continue.

In July, BR gained parliamentary approval for its international terminal at King's Cross and the redevelopment of 130 acres of nearby under-used land. BR's attempts to pressure the four MPs in the Private Bill committee "verged on being a contempt of this House." Such lobbying and 'unattributable' press briefings amounted to 'misinformation', the committee's report continued.

The committee attached conditions and amendments to the Bill and deleted a clause which would have allowed developers to demolish any buildings, listed or not. In addition, a satisfactory answer to traffic problems would have to be found before the Bill gets Royal Assent.

Irish Pictorial

▲Withdrawn CIE 'C' Class No.208 en route to Vic Berry's at Leicester for cutting up on 27th July. *A.O. Wynn*

▼The Irish Traction Group's 'Last Resort' railtour at Bangor with NIR 101 about to return to Belfast. NIR was at the other end of the train having hauled it on the outward journey. *Steve Turner*

Safety & Accidents

THE CLAPHAM AFTERMATH.

The British Railways Board submitted a progress report to the Department of Transport on 19th February. In the report, BR said that it had made progress on all but two of the 71 railway recommendations in the report by Sir Anthony Hidden QC, published on 7th November 1989. The increased External Financing limit for 1990–91 announced on 26th July was to help BR maintain its investment programme and to meet Hidden Report recommendations. BR published a second progress report in mid-August, Fifty-two of Hidden's recommendations had been put into effect.

Legal repurcussions continued. In May, the Director of Public Prosecutions announced that there would be no prosecutions of individuals connected with the tragic event. However, in September an inquest decided that those who died were unlawfully killed. On 20th November the Department of Transport announced that the Railway inspectorate would be prosecuting the British railways Board for alleged breaches in Sections 2 and 3 of the Health and Safety at Work Act 1974: it had failed to ensure the safety of its employees and had put passengers at risk.

SAFETY MEASURES

Installation continued of cab radios during the year. Two other measures realting to safety reserve special mention:

Automatic train Protection (ATP).

February saw the awarding of contracts worth £10 million to develop and supply two ATP systems. The Clapham and Bellgrove accidents merely precipitated matters as BR had been investigating such safety systems, for installation between London Marylebone and Aylesbury/Bicester, and on the Class 165s to run on the route. ACEC Transport received the other order for its TBL Track Beacon system for use on the London Paddington–Bristol route.

Data Recorders.

BR confirmed in October that it had chosen the 'Teloc 2200' 'black box' for installation in part of the EMU fleet operated by NSE. Hasler (GB) would supply more than 500 recorder at a cost of £3 million in this initial contract.

THE BELLGROVE AFTERMATH.

The Railway Inspectorate's report on the Inquiry into the accident at Bellgrove Junction, Glasgow, on 6th March 1989 was published just over a year later on 15th May 1990. The immediate cause of the accident had been that the Springburn bound train passed a danger signal at Bellgrove Station.

The inspectorate recommended the speedy introduction of a system of ATP. Whilst calling for checks on certain operating procedures and the performance of new drivers, the report confirmed the basic safety of single-lead junctions. After the report's publication, Scotrail said that it was examining the siting of the signal at Bellgrove station and introducing trap points at the junction. Wording in the rule book might also be clarified.

BRIDGE SAFETY.

In May BR ordered extra safety checks on over 500 bridges as a result of the Glanrhyd Bridge Collapse which occured on 19th October 1987. The safety checks immediately followed a Railway Inspectorate report which criticised the lack of knowledge amongst engineers about the effect of flooded rivers on bridge foundations. Following the February 1989 collapse of the Ness Viaduct BR had instigated a 13-point standard inspection and assigned a flood safety level to each bridge.

▲Class 47/4 No. 47461 was damaged after a shunting accident at Liverpool Lime Street on 18th November 1990, when it hit BG 92020 whilst backing onto the stock of the 13.30 to London Euston. The driver was in the other cab at the time and was not injured. The 47 was not so lucky and never worked again.
Richard Bolsover

▲A close-up of accident damage sustained by 31107 whilst working in an engineering occupation on the Scarborough line near Malton on 4th February. The photograph was taken at York LIP after the locomotive had been made fit to travel to Doncaster for repairs.
B.J. Nicolle

ACCIDENTS

Luckily, there were no major accidents of the Clapham or Purley magnitude during 1990. There were however a number of smaller accidents involving passenger trains as follows:

●**1st March, Stourbridge.** The 14.46 shuttle from Stourbridge Junction to Stourbridge Town crashed through the buffer stops at Stourbridge Town. The accident was similar to that on 21st January 1989. The Class 121 power car involved was 55034.

●**1st August, Reading.** The 07.02 Tonbridge–Reading DMU collided with the eight-coach 09.24 Reading–London Waterloo, about to leave platform 4b. The driver of the Tonbridge train was trapped. Forty passengers suffered injury or shock.

●**3rd August, Stafford.** The 22.18 Manchester–Penzance was hit from the rear end at Stafford by a Class 310 EMU No. 310 102 forming the 22.36 Stoke–Soho carriage sidings ECS. The driver of the EMU was killed.

●**23rd August, Hyde.** The 09.33 Rose Hill–Manchester Piccadilly DMU (LO 265 – 51913/54497 with 51913 leading) collided with the 09.36 Manchester Piccadilly–Sheffield (CH 351 – 51418/59688/53977) on the single-lead junction 200 metres to the north of Hyde North Junction. 25 people were injured.

●**23rd October, Milngavie.** Three rail staff and several passengers were injured when the 17.39 Springburn–Milngavie EMU struck a stationary and empty three-car Class 303 EMU at the terminus. The incident followed a week of engineering work in which Westerton Junction, which takes the Milngavie branch off the Aidrie–Helensburgh main line, was converted to a single-lead junction. These track alterations were part of the £18.5 million North Clyde scheme to improve track & signalling and reduce operating costs.

DOOR SAFETY.

By December there was growing concern about the number of people that had died by falling from high speed trains. A succession of such deaths in 1990 particularly on the West Coast Main line at Tamworth brought matters to a head. John Prescott, opposition transport spokesman pressed the government into admitting that there had been 92 deaths and 68 serious injuries in 1985–89 alone.

Following an incident on 30th October 1990, in which a BR guard fell to his death, a memo was sent to depot managers asking them to check doors, locks and hinges.

◄The scene at Reading on 1st August showing vehicles 51062 (Class 119 unit L 576) and 76644 (Class 423 unit No. 3117) entangled after the collision.
Duncan Street

LICKEY INCLINE DERAILMENT

In the early morning of 17th November Class 37 No. 37197 tried to bank the 01.00 Gloucester to Bescot Speedlink service up the Lickey incline. Unfortunately it lost its grip on wet rails and the whole train slid back over the catch points, derailing itself and four tankers.

▲37197 plus the last tank wagon as derailed. *Stephen Widdowson*

◄It was dark by the time rerailing commenced. *Don Gatehouse*

▼The laying of the first replacement sleepers on the Sunday. *Don Gatehouse*

he year was a difficult one for LUL with property development at a standstill and fewer travelling due to the recession. Measures were taken to cut the system's 'overspend' by reducing costs.

Parts of the system appeared cleaner and statistics showed that new technology and greater safety investment were combining to reduce crime. Automatic ticket gates became more acceptable to the travelling public and fraudulent travel was reduced.

There remained a huge gap between people's overcrowded and costly jouneys by Underground in 1990 and the promises of better things to come. Investment was authorised to increase sharply but this was against a background of years of neglect.

LONDON REGIONAL TRANSPORT/LONDON UNDER-GROUND ANNUAL REPORT 1989/90

In 1990 London Regional Transport decided to become London Transport (LT) and to re-draft the red roundel as its corporate symbol. For the first time, the Annual Report included a section on safety. In the specific case of the Fennell Report into the 1987 King's Cross fire, practically all of the 27 recommendations for action by LT or London Underground had been, or were in the process of being implemented.

Sales reveune for the London Underground remained the same as the previous year in real terms at £503.6 million. Industrial action in the summer of 1989 affected both sales revenue and passenger volume.

Inflation and additional staff to meet safety requirements increased costs. The resulting profit on operations, down on 1988–89, was insufficient to cover depreciation and renewals of £153.7 million. From this came a loss before grants of £123.6 million. Loss after grant was £20.7 million.

Investment expenditure during the year totalled £703.3 million. Major items were continuing Central line modernisation and safety improvements.

THE YEAR IN DETAIL

Expansion of the system was again in the news this year. The possibility of the Northern Line extending beyond Mill Hill East to serve a sports stadium at Copthall was announced in July. This would use part of the existing trackbed, once part of the GNR towards Edgware. Another extension, that of the East London Line announced last year, is to get £50 million private funding from developers London & Edinburgh Trust and Grand Metropolitan, although a substantial input from the government is still needed in order for a go-ahead.

Perhaps the most ambitious scheme to date, the East-West Crossrail from Liverpool Street to Paddington, a joint project between London Underground and Network South East, was approved by Cecil Parkinson, with construction to begin in 1993. However, the Jubilee Line extension, also announced last year, was feeling financial problems which may cause a reduction in the number of stations to be built on the line.

Changes to the underground map are afoot, which will redesigned to enable easy incorporation of new extensions to the system as they appear. Two new colours appeared during the year, salmon pink for the Hammersmith & City and orange for the East London Line.

Service alterations included a useful extension of all Uxbridge an Amersham trains beyond Baker Street to Aldersgate in May, a facility previously only available during the peak hours. Fairlop, on the Central Line, opened at weekends from 21st April, while other station news included a £1 million facelift to St Johns Wood and the announcement of plans to enlarge Tottenham Court Road, Holborn and London Bridge, presently very congested. The first two will be on the proposed Crossrail route referred to above. Work has also started on a new station and bridge at Hillingdon, to replace the present wooden station. Mention should perhaps also be made of High Barnet, winner of the LU Station Garden Competition for the fourth consecutive year.

An interesting development is the setting up of a new power company, MetroPower, with the intention of supplying electricity for both the Underground and commercial sale. This new company is a joint venture between London Underground, Scottish Power PLC and VEBA Kraftwerke Ruhr AG (VKR), the latter one of Germany's largest generators and distributors of electricity. The underground's existing electricity generating stations at Lots Roads and Greenwich will will be leased to the new company and re-equipped for their new roles.

A new equipment overhaul workshop was officially opened at Acton on 2nd October. With the gradual reduction of train overhaul being undertaken at Acton Central works, most of it having being transferred to the various Underground depots, it has decided in 1984 that a purpose-built facility was required for associated equipment, much of it of a specialist nature. The following activities are undertaken;

- The fitting of new wheels and the overhaul of axle bearings and drive gears.
- Seat repair and upholstery.
- Repair and overhaul of electrical and pneumatic equipment.
- Traction motor overhaul.
- Sheet metal work, welding and blacksmithing.
- Repair and servicing of electronic equipment.
- A machine shop to manufacture replaceable parts.
- General workshop support.

1990 was definitely a year for the enthusiast. Following last year's steam workings celebrating the centenary of the Chesham branch, further steam runs were organised between Harrow-on-the-Hill and Amersham on 21st/22nd and 28th/29th July, with Metropolitan No. 1, GWR 9466 and BR Standard 2–6–4T 80080 performing the honours. It was also intended that 'SARAH SIDDONS', the former Metropolitan Railway electric locomotive, would provide the necessary air pressure for braking purposes. However, repairs that were required could not effected in time, resulting in the substitution of battery loco L44. Passenger accommodation was provided by two BR departmental coaches (DB 977547/977588), on long-term loan to LU and 4-car EMU 305 315 from the LT&S section of Network South East.

The runs were a great success, with most trains running fully-booked. Several special mid-week runs were also made, including an evening trip up the Stanmore branch on the 26th. with No. 1 and L44. Even more remarkable was the appearance of No. 1, in steam, with L44 again, sandwiching the two departmental coaches on the Circle Line en route to the openday at Upminster on 5th August, where they performed on a shuttle service to and from Upney.

There were other open-days to enjoy; first off the mark was the Piccadilly Line depot at Northfields on 27th May. There was no steam on show, but plenty of tube stock to clamber about on, while 'SARAH SIDDONS' was also present, as was some preserved surface stock, namely R49 DM car 22679 and Q35 trailer 08063. Northern line 1956 stock 4-car set 1008+2008+9009+1009 provided a shuttle service between Acton Town and Northfields station.

The Central Line's Ruislip depot opened its doors to the public on 28th October. 'SARAH SIDDONS' was again on hand, as was No. 1, this time at the other end of a two coach set with 'Deltic' D 9000 – some combination! Sister D 9016 ws also to be seen.

Finally, Morden depot, on the Northern Line, was opened

►The first contracts for the complete refurbishment of over 14 trains were announced in April, with the Coventry-based engineering firm, Tickford, in association with Vic Berry at Leicester winning a £54 million contract to deal with the 1967/1972 stock. Victoria Line driving motor car 3158 is pictured at Vic Berry's yard on 5th August. *John Stretton*

◄The new Central Line stock was unveiled in mock-up form in April at DCA design consultants, warwick. A number of features have been incorporated into the design, including a better quality public address system, end car windows and improved lighting. Dot-matrix destination displays are also a feature. *Colin Marsden*

▼The interior view showing the deep windows and improved handrails. *Colin Marsden*

over the week-end 3rd/4th November, access provided by a 4-car set of 1938 stock. As might have been expected, all displays of undergound stock were, confined to tube gauge, with several visitors from other lines. However, outside on a low-loader was Brighton 'Terrier', SUTTON from the Kent & East Sussex Railway, and inside nearby was a representative from London's other underground line, the Post Office Railway, in the shape of 532, 'THE LONDON FLYER', built by Hunslet and Greenbat in 1982. The event also provided an opportunity for Network SouthEast director Chris Green to hand over the five cars of Isle-of-Wight stock to London Undergorund managing director Denis Tunnicliffe, which will provide a second heritage train.

The first heritage train unveiled on 19th July, in fact a six-car train of Northern Line 1959 stock (1044+2044+9045+ 1045+1030+2030), refitted and painted to 1920s style (and very nice too). It continues in daily service and is also available for private hire.

This unveiling was part of the outgoing centenery celebrations of the 'Tube', the then Prince of Wales opening the City & South London Railway between King William Street and Stockwell in 1890. A special exhibition is being staged at the London Transport Museum at Convent Garden, to reopen until October 1991.

Another, less spectacular, event was the unveiling of a commemorative plaque by transport secretary Cecil Parkinson, to celebrate 21 years of the Victoria Line on 7th March – the line having been opened from Walthamstow Central through to Victoria on that day in 1969. At Arnos Grove, Piccadilly Line, part of the station building, itself a listed structure, was reopened on 16th February to house an exhibition on the life and work of architect Charles Holden, designer of many of the underground stations as the system expanded during the 1920s and 30s.

A new – and welcome – livery for trains was announced in July; red front, white with blue skirt, interesting in view of British Rail's seeming obsession with yellow fronts. The effect is more than merely cosmetic as a number of internal improvements are also being made such as better lighting and the use of fire-resistant materials. The scheme will take up to four years at an estimated cost of some £40 million. The first contracts were awarded in April. Vic Berry, in association with Tickford were tackling the 1967/72 stock while the C69/77 stock was to be handled by RFS Industries, Doncaster. Meanwhile, a mock-up of part of a new Central Line car was to be seen in April, commissioned by BREL and built by DCA Design consultants, Warwick. It was subsequently moved to feature in the Tube Centenery Exhibition at Convent Garden. The 85 new trains will be introduced between 1991/5.

The District Line experienced well-publicised problems in July, when a motor broke loose from its mounting in a train of D Stock and subsequently caused a severe reduction in the service. Other members of the fleet received necessary modifications.

ACCIDENT AT CHORLEYWOOD

On 16th May, a runaway wagon killed four track workers between Chorleywood and Rickmansworth on the Metropolitan line of the London Underground. An internal inquiry found that none of the three braking systems (parking brake, rail anchor or wheel scotches) were used to secure the wagon which had been left unattended at Chorleywood station. The inquiry recommended improved management, procedures and communcations.

▲The first so-called heritage train was launched at East Finchley on 19th July and was a six-car train of Northern Line 1959 stock renovated to 1920s-style. It was shown off together with a train of 1972 Mark 2 stock wearing the new corporate livery of red, white and blue. *Colin Marsden*

◄At the Morden depot open-day, five cars of Network SouthEast Isle of Wight stock were handed over to London Underground with the aim of creating a second heritage train. The stock had originated in London Underground service, having passed to British rail in 1967. Three of the cars have been renovated to some extent already, including DTSO 27 carrying its pre-1930 number, 1789. *Kevin Lane*

LT OPEN DAYS

▲The scene at the London end of Harrow-on the-Hill station on 28th July, one of the four days of steam running between Amersham and Harrow-on-the-Hill, with GWR 9466, Metropolitan No. 1 and battery loco L44 on arrival from Amersham. This photograph shows the typical crowd that attended the event.
Kevin Lane

◀Northern Line 4-car set of 1956 stock 1008+2008+9009+1009, complete with balloons and special destination blinds, stands at Acton Town working the shuttle from Northfields in conjunction with the open day at the depot on 27th May.
Kevin Lane

European Scene

AUSTRIA

1990 started off with lots of extra trains being laid to convey people over reopened border crossings following the collapse of communism in Czechoslovakia. However, once the New Year holiday period was over, traffic flows levelled off.

Wien (Vienna) is undoubtably a fast growing area and more and more trains are being laid on for commuters. The extension of the VOR tariff to the Wulkerprodersorf/Eisenstadt area also bought more people to rail. Overcrowding on some routes in the Wien area has led ÖBB to experiment with double-decker stock and some carriages were borrowed from other railways for these tests.

In the south of the country the main event was the opening of the new automated marshalling yard called Villach Süd and located at Fürnitz on the line to Arnoldstein. This led to the closing of various small yards in the area and a reduction in status of others.

During the summer, traffic around the Innsbruck area from Germany to Italy etc. was disrupted when the railway at Kufstein had to be closed. The problem lay in a weak structure supporting a motorway which spanned the railway. Trains from Germany had to be diverted via Garmisch Partenkirchen and the Karwendelbahn.

On the traction front ÖBB was hard pushed to run all its services and assitance was provided in many ways. One of these involved DB Class 111s working through to the Hungarian border at Hegyeshalom and CSD Class 781s taking over some freights between Breclav and Hohenau thus releasing ÖBB Class 1063s. The same type of diesel loco as CSD 781 was also working in another part of the country in the form of Hungarian M62s which GySEV loaned for working from Wiener Neustadt and Graz. A new ÖBB shunting loco appeared – Class 2068, which started taking over from Class 2067 on shunting and short trip work.

On the preservation front the new relations with Czechoslovakia saw CSD types 475.1, and 498.1 working on ÖBB to cover Austrian loco failures. A major new museum line was opened when a society introduced steam services on the former ÖBB narrow gauge line from Kienberg to Lunz am See.

BELGIUM

The reorganisation of SNCB in recent years could be seen to be having an effect with many surplus locos heading for the scrapyards, in particular Class 59 and 60 diesel locos. However, some of each type were saved by preservationists. In addition the SNCF hired some Class 59s for use on construction trains in France and Italian contractors bought several Class 60s for further use.

The only electrification in the year saw the line from Namur to Dinant finally go live after having been put off for some time whilst the scheme was reassesed. To determine future needs SNCB tested an SNCF Sybic loco and ran some high speed tests with one of its own Class 18s.

The arrival of the Channel Tunnel and TGV Nord meant that SNCB has to build a new depot for these trains and a site at Forst was chosen which meant closing the loco depot that served Brussels Midi. The affected locos were all transferred to Schaerbeek as were the two Royal Train sets which had also been housed at Forst. An innovation during the summer was an SNCB loco working through to Thionville via Luxembourg on a car sleeper train from Schaerbeek.

Preservation in Belgium saw several interesting developments. The longest preserved line in Europe must surely be the Vennbahn (55 km!) which ran on Sundays and holidays during most of the summer. The famous Class 1 pacific was steam tested but was not used during 1990. Another new museum line was Dinant to Givet which was operated at weekends by the Chemins de Fer des Trois Vallées organisation.

DENMARK DSB

Afer a lot of teething troubles the DSB eventually brought its new IC3 DMUs into service and all the old Lyntog sets were finally laid up.

FRANCE SNCF

1990 was once again dominated by the TGV. On 18th May, unit 235 shortened to three trailers and with additional streamlining and a rear spolier, reached 515.3 km/h (320 mph) near Vendome on the TGV-Atlantique Tours branch. This section of new line opened to passengers in September and Tours–Bordeaux was upgraded to 220 km/h over much of its length, reducing Paris–Bordeaux times to 2 hours 58 mins. non-stop. One return train per day is extended from Bordeaux to Toulouse giving a Paris–Toulouse time of 5 hours 10 mins – almost an hour faster than via the "classic" Limoges route.

In January, SNCF announced their next 5 year plan with investment totalling FF 100 billion over the next 5 years.

Civil engineering works on the TGV-Nord (Paris–Lille–Channel Tunnel), Paris Interconnexaction by-pass line and TGV-Rhone-Alps (Lyon by-pass) lines made significant progress. The announcement of the TGV-Mediterranée (Valence–Marseille/Fréjus) route provoked protests particularly in the areas around Avignon and Aix-en-Provence, Protestors blocked SNCF tracks, delaying trains on many occasions.

1990 was a year of staff and motive power shortages, partly due to the late arrival of Sybics, leading delays to freight services, Remedial measures included increased use of foreign engines over SNCF metals, particularly SNCB class 12 on freights to Lille and greater use of DB class 181s on the Metz–Saarbrücken line. SNCF also decided to buy 44 NS class 2400 diesels and hire 10 SNCB class 59 locos for TGV-Nord tracklaying in 1991–93 (q.v.). Most surprising was the decision to test FS class 491 25 kV electrics (spare due to late-running Sardinian electrification) in the Mohon area during November with a view to using them in multiple on freight over the Thionville–Dunkerque route.

28 "Sybic" electrics arrived during 1990 and in October, SNCF ordered a further 220 from GEC-Alsthom at a cost of FF 4 billion. The Sybics first went into service on Paris–Vallorbe international expresses then started to displace class BB 25100 on freight prinicpally between Dijon and Thionville. This allowed BB 22200 locos to be cascaded to Paris–Clermont Ferrand services when electrification of theline was completed in March. In June, an accelerated morning train brough Clermont Ferrand–Paris down to 3 hours 8 mins. Another significant acceleration was on the Bordeaux–Marseille route where a pair of trains were introduced calling only at Toulouse and Montpellier.

Double-deck class 20500 EMUs continued to be delivered to Les Jonchérolles depot for a services on Paris RER line D (Chatelet–Gare du Nord–Orry-la-Ville). During the year, approval was granted to build twin tunnels from Chatelet to Gare-de-Lyon low-level, thus interconnecting the Orry-la-Ville line to south-eastern suburban services. The go ahead was also given to the "EOLE" project (Est-Ouest Liaison Express) to create a new RER line by diverting certain Gare de l'Est suburban services via a new tunnel from Pantin to St Lazare, serving the Nord and Est termini with a common underground

◄The CFTA, an independant organisation which runs a number of secondary lines in France took delivery of three new four-wheeled railcars known as type A2E ('Autorail à 2 essieux'). Two of these, Nos. X 97151 and X 97153 are seen at Paimpol, Bretagne during August with a service for Guingamp. *David Haydock*

►With the collapse of communism in East Germany and the opening of frontiers, Deutsche Reichsbahn (DR) locos started penetrating deep into DB territory. Here Russian-built Class 132 diesel electric No. 132 592-7 is seen at Hamburg Altona with the 15.32 for Wittenberge on 19th September. *Peter Fox*

station.

Final deliveries of BB 66700 and reception of the first BB 64700+TBB 64800 "master and slave" units, both conversions for heavy shunting, started to take their toll on numbers of class A1AA1A 62000.

From May, services on former "Réseau Breton" lines Guingamp–Paimpol and Guingamp–Carhaix were taken over by two-axle, one-man-operated A2E railbuses built by Soulé, with the aim of reducing operating costs substantially.

Reorganisation of freight services in June brought productively increases through heavier trains and longer trunk hauls. At the same time, SNCF pursued its policy of "Fercamisation" – transferring small freight flows to road and closing lightly trafficked rail lines. Also victims of the economy drive were the Clamécy–Corbigny and Bellegarde-Causes passenger services which were replaced with bus links. Of note was the introduction of "Semi-Rail" road trailers mounted on rail bogies, between Lille and Lyon.

GERMANY

The eastern half of the country was affected by the removal of the "Iron Curtain" and many new train services had to be introduced linking the two halves of the country. This included the re-openeing of certain cross-border routes. For a period a new IC train between Berlin and Hamburg was worked by a former DB Class 601 DMU hired by the DR from Italy! DB locos started working through on new IC/IR services to such places as Erfurt, Jena, and Berlin. This was due to the e.t.h. supply from DR Class 132 diesels not being suitable for the modern DB air-conditioned stock. A programme of rebuilding Class 132 was announced but an interim solution saw services double headed with a 132 leading a 119, the latter purely there to provide the e.t.h. supply. In the Berlin area, services were introduced to link up parts of the city previously cut by the wall. One such service was a shuttle worked by DR 118s between Wannsee and Potsdam pending extension of the S-Bahn. Freight traffic in the eastern half of the country plumetted as factories were closed, resulting in DR laying up some 500 locos by the end the year as some 800 feright trains were deleted from the timetable. DR drivers went on strike on 25th November, complaining that their colleagues on the DB were paid 3–4 times more for the same job. Karl Marx Stadt reverted to its former name of Chemnitz. This has an effect all over the country as not only station signs in Chemnitz itself had to be altered but destination indicators and posters everywhere else.

In the western part of the country DR, Class 132s started working through to Hamburg, Nürnberg and Regensburg amongst other places and a Class 112 had a diagram to Pader-

born. The DB itself was busy testing the new ICE power cars which were being delivered to AW Opladen and tested in the area at the head of rakes of ordinary coaches. During the year the new ICE depot at Hamburg Eidelstedt was completed.

An innovation with the summer timetable was the introduction of a Lufthansa shuttle train between Stuttgart and Frankfurt/M Flughafen which saw 111 049 being repainted in Lufthansa Livery. The summer timetable also saw the introduction of full S-Bahn services around Köln.

DB received three Class 240 diesel from MaK which went on test duties before being allocated to Hamburg for normal service in the area. Shortage of S-Bahn sets in the Ruhr saw EMUs returning to the area after a gap of some years when some Class 420s were transferred in to help out. Towards the end of the year there was a very heavy build up of freight traffic as USA and British military forces moved equipment out of Germany in readiness for the Gulf War. Over 600 special trains were run to North Sea ports.

GREECE

Greece recived some new stock and some not so new stock in 1990 – in both cases from Germany. The new stock was a fleet of high speed trains for use between Athens and Thessoloniki whilst the old or not so new stock was a batch of second-hand diesels from the DB in the shape of refurbished Class 221s. Interestingly the locos were refurbished in Italy.

ITALY

Two names were in the news "Settebello" and "Pendolino". The former famous EMUs were all taken out of service when the new tilting trains came into use. Test running of the Italian answer to TGV/ICE took place when FS unveiled its ETR500 prototype. Old locomotives of Class E428 continued to head for the scrapyards as new locos of Class E404, E453, E454, and B652 entered traffic. In Palermo traffic stagnation in the streets led to the reopening of several freight lines to suburban passenger trains.

NETHERLANDS

The year started with a storm on 25th january which badly interrupted train services as it also did in Belgium, France and the UK. During the year NS brought into traffic its new series of EMUs of Class 4200 and more deliveries of Class 6400 diesel locos allowed most of the elderly 2400s to be withdrawn at the rate of 5–6 a month. NS had a scoop later in the year announcing the sale of some 44 2400s to SNCF for use on construction

▶Similarly on 19th August DR Class 112 diesel-hydraulic is seen at Altenbeken with the 12.57 to Halle. *Ian Futers*

▼In East Germany, the branch line to Schierke of the Wernigerode–Nordhausen narrow gauge line had previously not been open to passenger service as it was in a sensitive border area which had been banned to foreigners. This line re-opened in 1990 and there were hopes that at some time in the future it would re-open to its former mountain terminus at Brocken. Most trains on this narrow-gauge network are steam-hauled, but there is the occasional diesel-hauled passenger utilising former Class 112s converted for narrow-gauge use with new six-wheeled bogies. 119 863-2 is seen on 3rd August about to leave Schierke with the 16.40 additional service to Wernigerode. *Peter Fox*

trains in France. On the preservation front former BR Class EM2 NS 1501 was overhauled and a ceremony held where it was renamed "DIANA".

LUXEMBOURG

Electrification of the line north from Luxembourg continued and CFL took delivery of its first new EMUs of Class 2001. The overhaul, of 2–10–0 5519 at Pétange continued very slowly.

NORWAY

The only news that filtered through was the testing under NSB conditions of DB Class 240 and NS Class 6400 diesel locomotives.

PORTUGAL

The opening of the new bridge over the Douro took another step nearer to completion when the old loco works at Campanha were closed and new facilities opened for both broad and narrow gauges at Custois. CP closed several branches from 1st January, some of which had lost their services much earlier but became officially closed on this date. A restructuring plan was announced which envisaged the reduction of freight facilities from 126 depots to 18. The only locos acquired during the year were second-hand Alco diesels from Spain.

SPAIN

The major development in Spain is the new high speed line from Madrid to Sevilla. During 1990 construction continued and the first tangible signs appeared. In Madrid the old Atocha terminal was stripped out and full refurbishment started as it will be the standard gauge terminal in Madrid. At the end of the line, construction of the new station in Sevilla continued at Santa Justa. This will be a dual gauge station handling all traffic for the city and thus allowing San Bernado and Plaza de Armas to close.

RENFE got its first standard gauge locos when some 319.2 GM diesels were rebuilt to standard gauge for use on work trains on the new line. RENFE started yet another new livery scheme for suburban services which saw traffic grow at a fast rate so much so that extra funds had to be pumped in and new double deck trains ordered.

SWEDEN

A big change in Sweden was the setting up of a seperate infrastucture organisation "Banverket", leaving SJ to run passenger and freight trains without the traffic overheads. Banverket acquired many permanent way machines etc and certain locos and shunting tractors from SJ all of which were renumbered into a new series. SJ entered the high speed train stakes with the delivery of its first X2 tilting train EMU for service between Stockholm and Göteborg which should bring the time down from 4 hours to 2 hours 55 minutes. Other new stock in Sweden saw the Stockholm Roslagen line getting new EMUs to replace its old stock some of which was over 50 years old. In Blekinge a Danish IC3 set was tried out as a possible replacement for the old double decker DMUs in that area.

After the good news comes the bad – line closures. SJ withdrew passenger services from several lines notably Skelleftea–Bastuträsk and Jörn–Arvidsjaur. Towards the end of the year the Swedish military announced it no longer needed the reserve of some 150 steam locos which will all be offered for preservation before scrapping commences.

USSR

The event worth mentioning here was the running of a steam hauled special train through the Baltic states using several classes of steam locos.

◄New double-deck push-pull suburban stock is now in use in Spain. This set is seen at the new Madrid Atocha station on 7th December. *D. Trevor Rowe*

►*SZD 2–10–0 No. L 0312 seen with the 'Baltic Coast Express' railtour at Valmeira on 6th June.* *L.J. Kenwars*

SWITZERLAND

The main event of the year has to be the start up of the Zürich S-Bahn which commenced with the summer timetable. A new underground section means that Zürich HB is no longer a termial and SZU line has been extended underground to the HB. 23 routes have been established and a big increase in ridership was expected. Unfortunately not enough of the new Class 450 locos and double deck sets were available for the start of the service so for a while some strange train formations were to be seen. A new depot was built at Oberwinterthur to service S-Bahn sets.

The Brunig line took delivery of the last of its new locos and similar ones are also on the BVZ and FO.

On the steam/preservation front the most pleasing thing was the return to steam of A3/5 4–6–0 No. 705 which performed various tours in connection with the Jura centenary. Of second importance was the arrival in Switzerland of some steam locos from Vietnam. These were rack tank engines and are intended for the Furka Bergstrecke.

▲The first of the SBB's new express locomotives of Class 460 No. 460 000-3 seen at the ABB works in December. *ABB*

◀The SBB's narrow gauge Brunig line benefitted from the introduction of the new Class 101 locos into service in 1990. 101 966-0 is seen at Interlaken Ost on 23rd June *E.H. Sawford*

▼The Zürich S-bahn opened for service in 1990 together with the new Class 450 single-ended locos and double-deck push-pull stock. 450 013-8 is seen at Zürich HB on 4th July before forming the 14.38 service to Oerlikon and Hinwil *G.B. Wise*

A Class 601 former Trans-Europe Express DMU was hired from Italy by the DR for their new 'Max Liebermann' Intercity service from Berlin to Hamburg. The cost was paid for with a steam locomotive of Class 01.5! The unit is seen stabled midday at Hamburg Altona depot on 19th September
Peter Fox

▼Main-line steam still surviving in Poland. PKP Class Pt47 2–8–2 No. Pt47 65 at Wolsztyn with the 09.45 Leszno–Zbasynek service on 18th November
Graham Scott-Lowe

▲ The NS took delivery of a new class of four-car Inter-City EMUs during 1990. Designated Class 4200, they are are similar to the three-car units of Class 4000 nicknamed 'Koplopers'. *NS*

◄ Ex DB Class 221 diesel hydraulics started work in Greece during 1990. OSE A411 is seen at Lianolokladi on train 503 to Thessalonik1 16th September. *Philip Wormald*

◄ The CFL (Luxembourg Railways) took delivery of its first new design of EMU with the delivery of Class 2000, based on the SNCF Z2 series. No. 2001 is seen on the 13.35 Luxembourg–Esch-sur-Alzette.
D.W.G. Beynon

Light Rail Transit

Light Rail progress continued to be a major factor in 1990. With construction under way on two extensions of the DLR, one extension of the Tyne and Wear Metro and the commencement of construction of Metrolink in Manchester, the building contractors were being kept busy. A further major step forward occurred in Sheffield in December when Roger Freeman, Minister for Public Transport officially opened the South Yorkshire Supertram project and announced that the Government had agreed to finance virtually the whole of the scheme.

As in recent years the number of cities reported to be considering Light Rail for future transportation plans crept higher, but inevitably there has been a slowing down of this process. Understandably when one considers that vast amounts of money have to be expended before any of the projects even get to the 'starting line', a number of schemes will not materialise. However currently approximately 40 studies are in force.

TYNE & WEAR METRO

The Tyne and Wear Metro celebrated its 10th Anniversary in August 1990.
Balfour Beatty Construction Northern Ltd were awarded the design and build contract for the extension from Bankfoot to Newcastle International Airport in May 1990 and work commenced on 8th June. The £12 million scheme was expected to be completed by summer 1991. The contract involved trackworks, overhead lines, a second platform at Bankfoot and new station at Callerton. It is forecast that 2 million passenger journeys will be undertaken each year. No new rolling stock will be needed to serve the extension. Installation of the signalling system was commenced by Westinghouse. The extension has not qualified for section 56 grant and funds have been obtained from the sale of the PTA Busways company – £5 million, a contribution from the Airport of £2.44 million and use of revenue funds £3.2 million. A £200,000 feasibility study commenced in May by Steer Davies & Gleave to evaluate possible routing for a further extension to Washington and Sunderland. The Bank of America has been commissioned as financial advisers. Sunderland Council have also suggested an isolated Light Rail scheme for the Borough.

At the end of the year Newcastle City Council proposed street running extensions to the Metro to serve the West End area radiating from St James Station to Scotswood, Elswick etc.

Unfortunately theft and vandalism is causing a big problem to Metro and therefore a further £100,000 investment in CCTV cameras to combat vandalism and hooliganism was approved in late 1990.

The Metro Day Rover ticket was abolished on 1st October 1990.

DOCKLANDS LIGHT RAILWAY

Work on the £240 million Beckton extension commenced in February 1990 with Mowlem and Taylor Woodrow being awarded a £116 million contract for construction of double track, 11 stations and 8 other major structures, Balfour Beatty Construction being responsible for track construction between West India Dock and Preston Road. Forty-four vehicles were to be supplied by BN Belgium and Hawker Siddeley Rail Projects, and an automatic fare collection system from Westinghouse Cubic. Ballast mats and accoustic pads will be installed to reduce noise and vibration. Poplar Station is to take on a new role when the Beckton extension opens and during 1990 work started to completely rebuild this site.

Work on the tunnel section of The Bank extension was virtually completed in 1990 and clearance tests etc carried out. The actual tunnelling was completed at the end of January.

However problems were experienced with the foundation o the Mansion House.

As the original signalling installed by GEC General Sign: was designed to cope with the original lower passenger ride ship it was decided in 1990 to completely resignal the networ at £30 million using the SEL Alactel (Canada) Seltrac movin block system. The equipment will enable the Docklands ligh Railway to reduce headways from 7½ min to 2 min.

All ten BREL built cars had been delivered by June but a the original eleven vehicles are unsuitable for tunnel opera tions to Bank it was announced that it is proposed to sell thes cars. A further order for 26 vehicles, worth £20 million wa placed in October with BN. There are plans to operate th system exclusively with two car operation.

A further Bill was deposited in Parliament with the conser of the DTp in November for an extension of the Dockland Light Railway from Island Gardens, under the Thames t Lewisham via Greenwich in South East London. The Bill w allow LT to offer a contract to design, build and operate th section to the private sector. An interesting side effect of th would be the cross charging between LRT and the successf Private Company for vehicle mileage over each other's opera ing territory! It is expected to cost £130 million for this exter sion.

The 1989 Bill for North Quay junction has completed th Commons Reading and by December reached the Lords.

The major Private Secor contributor to the DLR fund: Olympia and York were understood to be very critical of th time it takes to implement improvements on the railway. How ever during 1990 large scale upgrading work continued.

MANCHESTER METROLINK

Manchester is now undoubtedly leading the way in the U.K Light Rail Construction work on this project started on 14t January on BR tracks at Cornbrook Junction to form an under pass to carry trams from Altrincham under the BR Manches ter–Warrington–Liverpool line. This construction will includ a future junction for the line into Trafford Park. Tracklayin was officially inaugurated by Roger Freeman Minister for Pub lic Transport on 6th June in Long Millgate by Victoria Station This "official" piece of track was later removed. Ri59 typ tram rail with 42 mm groove was received from Luxembour via Goole Docks in August and stockpiled near Balloon Street

A prototype body shell of a Metrolink vehicle arrived from Firema of Italy on 25th March and was displayed to the publi during April and May. This "vehicle" later in 1990 displaye the intended livery of two tone grey with aquamarine relie together with the encircled geometric 'M' logo. This logo wi be carried on all vehicles and stations.

By the close of the year tracklaying in Manchester Cit Centre was well advanced although problems had been en countered using the polymer infill technique and obviousl new skills for the UK are being learned very much in th critical view of the public. Work on the city centre streets wa suspended for the Christmas shopping period and three majo thoroughfares were resurfaced and opened for motor traffic Construction of the viaduct alongside the G-Mex centre wa commenced towards the end of the year.

Thorn EMI was appointed in October to supply the far collection equipment, based on that company's Tollpoint rang of passenger operated machines.

The two Bills deposited in Parliament in November 198 and 1988 both received Royal Assent in 1990, and a furthe Bill was deposited in November 1990 covering cetain diversio nary work in Oldham town centre. The other two Bills pre sented in 1989 were still making their way through the Par liamentary procedures.

SOUTH YORKSHIRE SUPERTRAM

On 22nd February, Michael Portillo informed the promoters that although the project met the Department of Transport's criteria, no funds could be found for even a limited start in 1990/91 thus putting an end to any hopes of having a service in place for the World Student Games in July 1991. This came as a great disappointment to all concerned and it was not until 11th December that Roger Freeman, Mr. Portillo's successor announced the government funding for the scheme. The Government agreed to cover 50% of the £230 million cost under the Section 56 grant with the remainder covered by credit approval to borrow. Other contributors announced at the same time are Sheffield City Council, Meadowhall Centre and Sheffield Development Corporation.

It had already been announced that South Yorkshire Passenger Transport Executive had chosen Balfour Beatty to build the infrastructure and Siemens Duewag the vehicles. A mock-up vehicle was built at Duewag and demonstrated in the Sheffield City Centre for a week after the minister's announcement, when a majority of visitors were noted as supporting the scheme. A model of the vehicle had also been exhibited at the press conference showing it to be a three-section design with all four bogies powered. There were to be 100 seats and room for 150 standees. Level access would be provided from low platforms to low floor entrances.

Detailed design work for line 2 (Sheffield City Centre–Meadowhall) started immediately after the minister's announcement so that construction would be able to start in August the following year.

An Integrated Strategy for transportation and the environment in the Sheffield City Centre was accepted by Sheffield City Council in April which of course involves the Supertram project.

MIDLAND METRO (WEST MIDLANDS PTE)

The second Metro Bill deposited in Parliament in 1989, completed the third Reading in the Commons by the end of 1990 and now awaits transfer to the Lords. A further Bill, Midland Metro North Bill was presented in November 1990 covering Wolverhampton Town Loop, Merry Hill Extension and various route amendments.

Travis Morgan Railways received a £¼ million contract to work on detailed engineering requirements for Metro Line 1 – from Snow Hill to Bilston Street Wolverhapmton. Transport Design Consortium were appointed to set design standards. TDC's brief includes vehicle interior and exterior layout, stops, information system and Metro identity.

WMPTE submitted its formal bid to DTp for capital grant to build line 1 and encouraging Roger Freeman when officially opening the South Yorkshire project suggested that "if it proves satisfactory we will be ready to consider paying grant aid towards the cost of developing the scheme as soon as possible".

WMPTE announced that it plans to sell by competitive tender the right to design, build, operate and maintain the first line. this 'total concession structure' was recommended by Merchant Bankers Chartered West LB Ltd. This arrangement is similar to Greater Manchester Metrolink project and is understood to meet Government requirements, although it has not operated entirely satisfactorily in Manchester.

G. Maunsell & Partners have been appointed to carry out engineering feasibility studies and produce parliamentary plans for the next phase of Midland Metro.

ADVANCED TRANSPORT FOR AVON

Many problems occured during 1990 paricularly with public objections revolving around a cyclepath and footpath on the proposed Yate Line. The estimated cost of the lines from Portishead, through the City Centre and Bradley Stoke and Yate with rolling stock was quoted as £192 million in May and it was confirmed that section 56 grant was essential, official application for which was made in October.

Bristol's controlling Labour group decided in January to continue to block the scheme, but changed its policy in June to back to project. Avon CC & ATA signed a joint venture agreement in September with the aim of establishing the Metro and as the City Council and Avon CC have a fundamental role in the grant and planning processes it is hoped that the future looks good.

Badgerline,the major bus operator in the area acquired a 10% stake in the project in May. In September it was announced that Badgerline would operate the system on behalf of ATA for an agreed percentage of operating costs.

The two Bills introduced in Parliament in 1989 had both reached second Readings by the end of the year. Consultants working on the project are Kennedy Henderson (lead), Foster Wheeler (Project Management) and Peat Marwick McLintock (Finance).

CROYDON & KINGSTON-UPON-THAMES

Two seperate Light Rail schemes, both promoted by the local Boroughs together with London Transport completed studies, and recommendations that the proposals should go ahead were accepted in 1990.

The second stage Croydon study report was conducted by MVA Consultancy and submitted to Croydon Council in early 1990. the cost was shown as £80 million (1989 prices), with estimates that an operating surplus of £2.8–£4.3 million annually is likely. This surplus together with private developer contributions, government grant and savings in BR costs should be sufficient to enable the funding of the project.

A consortium of consultants including MVA Consultancy and Kennedy Henderson led by G. Maunsell & Partners was appointed in July to identify routes, prepare preliminary design, economic feasibility etc. A working party made up of local councillors and officers has been set up and visited Holland towards the end of 1990, to see the LRT systems in Den Haag and Amsterdam.

The Kingston scheme has Ove Arup as Consultants and the three line proposals are Kempton Park–Kingston (6 miles upgraded BR line) Kingston–Tollworth–Chessington–Epsom (mixed BR and new alignment) and Kingston–Surbiton (Tramway).

CLEVELAND

Consultants Steer Davies & Gleave undertook Stage 3 of the LRT study and towards the close of the year the County Council announced that it intended to take the proposals to public consultation. Four options were identified including a core section of 7.5 km between Middlesbrough and Stockton. Different choices then link this to Yarm and Saltburn (35 km) Hardwick–Ormesby (18 km) Coulby Newham (15.4 km) Ingelby Barwick (13.6 km). A mix of alignment is necessary. The initial capital cost for whichever option is agreed to first would be approximately £60-70 million.

NOTTINGHAM

The studies by Scott Wilson Kirkpatrick, Kennedy Henderson, and Peat Marwick McLintock for Nottingham Development Enterprises announced in June showed the re-use of the abandoned ex GC railway viaduct between the BR station and Weekday Cross linking to street based line via Market, Goldsmith and Waverley Streets to join the BR "Robin Hood" line alignment to Hucknall and Babbington. Three alternative routes were to be evaluated between Weekday Cross and Market St. and two to the BR right of way between Wilkinson St or Bobbers Mill.

The original plan was to run through the disused tunnels either side of the former Nottingham Victoria Station but this proved to be impossible under the Victoria Shopping Centre because of lack of headroom in the underground car park, and therefore a new deep level tunnel costing £23 million would have been necessary.

SHEFFIELD GETS THE GO-AHEAD

On 11th December, Mr. Roger Freeman Minister for Public Transport finally gave the go-ahead for the South Yorkshire Supertram scheme.

▲An artist's impression of the vehicle to be built by Siemens-Duewag in Düsseldorf Germany was released. The vehicle has a very stylish appearance and is designed with passenger comfort in mind.

South Yorkshire Supertram Ltd

◄A mock-up of one end of the tram was displayed for public comment outside Sheffield Cathedral for a few weeks. In this view looking towards the cab, two different types of seat can be seen. The seats on the right which are of the same type as those used in recent vehicles built for Stuttgart, Germany were very comfortable and were preferred by almost everybody. Note that the seats line up with the windows (and do so throughout the vehicle) – BR please note.

Peter Fox

◄Another view of the mock-up. On the left a tip-up bench seat can be seen. We understand that this is not to be incorporated in the actual vehicle, which will have space for push-chairs etc. in this area which is between the two sets of doors. *Peter Fox*

TRACKLAYING IN MANCHESTER

▲The first of the new generation of tramway rail was laid in Manchester during 1990. This view shows tracklaying in Balloon Street, just up the hill from Manchester Victoria station. *Peter Fox*

▶Another view of tracklaying, this time in High Street. A station will be located in this area. *Peter Fox*

THE MAN LOW-FLOOR TRAM

▶What was claimed to be the world's first completely low-floor light rail vehicle was built by MAN and operated in Bremen, Germany. A launch was held in Nottingham for the benefit of the British market, but only photographs were to be seen in Britain! The photograph shows the vehicle operating in Bremen during August. The legend on the side reads (translated into English) "1890–1990 The first of the new generation of electrics". *Peter Fox*

WEST YORKSHIRE

This area continued to show a very confused picture although towards the end of the year a major public consultation exercise was conducted entitled 'Think Leeds Talk Transport' and initial reaction appeared to favour street level LRT as the way forward.

Massive environmental objections to "Briway" were encountered and subsequently Leeds City Council decided to reject this mode.

LOTHIAN

During the year Lothian Regional Council, the Scottish Office and Edinburgh Borough Council commissioned MVA Consultancy to undertake a Joint Authority Transportation and Environmental Study which includes the plans for the Metro System. The underground section for the City Centre was expected to be extended to Cameron Toll West due to the conflicts expected between the LRT system and car parking requirements. The public consultation exercise completed in early 1990 gave the Metro Development Group a mass of feedback which needed evaluation.

Discussions were also conducted with BR Scotrail as part of the proposed system would use BR alignment or reopen ex Railway infrastructure.

Consultants involved in the varying studies include Steer Davies & Gleave, Halcrow Fox Associates, Mott MacDonald & MVA Consultancy.

STRATHCLYDE

In March 1990 the Stratclyde PTE reported its Public Transport Development Study to the Highways & Transportation Committee of the Strathclyde Regional Council. Amongst other items the report urges that the provision of a light rail transit (Metro) network be agreed in principle. The full council approved the PTE strategy in April and therefore the study has continued. A total of 12 lines have been identified for either conversion from heavy rail or to be built on a new alignment, totalling 100 km – 57% segregated, 9% segregated surface alignment 34% Unsegregated.

OTHER SCHEMES

Various other areas are in the process of evaluating Light Rail proposals but not at stages that make them of value to the 1990 Review. These include Belfast, Cambridge, Cardiff, Chatham, Chester, Chelsford, Exeter, Hull, Liverpool, Milton Keynes, Norwich, Preston, Plymouth, Reading, South Hampshire, Southend, Swindon, Stoke and a scheme in North London. It is known however that certain earlier proposals have now been shelved including Aberdeen, Bedford, Gateshead, Leicester, Swansea, St Albans.

EUROPE

New vehicles have been delivered to a number of cities during 1990, the most notable being a new MAN-built low floor articulated car delivered to Bremen in January and presented to the public in February. a similar vehicle was also received in München in December.

BN also built a prototype low floor vehicle known as "LRV 2000". This was tested on 14th March at Brugge test track and in Brussels in August.

The following cities received new vehicles:
Bern, Oslo, Rome, Lausanne, Basel, Wien (Vienna), Amsterdam, Goteborg, Essen, Darmstadt, Freiburg, Napoli light Metro.

Now that many barriers between former West and East have been broken certain transactions are taking place such as the loan of Essen LRVs to Erfurt in April/May. CKD Tatra and other former Eastern Bloc manufacturers are attempting to get a foothold in the "west" and early in the year rumours were rife that a TATRA product was to run in Blackpool. Unfortunately this did not materialise.

A large number of extensions were recorded in 1990, the following being examples.

Antwerpen	Maas Tunnel opened 21st September.
Amsterdam	To Amstelveen 30th November. Extension to Diemen 6th July.
Bielefeld	opened new subway in February.
Köln	work started on a new subway in Merheim in October.
Trondheim	In March the city council voted to restore operation on the Grakellbanen from 18th August.
Grenoble	2nd route opened 1st September.
Stuttgart	Stadtbahn U5/U6 opened 3rd November.
Genova	Light metro opened 13th June.
Rotterdam	New work started 28th April on Sneltram to Capelle a/d Lissel and Oostgaarde.
Stockholm	Ground breaking for new route from Norrmalstorg to Djugarden on 18th April.
Den Haag	Work started on extension to Voorburg.
Düsseldorf	Short 500 m extension to Hellriegelst.
Graz	Short 500 m extension to Eggenberg.
Paris	Construction commenced on the new Bobigny to St. Denis route.

In Belgium the Vicinal undertaking was split up on 31st December and was merged into the transport organisations VVM (Flemish) SRWT (French)

A feasibility study on re-introduction of light rail in Hamburg was announced in October, whilst in München it is understood that three road projects have been cancelled to release DM 2000 million for public transport investment.

INDUSTRY

AEG reached agreement to acquire the rolling stock activities of MAN-GHH and also formed a joint venture with VEB LEW Hans Beimer.

ABB Traction bought the rolling stock builder Hagglund & Soner from ASEA.

Hainje (Netherlands) became part of Berkhof. ABB and Herschel merged to create ABB Herschel AG.

CKD Tatra & BREL signed a co-operation agreement on 11th April.

PARLIAMENT

The House of Commons Transport Committee turned their attention to The Light Rail Option in 1990, and received submissions from many sources including the Department of Transport, the PTE Group, Consultants, Manufacturers and even from certain well known anti-Light Rail activists. The Committee members also visited Manchester, Sheffield, Leeds, Newcastle, Essen, Wien (Vienna) and Prague. Their findings were to be made known in 1991.

AMSTERDAM'S AMSTELVEEN LINE OPENS

On 30th November, the new Amstelveen line opened in Amsterdam. It is served by 2.35 m wide city trams (with a low-floor centre section) that run over an existing street route through the city centre, and 2.65 m wide light rail cars (sneltrams) that link up with the existing classic metro (served by 3 m wide cars) to reach Central station. These sneltrams run on overhead on the joint running sections and on third rail on the existing Metro sections.

▲Station Zuid WTC provides level interchange between southbound cars, although the sneltram to the right is at a high platform. Note that car 56 has its running board extended, since this platform can also be served by 3 m-wide metro trains.
M.R. Taplin

◄A city tram pulls away from the low-level section of an island platform. Sneltrams must have their running boards folded to align with the high platform. *M.R. Taplin*

►The sneltram is running on third rail at Station Zuid WTC, with pantograph folded and running board extended. *M.R. Taplin*

◄The interior of the new low-floor Bremen car (see page 101). It can be seen that whilst the floor is at the low level, it is necessary to step up to reach the majority of seats, thus defeating the object. *Peter Fox*

Preservation Scene

◀'DUCHESS OF HAMILTON' bereft of numbers and nameplates restarts its test train from Derby to Sheffield after being brought to a stand near Woodhouse station. No. 46229 made a characteristically clean get away with its eleven coach train up the rising 1 in 50 gradient.   *Les Nixon*

▶The beautifully restored KING EDWARD I was used intensively on specials from Tyseley to Stratford on Avon over the Easter weekend. Complete with a matching rake of chocolate and cream coaches No. 6024 evokes memories of the past as it storms past Earleswood on 15th April.   *Bryan Hicks*

▶▼It is many years since the Worth Valley ex-London Transport and GWR pannier tank No. 5775 has turned a wheel in the garish orange livery it wore for its appearances in the film "The Railway Children" 2 years ago. It was back in action however in 1990 and it is pictured here battling upgrade towards Oakworth on 31st March.

David C. Rodger

▼It is not so long ago that we reported the movement of Schools No. 30926, as a kit of parts from Sail and Steam, Brightlingsea to Grosmont. Looking as good as new it was returned to traffic in the autumn although it proved to be not entirely suited to the steep bank to Goathland. 'REPTON' is pictured making a spirited run at the bank near Esk Valley on 6th October.

David C. Rodger

LOCOMOTIVES – STEAM

1990 was truly a vintage year for steam enthusiasts with the return to main line service of no fewer that eight locomotives. Representing the GWR was the welcome return of No. 6024 'KING EDWARD I' and for the Southern King Arthur 4–6–0 No. 777 'SIR LAMIEL'. For the LMS came a brace of Pacifics, Nos. 6203 'PRINCESS MARGARET ROSE' and 46229 'DUCHESS OF HAMILTON' whereas firm favourites from the LNER camp were No. 4472 'FLYING SCOTSMAN', reappearing in steam after its trip down-under, along with John Cameron's newly renamed A4 No. 60009, 'OSPREY'. Last but certainly not least was the long awaited and quite remarkable return to main line traffic of No. 71000 'DUKE OF GLOUCESTER'. It will be some time before we again see such a galaxy of power return to the main line in the space of

less than 12 months.

However the preservation lines were determined not to be outdone and they too did their bit to bring long retired locomotives back into service. It is difficult to select one to head the list but many were pleased by the appearance of two first timers on the NYMR in less than three months. The steaming of a 4–4–0 in the shape of Schools No. 30926 'REPTON' and three-cylinder Class Q7 0–8–0 No. 63470 were significant milestones in the preservation movement. Meanwhile yet another Bulleid Pacific, Merchant Navy No. 35005 'CANADIAN PACIFIC', was in steam for the first time on the Great Central Railway. The Severn Valley Railway can always be relied upon to appear in the preserved section notes; in 1990 they steamed Stanier Mogul No. 42968 for the first time and it was expected to enter traffic in 1991.

The Port Line Project Group successfully returned Battle of Britain lightweight pacific No. 34072 '257 SQUADRON' to steam in time to travel to the south east to take part in the 50 year Battle of Britain celebrations. Although the engine was not allowed to work trains over electrified lines it was the first Bulleid to put in an appearance at Folkestone for many a year.

One of the more unusual locomotives to be placed in traffic during the year was the Greek but American built class S160 2–8–0 No. 'FRANKLIN D. ROOSEVELT' on the Mid Hants Railway, resplendent in Longmoor military blue. Inevitably one of the more memorable events of the year was the pairing of this locomotive with their WD 2–10–0 No. 601.

The former GNR 0–6–0ST No. 1247 was also returned to traffic by the Humberside Locomotive Preservation Group whilst Collett 0–6–0 No. 3205 made a welcome return to service on the West Somerset Railway.

Significant amounts of money were raised to secure the return to steam of class B12 4–6–0 No. 61572 on the North Norfolk Railway, while sums of around £500,000 were being seriously considered for the construction of a brand new Peppercorn Class A1 Pacific by a Polish firm. The inaugural run of this locomotive will be surely be the event of the decade!

◀After years of dereliction at Steamtown, the restoration of Merchant Navy No. 35005 'CANADIAN PACIFIC' at Loughborough made rapid progress with the locomotive working its first train for almost 25 years in November. The immaculate locomotive, complete with a 71A, Eastleigh, shedplate is pictured outside the shed on 3rd December 1990. *Les Nixon*

◀'SIR LAMIEL' made a welcome return to mainline duty but without the smoke deflectors which adorned the Class in their BR days. The little 4–6–0 is a competent performer and it was certainly going well with the southbound Cumbrian Mountain Express on 26th May. No. 777 heads a ten coach train on the final pitch of the climb to Ais Gill Summit. *Les Nixon*

▼Complete with a 66A, Polmadie, shedplate Princess Royal No. 46203 'PRINCESS MARGARET ROSE' climbs past Orgreave on the former Great Central main line with the first of the two memorial trains which ran between Derby and Sheffield on 2nd June. Richard Levick was tragically killed in a workshop accident at Butterley in 1989 and it was particularly appropriate that these trains should be hauled by 46203 since he was instrumental in rescuing the locomotive from Butlins at Pwllheli. *Les Nixon*

Judging by the number of photographs submitted to 'Todays Railways Review of the Year' DUKE OF GLOUCESTER was the most photographed preserved steam locomotive in 1990. The return to main line duty of this fine engine is undoubtedly one of the major achievements of the preservation movement in recent years. In these pictures we recall two of its memorable outings.

▲Many enthusiasts eagerly awaited the ultimate challenge to No. 71000, namely its run over the Settle and Carlisle line. They were not disappointed with two quite exceptional runs recorded on its two southbound trips. The Duke is seen here picking up speed near Lund's on the approach to Shotlock Tunnel with the northbound Cumbrian Mountain Express on 17th November.   *Les Nixon*

▼On a sunny 7th April No. 71000 made its inaugural return to revenue-earning main line duty when it headed the Red Dragon excursion from Didcot to Derby. The immaculately turned-out pacific produced a fine smoke effect as it sped its eleven coach train north through Oxford.   *Martin Loader*

▲The Great Western weekend on the Gloucestershire and Warwickshire Railway in mid-October was a huge success raising over £20 000 for the line. The star attraction was undoubtedly NRM's CITY OF TRURO seen here near Winchcombe on a substantial train of 14th October. *David C. Rodgers*

▼The Swanage Railway was host to two 'foreign' locomotives during the summer. The East Anglian Railway Museum's N7 0–6–2T made the first visit of the Class to Dorset and it is seen here running round at Swanage alongside GWR 0–6–2T No. 5619, on loan from the Telford Steam Trust. Also in the picture is dismantled ex-Midland Railway half cab 0–6–0T No. 1708. *Les Nixon*

▶Adams Class T3 4–4–0 No. 563, the prototype HST power car and Class EM1 (Woodhead line) electric No. 26020 arrive at Swindon in the second convoy from York on 16th March. These were just a few of the exhibits which appeared at the National Railway Museum on Tour display which opened on 10th April.   *Mike Goodfield*

Perhaps one of the more remarkable events of the year was the importation of no fewer than FOURTEEN 5'0" gauge steam locomotives from Finland. The locomotives were taken to temporary holding location at Sudbury in Suffolk. Their precise destination is unknown but one Class TK3 2–8–0 is destined for the proposed Frontier City Theme Park at Newquay.

Out of traffic pending a full internal examination of the boiler was Castle No. 5051 'DRYSLLWYN CASTLE'.

DIESELS

ETHELS (former Class 25 Electric Train Heat Ex-Locomotive) were universally detested by both photographers and travelling enthusiasts because of their appearance and noise respectively. Almost £8000 was raised by a fund promoted by the magazine 'Steam Railway' for the conversion of a BSK coach into a generator vehicle. A contract was awarded to the Kilnhurst Works of RFS Engineering. It was initially hoped that it would enter service before the end of 1990 but ETHELS were still with us at the end of the year.

The appearance of BR Class 37 No. 37511 at the head of four trains running over the NYMR on their April diesel day provided a most welcome counterpoint to the preserved diesels.

The future of diesel events on preserved lines was the focus of attention of a number of railways particularly following incidents of mindless vandalism on the SVR. Two railways, the Great Central and the Kent and East Sussex, announced their intention to abandon all-diesel days for the 1991 season.

▲The final chapter of the Dinting story was written over the Easter weekend when the final public steamings took place. On the last day, 16th April, shuttle services on the short demonstration line were operated by LNWR 'Coal Tank' 0–6–2T No. 1054 and Barclay 0–4–0ST TINY, to the sound of exploding fog detonators on the last day, 16th April.   *Les Nixon*

◀The weekend of 8th and 9th Septmeber was a gala event on the Leighton Buzzard Railway. Guest visitor was Orenstein & Koppel 0–4–0WT No. 22 'MONTALBAN' on loan from the West Lancashire Light Railway. On 2nd September it was used in service double headed with sister O&K locomotive, 0–6–0WT No. 5 'ELF'. They are seen here about to depart from Stonehenge works with a service to Page's Park.
Mervyn Turvey

ACCIDENTS

It is always sad to record accidents but alas no fewer than three serious events occured during the year. In two, fatal injuries were sustained. A passenger on the eastbound North Wales Coast Express was killed instantly while leaning out of a coach passing through a tunnel while Peter Wilks of Romsey, a trainee footplateman on the Mid Hants Railway met a similar fate while pushing coal forward in the tender of WD 2–10–0 'STURDEE'. The third accident occurred at Eldroth on 23rd June when Class 5 No. 44871 blew a washout plug during its light engine movement from Carnforth to work the Middleton Pioneer excursion over the Settle & Carlisle. One member of the footplate crew was quite severely scalded.

Perhaps some accidents are inevitable but it is to be hoped that these deaths will serve to improve the safety aspects of the industry.

On a slightly happier note the memorial train of Richard Levick's death at Butterley in 1989 was an outstanding success with his 'adopted' locomotive 'PRINCESS MARGARET ROSE' providing the motive power for two round trips between Derby and Sheffield on 2nd June.

NEW OPERATIONS

The long promised extension of the Great Central Railway south to the former station of Belgrave and Birstall came to fruition on 16th November when it was formally opened with a steam push-pull shuttle from Rothley. The old platforms of the station survive but passengers are presently not allowed to alight pending complete redevelopment of the terminus. The new station will eventually be designated Leicester North. Meanwhile a separate company was set up to deal with the northern extension of the GCR. Financed jointly by GCR, Nottinghamshire County Council and Rushcliffe Borough Council a start has been made on the purchase of 9 miles of track. The County Council has made available an 11 acre site at Ruddington for the establishment of a Beamish-style transport heritage centre. Steam did however return to this area in 1990 when class Y7 No. 68088 gave brake van rides at the

Yet another locomotive to visit the KWVR for the first time was the NELPG Class P3 No. 2392. The sturdy 0–6–0, built for heavy freight duty, was ideally suited to the steeply graded branch. On a very wet 24th August the locomotive runs round its train at Oxenhope. *Dr. WEA Davies*

British Gypsum Works Open Day whose factory is adjacent to the BR line.

The first standard gauge preservation line in Cornwall got off to a fine start on 17th June when No. D 3559 and Bagnall 0–4–0ST No. 19 double headed the first passenger train over the branch.

TWERPS, the amusing initials of the Tunbridge Wells and Eridge Preservation Society, became an operating railway during the year when it ran its first demonstration trains over a ½ mile section of disused line.

The Scottish Railway Preservation Society finally completed the 1¾ mile of line from Birkhill to Manuel in January making the long awaited link with British Rail.

The Strathspey Railway made another significant step in their long term bid to extend rails to Grantown on Spey when they bought another 1¼ mile of trackbed.

On the Isle of Wight Railway track was laid on the Haven Street to Ashey section and the trackbed acquired east to Smallbrook Junction where it was hoped to eventually build a station to connect with trains on the electrified BR Ryde–Shanklin line.

Yet another line was the subject of a preservation bid during the year. Following the cessation of BR traffic to Radstock, a group known as the Somerset and Avon Railway was formed with the long term objective of re-opening the 8 mile line from Radstock to Frome as a tourist attraction.

British Rail also announced their intention to sell 2½ miles of the surviving southern section of Colonel F.H. Stephen's East Kent Light Railway between Tilmanstone and Sheperdswell. A price of £32,500 was attracting the interest of a preservation group.

The Duke of Westminster formally opened the 1¾ mile Deeside extension of the Llangollen Railway.

The Bluebell Railway's long term objective of reaching East Grinstead received a shot in the arm when over ½ mile of track was commissioned from Horsted Keynes to Horsted House. The Society also managed to secure the purchase of a further mile of trackbed to the southern portal of Sharpthorne tunnel.

As a prerequisite to the sale of the trackbed by BR a Light Railway Order has been applied for the proposed 11 mile Grimsby and Louth Railway. A line to receive an LRO during the year was the ¼ mile line at Mangapps Farm in Suffolk.

Up in Ayrshire the Scottish Industrial Railway Centre at Minnivey held their first ever public open day on 23rd June.

The latest National Garden Festival was held at Gateshead and, as now seems customary, the site was well served by a steam operated narrow gauge railway. The locomotives hired to work on the line included 'NORTHERN ROCK' and 'RIVER IRT' from the Ravenglass and Eskdale Railway along with 'JOHN SOUTHLAND' from the Romney Hythe and Dymchurch line.

The Midland Railway Centre at Butterley commenced the short extension of their line from Ironville to Riddings Junction which in the long term could allow interchange of passengers with British Rail.

Although the Somerset and Dorset has now been closed for close on twenty five years its passing is still much lamented and a scheme was launched to reopen Midford station and to relay a short length of track.

A pleasing development which will affect the future of the Swanage Railway was an announcement by British Rail that in principle they could agree to the Railway using the bay platform at Wareham from 1992, a move which would presumably involve the joint use of track from Worgret Junction.

CLOSURES

Although most of the preserved lines seem to go from strength to strength each year, there are inevitably one or two which fall on hard times or even close. Such was the fate in 1990 of the ¾ mile 1'11½" gauge Knebworth and Wintergreen Railway which finally closed its doors after 20 years of operation.

One of the first main line duties for 'FLYING SCOTSMAN' following its successful tour of Australia was a short season of trips around the Cumbrian Coast to the BNFL nuclear reprocessing plant at Sellafield. No. 4472 is pictured passing Askam on its first outing on 7th May. The photographer was most annoyed that one of the few daily Barrow–Carlisle service trains contrived to creep into the picture at the critical moment!

Les Nixon

MUSEUMS

Sadly the prediction made in Volume 3 of 'Today's Railways Review of the Year' that the unique museum at the former Wolferton station close to the Sandringham estate might close came true in 1990 when the contents were sold at auction.

The SVR opened a new small museum in the old warehouse at Kidderminster in August as a preliminary to a major £170,000 conversion and redevelopment which commenced in October.

However the most significant museum development of the year was of course the complete closure of the traditional Leeman Road exhibition hall of the National Railway Museum at York (formerly York Steam shed) for "repairs". These so-called repairs included the virtual demolition of the building and also involved the removal of one of the two turntables. These acts displeased many enthusiasts who took the view that the former engine shed was an exhibit in its own right. Many of the exhibits were temporarily moved south as part of the "National Railway Museum on Tour" display based at Swindon. Other exhibits were moved across the road to the Peter Allen building as part of The Great Railway Show. This display won the Yorkshire and Humberside Tourist Board's White Rose Award for the best development of a visitor attraction.

The last trains were run at Dinting over the Easter weekend following the protracted dispute with the owner of the site Jack Warburton. Agreement was reached over the removal of that part of the track which the preservation group had laid during their tenancy. The Keighley and Worth Valley Railway reached an agreement with the Dinting Group for the relocation of the centre at Ingrow. Two of the locomotives from Dinting, the NRM's 0–6–2T No. 1054 and No. 45596 'BAHAMAS', were formally welcomed on 27/28th October when they operated trains over the line.

A rather less publicised move however concerned the Great Yorkshire Railway Preservation Society which moved from Starbeck (Harrogate) to Murton on the former Derwent Valley Light Railway. Here the Yorkshire Farming Museum has consented to the use of a short stretch of line. In the long term it is hoped to move to Layerthorpe station.

Wrabness signalbox moved to the Colne Valley Railway.

ANNIVERSARIES

The centenary of steelmaking at Scunthorpe was celebrated in fine style when BSC agreed to the running of a steam-hauled passenger train over the track around the perimeter of the site on no fewer than 98 occasions. The locomotive used, a Barclay 0–6–0ST 'SALMON' built in 1942 painted green and lettered "APPLEBY FRODINGHAM", was on loan from the Rutland Railway Museum.

The Buckinghamshire Railway Centre at Quainton Road celebrated its 21st anniversary on 5th May.

Perhaps the most notable centenary was that of the opening of the railway bridge over the Firth of Forth. The bridge was lit by spectacular floodlights in October while John Cameron's A4 No. 60009 "OSPREY" operated several commemorative trains over the bridge during the year.

At the other end of the spectrum, 1990 was also the centenary of the narrow gauge Fairbourne Steam Railway.

The 25th anniversary of the closure of the Aviemore–Forres line was celebrated in fine style at Aviemore when there was an unprecedented demand for tickets to travel to Boat of Garten at a price pegged to the estimated 1965 cost of 40p.

Yet another notable preservation anniversary was celebrated when two of our very first preservation lines, the Middleton Railway in Leeds, and the Bluebell celebrated their 30th birthdays. To celebrate the Yorkshire event a special train was run over the Settle & Carlisle line while back in Leeds the NRM's former GNR 0–6–0ST No. 1247 was the star attraction for the summer.

The Tal-y-llyn Railway celebrated its 40th anniversary of preservation by operating an all night train service over the weekend 23rd/24th June.

FINANCE

One of the greatest surprises of the year was the decision by Peak Rail to sell off the majority of its Buxton site, including the ex-Midland Railway goods shed to the Buxton Mineral Water Company for a sum in excess of £350,000. The sale means that track relaying of the Matlock end of the line could continue with a reopening target date of Spring 1991. Peak Rail were also fortunate in receiving a £119,000 derelict land reclamation grant for work on bridges and laying of ballast at Darley Dale. Last but not least the Society also received nearly 3 miles of track from Hams Hall power station. The acute lack of covered accommodation at Darley Dale was temporarily solved when Peak Rail acquired a six-month lease of the 1872 Midland Railway goods shed at Matlock from Derbyshire Dales District Council. Would 1991 be Peak Rail's big year?

By comparision the appeal to restore class B12/3 No. 61572 to working order realised £35,000 in just six weeks, although it was stated that restoration to main line order was not at that time being considered.

The Gloucestershire and Warwickshire Railway held a very successful steam celebration weekend on 13th/14th October when visiting locomotives (appropiately with a distinct GWR flavour) included Prairie tank No. 6106, Castle No. 5080 'DEFIANT' and 'CITY OF TRURO'. The GWR week-

▶The steam-hauled passenger train for the celebration of the centenary of steelmaking at BSC Scunthorpe pictured on 19th June with Barclay 0–6–0ST 'SALMON' pulling a Metropolitan Railway coach from the KWVR and a goods brake van.   *Peter Fox*

DIESELS & ELECTRICS IN THE NEWS

◀After suffering from a spell of vandalism from so called modern traction enthusiasts the future format of diesel weekends on the Severn Valley Railway is under review. It will be a pity if scenes like this, recorded on the October weekend are to be denied enthusiasts in the future. No. D 9016 'GORDON HIGHLANDER' accelerates away from Bewdley with the 14.55 Bridgnorth–Kidderminster on 14th October.   *Tom Clift*

▼Resplendent in its newly acquired desert sand livery is Western No. D1035 'WESTERN YEOMAN'. The immaculately turned out locomotive was posed on the turntable at Didcot for photographers on 5th May.
          Mike Goodfield

In comparison with steam 1990 was a relatively quiet year on the modern traction front. Notable moves however included the transfer of Peak No. 45118 from British Rail, March to its new home on the Northampton Steam Railway. The externally immaculate locomotive is pictured on a low-loader ready to start its journey on 15th September. *Phillip Crumpton*

▲Preserved Class 84 No. 84001 poses in front of the banner at the entrance to the "Great Railway Show" at York which was opened at the begining of March to coincide with the closure of the main exhibition hall of the National Railway Museum for demolition. *B.J. Nicolle*

The 3-car Hastings DEMU 60016/8 and 60527 was moved to the Swanage Railway and was soon pressed into service when, during the summer months it was regularly in action on the last train of the day to Harman's Cross. The unit is delightfully turned out in BR green with small yellow warning panels. It is seen here accelerating away from Harman's Cross on 26th July. *Les Nixon*

Several class 127 parcels units were preserved during the year. Nos. M 55966 and M 55976 were the subject of a private purchase and were moved late in the year to Butterley. The units were moved to the old locomotive shed in mid-November although this picture was taken immediately after the heavy snowfall of 7th December. It is not the intention to convert them for passenger service, at least for the foreseeable future. The other unit sold into preservation was No. 55967 which was moved to the Swindon and Cricklade Railway. *Les Nixon*

◀A bucolic scene on the new extension c the K&ESR showing Terrier tank No. 1 'SUTTON' leading. P Class 0–6–0T No. 155 about to cross the River Rother near North iam on 23rd September. The train is passin the site of a proposed halt which will serv a nearby children's farm.   *D. Trevor Row*

◀Yet another preservation group to ope its doors to the public for the first time wa the Wensum Valley Railway whose head quarters are at County School Station in No folk. The station has been rebuilt and a sho length of line relaid over the last two yea by MSC staff and was reopened on 15t June. The station is owned by Brecklan District Council and the tracked leased t the Fakenham and Dereham Railway C Pictured here on 28th May are a Rusto 0–4–0 diesel and a former LMS brake van.
Ray Kir

▼The long awaited 2½ mile southern e: tension of the Great Central Railway to th former station of Belgrave and Birstall wa formally opened on 15th November. Th southern terminus, to be known as Leicest North, does not presently have run roun or station facilities and passengers are no allowed to alight. Pending redevelopmer of the site, shuttle trains from Rothley a operated by the resident 3-car DMU con prising two Class 127 power cars and Class 120 trailer although a push-pull stear service was in use on special occasions. Th was the scene at Birstall on 3rd December.
Les Nixo

The Bure Valley narrow gauge railway was launched with great publicity in June but after only five months it was up for sale, lock, stock and barrel. Continuing high interest rates have been suggested as the principal cause of failure. The future of operation of this charming eight mile 1' 3" line running on the trackbed of the former Wroxham–County School branch as far as Aylsham in East Anglia is far from secure although the total closure would seem unlikely. Here Romney Hythe and Dymchurch 4–6–2 'SIR WINSTON CHURCHILL' leaves Coltishall station on 16th September.
Michael J Collins

The Bodmin & Wenford Railway started its public service over the full three miles between Bodmin General and Bodmin Parkway (the connection with BR) on 17th June. Trains ran on a daily basis through the summer with motive power usually provided by ex BR Class 08 No. 3559 (ex 08444) and Bagnall 0–4–0ST No. 19 (ex Devonport Docks). Pictured here is the 16.00 departure from Bodmin General on 27th August.
Stephen Widdowson

BIRTHDAYS

▲ Drifting down to Aberdou
is 60009 'OSPREY' with th
Edinburgh–Perth specia
marking the centenary of th
Forth Bridge on 4th March.
T.H. Nobl

◄ Class A4 No. 60009 'OS
PREY' moves off the Forth
Bridge for Inverkeithing afte
the ceremony at which th
centenary plaque rededicat
ing the bridge was unveile
on 4th March. Class 47 No
47835 'WINDSOR CASTLE
hauled the General Man
ager's saloon and a freigh
wagon fitted with a platform
from which the ceremon
was carried out. *T.H. Nobl*

▲ The Middleton Railway in Leeds was one of the first standard gauge preserved railways in Britain. It celebrated its 30th birthday in fine style by obtaining the services of the NRM Class J52 0–6–0ST No. 1247 for a short season. In a modern setting which belies the interesting history of the line (it was opened in part in 1758!) the locomotive heads a train of two four-wheeled coaches up the branch on 23rd June. *Les Nixon*

The Talyllyn Railway has been in continuous operation now for 125 years, a milestone marked by the runing of a birthday train on 5th July. The train, hauled by one of the original locomotives supplied to line, 0–4–0ST No. 1 pauses at Nant Gwernol on the outward run. For Welsh linguists the headboard reads "Y Tren Pen-Blywdd 5 Gorffennaf 1865". *C.V. Harvey*

end attracted many visitors and raised over £20,000 for the railway.

Sir William McAlpine decided to sell his controlling interest in Steamtown to David Smith, owner of Class 8F 2–8–0 No. 48151. A total of 49,710 shares changed hands.

Fund-raising schemes were announced during the year to resurrect part of the Lynton & Barnstaple Railway. An Association has been formed with the intention of opening a new terminus station at Barnstaple and laying two miles of 2'0" gauge track to Sapper.

The current crisis in Local Authority finance had a major impact on the Birmingham Railway Museum when early in the year Birmingham City Council decided that it could no longer afford to support the museum. Fortunately the decision was partly rescinded later in the year when an agreement was reached for the council to pay the £58,000 annual rent for the remaining 19 years of the lease.

An anonymous supporter pledged £100,000 for the Great Central Railway for the construction of a double track section of line between Quorn and Rothley, complete with a controling signal box and passing loops at Swithland.

A £500,000 share appeal was launched by the North Yorkshire Moors Railway to fund additional covered accommodation, a turntable and it is rumoured, a washing plant.

Only £2,000 of the £20,000 needed to return MAUDE to traffic in its centenary year had been raised by late summer. There was however better news for the Bo'ness Museum Project when the Royal Bank of Scotland made a donation of £10,000 towards the cost of the completion of the Society's new carriage shed.

The West Somerset Railway's share issue launced in 1988 finally closed when it was disclosed that a sum of £383,000 had been successfully raised.

The aspirations of the North Staffordshire Railway at Cheddleton were raised when the regular sand traffic from Oakamoor through the Churnet Valley ceased. A public limited company has been formed to purchase the line from BR.

A worrying development for the preservation movement was the move by the Inland Revenue to claim back repayments where benefits are received by donors in respect of free entries, reduced fares etc. If appropiate legislation were introduced it could have quite far reaching repercussions for the preservation industry.

The Severn Valley Railway reported an annual turnover in excess of £2 million for the first time with a profit of £106,000.

The group which have beautifully restored King No. 6024 'KING EDWARD I' to main line order deservedly won the Steam Heritage Award for 1990 and the prize of £3,000 was formally presented at the NRM, York on the 4th May.

The Foxfield Steam Railway announced plans to raise £20,000 for the purchase of a 4 acre plot next to its Caversall Road site at Blythe Bridge, Staffordshire. The site will eventually be used to build a new platform and station building along with additional sidings and another museum building.

One of the first locomotives to be rescued from Barry, Class 4F No. 43924 was sold by the eight-man consortium ownership group to the KWVR for a sum reported to be in the region of £33,000.

WEATHER

The weather provided a few surprises during the year. The long hot summer eliminated steam from the North Yorkshire Moors Railway for a period while floods at Swanage put part of the line here under 4' of water on 3rd February. Upwards of £15,000 of damage was also caused by flooding at Dunster on the West Somerset Railway.

COACHES

The six Pullman coaches which have been in use as holiday homes close to the beach at Marazion in Cornwall for many years were up for sale in 1990. The coaches however are reported to be in poor condition; years of exposure to salt laden air has wreaked havoc on the frames, bogies etc.

The all maroon BN90 Mark 1 set of Flying Scotsman Enterprises was disbanded much to the disappointment of the photographic fraternity.

GENERAL

The first independent railway boiler shop in the UK, complete with a 30 ton capacity overhead crane was completed at Bridgnorth early in 1990. It was formally opened by the Duke of Gloucester on 29th October.

Following the success of steam hauled excursions over part of the London Underground network in 1989 another short season of excursions were again run over the line between Harrow and Amersham. Locomotives appearing included the Metropolitan Railway 0–4–4T, 0–6–0PT No. 9466 and BR Class 4MT 2–6–4T No. 80080.

Many enthusiasts were agreeably surprised by the decision of ScotRail to use A4 'OSPREY' for crew training trips during the early spring months. Volunteers from Edinburgh, Thornton and Perth depots were given 'hands on' experience on a circular route embracing Thornton, Dunfermline, Thornton, Ladybank and Perth.

More and more ambitious engineering projects are now being undertaken, mention having already been made of the proposal to build a completely new Peppercorn A1 pacific. A contract for the construction of a brand new boiler for Buckfastleigh 1366 class 0–6–0PT No. 1369 was signed with boilermaker Roger Pridham. Tenders were also invited by the KESR for the constuction of a brand new boiler for the 118 year old Terrier No. 3 'BODIAM'.

The shortage of train crews and the introduction of a week day 45 minute interval DMU service were the official reasons given for the abandonment of steam running out of Marylebone. The programme of White Rose railtours was cancelled although alternate excursions from Paddington with

It is not every day that a preserved steam locomotive carries the headlamp code for a Royal Train. Four lamps were however certainly needed on the Severn Valley on 29th October when a special train was run from Kidderminster to Bridgnorth to convey HRH Duke of Gloucester for the formal opening of the new boiler shop. Providing the motive power was immaculate Manor No. 7819 'HINTON MANOR'.

Chris Milner

steam haulage north from Didcot to Derby were tried with limited success.

In a remarkable U-turn-decision no doubt prompted by the sale of Steamtown, Carnforth, Peter Beet's collection of steam locomotives returned to Carnforth after a period of nine months at Crewe Heritage Centre. The collection includes Ivatt Class 2MT 2–6–0 No. 46441, SNCF 231 K 22 and a DB Class 01.10 pacific No. 01.1104.

An announcement which was certainly welcomed by enthusiasts who travel on main-line steam tours was the BR decision to raise the speed limit along the North Wales Coast from 60 to 75 mph. One wonders why such limits are imposed at all. Why cannot preserved steam locomotives run at line speeds (subject to any reasonable maximum limit that might be applied to individual locomotives for mechanical reasons) just as they do on mainland Europe?

As from October, the Cumbrian Mountain Expresses were rescheduled to be steam-hauled to and from Skipton rather than Leeds; a move apparently dictated by recent electrification developments.

The NYMR decided to adopt a policy of uprating its line to allow regular operation of locomotives with up to 22 tons axleloading. This will mean significant work on the strengthening of certain bridges.

TRANSFERS

Steam

Note: for convenience, locos are shown by BR number.

9	Vale of Rheidol to Brecon Mountain Railway
3802	Plym Valley to Bodmin and Wenford
4160	Plym Valley to West Somerset Railway
5080	Tyseley to Gloucester and Warwickshire Railway
5199	Llangollen Railway to MoD Long Marston
5553	Barry to Dean Forest
5619	Telford Horsehay Steam Trust to Swanage
6000	Hereford to Swindon
6023	Bristol to Didcot
6024	Birmingham Railway Museum to Didcot
6106	Didcot to Gloucestershire and Warwickshire Railway
6430	Dart Valley to MoD Long Marston
7229	Plm Valley to East Lancashire Railway
7752	Birmingham Railway Museum to Gwili Railway to Gloucestershire and Warwickshire Railway
7760	Birmingham Railway Museum to GCR
7820	West Somerset to Birmingham Railway Mus.
30120	Mid Hants Railway to Swanage (as 120)
30245	Mid Hants Railway to NRM (as 245)
30053	Swindon to East Anglian Transport Museum
30825	Sail and Steam to NYMR
32650	Tyseley to KESR (as 10)
34072	Swindon to Bluebell to Swanage
45596	Steamtown to KWVR
46201	Hereford to Crewe (as 6201)
44871	to Bo'ness and Kinneil Railway
47406	Buxton to GCR
48151	Crewe to Carnforth
49395	Tyseley to Butterley
58926	Dinting to KWVR (as 1054)
60009	Severn Valley to Markinch
60103	Southall to Crewe to Southall (as 4472)
63601	Dinting to NRM
65894	South Shields to KWVR (as 2392)
68009	GCR to Tyseley
68077	KWVR to BSC Scunthorpe
68846	to KWVR (as 1257)
69023	NYMR to East Somerset Railway
69621	Stour Valley to Swanage to Stour Valley
75078	KWVR to ELR
92214	Buxton to Butterley
92219	Buxton to Butterley
92220	West Somerset to Swindon
Cornwall	Birmingham Railway Museum–Crewe Heritage Centre
GMAM	(South African Railways Garratt) Plym Valley Railway to Glasgow Museum

Diesel

W 22 W	Didcot to Tyseley for Midline day event
D 306	GCR to Nene Valley Railway
D 9016	to Aberdeen on 29/4 for renaming/rededication ceremony
25235	Springburn to Bo'ness
25265	Buxton to Darley Dale
27024	Eastfield to Northampton Steam Railway
55009	NYMR–ICI Wilton

NEW TO PRESERVATION

Steam

3 x Class Hr I 4–6–2
3 x Class Tr I 2–8–2
5 x Class Tk 3 2–8–0
3 x Class Vr I 0–6–0T

These Finnish steam locos went to a temporary location at Sudbury, Suffolk. One is destined for the Nene Valley, and another for the Sellinge Steam Centre in Kent.

Diesel/Electric

D 2070	Queenborough Shipbreakers, Kent to South Yorkshire Railway
D 2229	British Coal, Manton to South Yorkshire Railway
D 3019	Gwaun-Cae-Gurwen disposal point to South Yorkshire Railway
08220	to Carnforth
12099	Booth-Roe Metals to Severn Valley Railway
33034	Eastleigh to Ludgershall
45108	to Crewe Heritage Centre
45118	March (BR) to Northampton Steam Railway
45133	Nene Valley to Butterley
51813	Class 110 to East Lancs Railway
51842	Class 110 to East Lancs Railway
52071	Class 110 to Lakeside & Haverthwaite Railway
52077	Class 110 to Lakeside & Haverthwaite Railway
55966	Class 127 parcels car to Midland Railway Trust
55976	Class 127 parcels car to Midland Railway Trust
55967	Class 127 to Swindon and Cricklade Railway
Class 485	5 vehicles Nos 2, 7, 27, 14 and 48 Isle of Wight to London Underground Ltd.

LOCOMOTIVES TO SWINDON

(for NRM on Tour exhibition)

PUFFING BILLY (1813) ex Wylam Colliery
LBSCR 0–4–2 GLADSTONE
NER Bo Bo No. 1
NER 2–2–4T no. 66 AEROLITE
GNR 4–4–2 No. 251
LSWR 4–4–0 no. 563
NER 0–6–0 No. 1275
LNWR No. 1439
LNWR No. 1868
LMS 2–6–0 No. 2700
GWR 4–4–0 No. 3440 CITY OF TRURO
LNER 4–6–2 No. 4468 MALLARD
GWR 4–6–0 No. 6000 KING GEORGE V
LNER Class EM1 Bo+Bo No. 26020
BR Class 9F 2–10–0 No. 92220 EVENING STAR
BR HST Power Car No. 41001

A total of 21 locomotives and 17 items of rolling stock were on display.

▲After a protracted period of restoration the first 9F to leave Barry for preservation finally returned to steam on 15th September. No 92240 rounds the curve near Freshfield Halt with the 16.50 Sheffield Park to Horsted Keynes on its first revenue earning trip.   *Phillip Barne*

▼Part of the National Railway Museum on Tour exhibition showing 9F No. 92220 'EVENING STAR', A4 No. 4468 'MALLARD' and Cra 2–6–0 No. 2700 inside the old No. 19 shop at Swindon.   *Mike Goodfiel*

▲St. Pancras masqueraded as Zürich Hautbahnhof on 16th December. The station might have looked convincing but the steam motive power was certainly not very Teutonic in apearance. Butterley locomotives No. 44932 (temporarily numbered 919318), and No. 80080 were brought down overnight for appearance in sequences for the film 'SHINING THROUGH'. *Chris Milner*

▼On a visit to the KWVR, Jubilee Class 4–6–0 No. 45596 'BAHAMAS' leaves Oakworth with an afternoon train from Keighley to Oxenhope on 25th March. This locomotive was to take up permanent residence on the Worth Valley later in the year. *Brian Dobbs*

Locomotives & Coaching Stock

LOCOMOTIVES – CLASS BY CLASS SUMMARY

Class 03

The two surviving members of this class continue to see use as required on the Isle of Wight, despite their on paper reallocation during the year to mainland Eastleigh. The other four members of this class still extant in BR ownership remained at the same locations as at the end of 1989 (03073 Chester, 03084, 03158 and 03189 March) awaiting disposal.

Class 08

Still numerically BR's largest class, the 442 locomotives in stock at the beginning of 1990 were reduced in numbers by 20 withdrawals during the year, although two examples were subsequently reinstated. Surprisingly, only one vacuum braked example, green liveried 08556 succumed, with other withdrawals being five air-braked only examples and 14 of the dual braked variant. All were withdrawn as surplus to requirements.

The two vacuum braked examples withdrawn in 1989 both passed to new owners during 1990, with 08202 going to work at G.G. Papworth, Ely and 08769 at MoDAD, Long Marston. Only two of the 1990 withdrawals were sold for further use during the year, with 08704 passing to A.F. Budge for use in Boston Docks and 08871 to Humberside Sea & Land Services for work in Grimsby Docks.

24 locomotives emerged from classified overhauls during 1990, all sporting the now standard class livery of BR General Grey. Six locomotives were overhauled by RFS Industries Kilnhurst, the remainder being completed by BREL Crewe. Due to the difficulties involved in transporting low speed locomotives large distances by rail to overhaul locations, most such moves to BREL Crewe since the spring of 1990 have been made by road.

Class 09

The number of officially named members of this class was doubled during the course of the year by the additions of 09008 'Sheffield Children's Hospital' and 09009 'Three Bridges C.E.D.'. Both were named at depot open days, with the former at Tinsley TMD on 29th September and the latter at Three Bridges on 27th August.

09012 was the first member of its class to be overhauled away from Eastleigh for a number of years, arriving at BREL Crewe on 3rd May in Mainline livery and departing on 1st October in General Grey livery. The 'Dick Hardy' nameplates carried by this loco were removed at Selhurst prior to despatch to Crewe, and by the end of the year still remained to be refitted. No other overhauls were carried out during 1990.

Class 20

The year started with seven members of this class being withdrawn during January and February, but then only two other examples were withdrawn up until the end of August. However, deliveries of Class 60 meant that further withdrawals were imminent and in the last four months of the year a further 23 locomotives were condemned. On the plus side, 20032 was withdrawn and reinstated twice, and 20138 (withdrawn in 1989) was also reinstated.

Although continuing their work on Humberside, class members in the FMYI pool at Immingham were transferred to Thornaby for maintenance purposes from May, whilst at the same time a number of the erstwhile Thornaby Metals Sector fleet were transferred to Eastfield for Railfreight Distribution use. In October a pool of 14 locos was created at Bescot to be used on engineering trains in connection with the Birmingham cross-city Electrification project. These locos predominantly saw use at weekends and on weekdays spent much of their time stabled at Bescot Yard.

Class 25

The celebrated Holbeck Depot training locomotive D7672 (TOPS No. 25912) was officially returned to traffic during the year, appearing initially as a pilot locomotive on Leeds–Carlisle services during the February "Enthusiasts Days" and later both as a pilot and unassisted on other charter services. However, as the year closed the future of this locomotive was uncertain as none of the business sectors was prepared to continue sponsorship.

Class 26

Although no classified repairs have been made to this class since 1988, withdrawals have been few indeed over recent years and restricted to accident and fire damaged examples. Early in 1990 the decision was taken to retain a number of this class for Civil Engineers' trains in Scotland into the twenty-first century, and as a result some further overhauls are expected in a couple of years time. A number of the class were painted in the attractive Civil Engineers grey & yellow colour scheme during the latter part of the year as a prelude of things to come.

Two examples of the class were withdrawn during the year (26023 & 26039), both after major component failures rendered repairs uneconomic.

Class 31

Scheduled overhauls recommenced on class 31/1 locomotives with the advent of the 1990–91 financial year in April. A total of twelve members of this sub class emerged from BRML Doncaster by the year end, eight for Departmental use and four for Railfreight Petroleum. These latter overhauls were necessary due to the late delivery of Class 60s and the consequent need for substitute motive power. A net 12 31/1s were withdrawn during the year, seven less than in 1989. 31299 was withdrawn and reinstated in March and then withdrawn again in November.

The five remaining members of sub-class 31/4 which had not been overhauled in recent years also passed through BRML Doncaster. 31464 was outshopped in July in Mainline livery, becoming only the second member of this class to carry these colours.

A new sub-class was created during the year, namely 31/5. This comprises class 31/4 locomotives allocated to the Civil Engineering function. The Electric Train Supply equipment is isolated and maximum speed is limited to 60 mph. By the end of 1990 31 locomotives had become so designated.

Class 33

A limited number of overhauls were scheduled for this class during the year, with six examples emerging from BRML Eastleigh. These locomotives are to be retained for a number of years for Civil Engineers trains on the Southern Region.

Only three locomotives were withdrawn during the course of the year, but with 33057 being withdrawn and then reinstated and overhauled, and also the return of 33035 (withdrawn 1989), the class ended the year only one down in strength from the end of 1989. However, cessation of a number of the Channel Tunnel construction workings and also arrival of a number of Class 60 locomotives is scheduled for 1991 and it is expected that a number of examples will then be withdrawn.

Withdrawn 33115 emerged from the Doncaster factory of RFS Engineering in February converted to a test vehicle for

high speed current collection in connection with the Trans-Manche Super Trains which will work the London–Paris/Brussels services through the Channel Tunnel. Fitted with TMST-type bogies, it began extensive testing on the Southern Region later in the year in its current guise of vehicle 83301, and is semi-permanently coupled to Class 73/2 73205.

Class 37

Overhauls continued on both refurbished and unrefurbished locomotives of all Class 37 sub-classes. During the year overhaul work was concentrated on the BRML workshops at Doncaster (57 examples) and Springburn (23) after completion of the final two examples scheduled for Plymouth Laira from the 1989–90 programme. Of these, 37293 was the final locomotive to receive classified attention at Laira, emerging after overhaul on 26th March, just before the end of the financial year.

No members of this class were withdrawn during 1990, reflecting the long term role of this class in BR's motive power plans.

Class 43

At the end of 1990 only 17 members of this class remained still carrying the old style InterCity livery. Locomotives which had been denamed at the time of repainting at last began to receive replacement nameplates in the new InterCity standard style towards the end of the year. Overhauls continued at Bristol Bath Road/St. Phillips Marsh and Leeds Neville Hill. The four locomotives with Mirrlees MB190 power units were amongst those overhauled at the former location, spending long periods of time out of service awaiting their own engines being overhauled due to the lack of any spare units. Some journals even reported these cars as withdrawn, but all had returned to service by the year end.

Class 47

A further 13 members of this class were withdrawn during 1990, and many others stored due to the downturn in freight traffic and cash shortages. The unique class 58 test bed 47901 was withdrawn in March, and 47406, 47407 (both August) and 47402 (December) from the prototype batch were also taken out of stock. Other withdrawals were of locomotives falling due for overhauls or those damaged by fire or collision.

53 locomotives received classified repairs during the year, 34 at BRML Doncaster, 11 at BRML Springburn and eight at Stratford DRS. The modification programme for equipping a number of InterCity locomotives with high capacity fuel tanks was completed during the year, along with a small programme of four locomotives which were equipped with multiple working for use on Departmental services. A new colour scheme for Parcels locomotives was introduced in April with the painting of 47474 in a grey and red scheme at Doncaster, and subsequently many Parcels sector locomotives have received this livery.

Class 50

Continued lack of replacement motive power for the Network SouthEast London Waterloo to Exeter services again reprieved many members of this class, although 15 examples were withdrawn during the year as and when major defects occurred. At long last some Class 47s became available as replacements towards the end of the year, hastening the demise of the "Hoovers", of which only 24 remained in traffic at the year end.

Class 56

This class remained intact during the year, despite fears at one time that the first withdrawals were about to take place. However, it is doubtful that 56042 will be seen in service again as this locomotive is stored off its bogies at Toton depot in a severely cannibalised state. The problem with this locomotive is that it was mounted on non-standard CP1 bogies and the cost of converting to standard proved to be prohibitive when

overhaul fell due.

Overhauls continued at BRML Doncaster, with 23 examples being completed during the year.

Class 58

Overhauls and repaints into Railfreight Coal livery continued at BRML Doncaster during the year, with fifteen examples being dealt with.

Class 59

The four locomotives ordered by ARC were shipped into the UK from Canada via Newport Docks in October. After testing they entered revenue earning service from November.

Class 60

After many delays the first members of this class to be formally accepted by BR for normal service were 60017 and 60018 on 30th October. By the end of the year nine examples were in traffic.

Class 73

Overhauls of this class were transferred from BRML Eastleigh to Selhurst depot during the course of 1990. The last two examples overhauled at the former were 73106 and 73202, completed on 18th and 19th April respectively. Surprisingly two class 73/0 locomotives were amongst those overhauled at Selhurst during the year, placing in doubt fears for the future of this sub-class.

Class 81

With four further withdrawals during 1990, only two locomotives remained at the year end, namely 81012 and 81017. They are engaged on e.c.s. duties at London Euston.

Class 85

Three further class 85/0 locomotives were converted to class 85/1 during the year. All locomotives of the former type were withdrawn from service other than two retained by InterCity for e.c.s. duties at Manchester (85018) and London Euston (85040). Of the latter sub-class, 85107 and 85111 suffered major failures and were also withdrawn from stock.

Class 86

Fitting of this class with Time Division Multiplex equipment continued during 1990, with only ten examples remaining to be done at the year end. The renumbering programme of a number of Class 86/4 locomotives as Class 86/6 was also completed and these latter locomotives had their electric train supply equipment isolated.

Overhauls continued at Stratford DRS, with 36 examples being dealt with during the year.

Class 87

The programme of equipping this class with Time Division Multiplex equipment was completed during the year and this equipment was put to use with the introduction of a large number of push-pull services on the West Coast Main line.

Overhauls were moved to BRML Springburn with the onset of the 1990–91 financial year, the first electric locomotive overhauls to be carried out at this location. Eight locomotives were overhauled at Springburn during the year, and three at Stratford (including thyristor-control-equipped 87101).

Class 89

The unique Brush prototype electric only saw occasional service during the year, usually between London King's Cross and Peterborough.

Classes 90 and 91

Deliveries of these two classes were completed during the year.

DEPARTMENTAL SECTOR LOCOMOTIVES

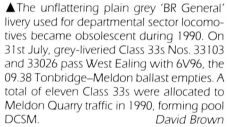

▲The unflattering plain grey 'BR General' livery used for departmental sector locomotives became obsolescent during 1990. On 31st July, grey-liveried Class 33s Nos. 33103 and 33026 pass West Ealing with 6V96, the 09.38 Tonbridge–Meldon ballast empties. A total of eleven Class 33s were allocated to Meldon Quarry traffic in 1990, forming pool DCSM.   *David Brown*

◄The 'Civil Link' livery incorporating a yellow bodyside stripe was generally acknowledged to be a great improvement on the previous plain grey. This livery is similar to that carried by the Class EM2 electric locomotives of the Manchester–Sheffield 'Woodhead' line whilst they were on the Netherlands Railways (NS) as Class 1500. Stabled at London King's Cross on 14th September is Class 31 No. 31541, the first Class 31/5 to receive this colour scheme.

Colin Marsden

◄The use of Class 50s on departmental workings was all but finished as 1990 drew to a close. On 5th April No. 50019 'Ramillies' passes Flax Bourton with an Exeter–Bristol engineers' train. This locomotive was withdrawn on 19th September after suffering a main generator flashover. It had spent its last year painted in blue livery.

Martin Loader

BR STOCK CHANGES 1990

LOCOMOTIVES

New

59101	AR	30/10/90
59102	AR	02/11/90
59103	AR	02/11/90
59104	AR	05/11/90
60007	IM	/01/90
60008	TE	22/01/90
60017	TE	30/10/90
60018	TE	30/10/90
60019	IM	06/12/90
60023	TE	08/11/90
60028	TE	09/11/90
60029	TE	26/11/90
60030	TE	22/11/90
60032	IM	03/12/90
60034	TE	12/12/90
90036	CE	25/04/90
90037	CE	30/04/90
90038	CE	30/04/90
90039	CE	31/05/90
90040	CE	31/05/90
90041	CE	31/05/90
90042	CE	05/06/90
90043	CE	18/05/90
90044	CE	25/05/90
90045	CE	01/06/90
90046	CE	08/06/90
90047	CE	15/06/90
90048	CE	27/07/90
90049	CE	26/10/90
90050	CE	14/11/90
91011	BN	28/02/90
91012	BN	11/04/90
91013	BN	25/04/90
91014	BN	10/05/90
91015	BN	31/05/90
91016	BN	14/06/90
91017	BN	03/07/90
91018	BN	06/08/90
91019	BN	08/08/90
91020	BN	17/09/90
91021	BN	25/09/90
91022	BN	27/09/90
91023	BN	08/12/90
91024	BN	09/10/90
91025	BN	24/10/90
91026	BN	09/11/90
91027	BN	19/12/90

Reinstated

* Subsequently withdrawn

08537	IM	05/07/90
08663	LA	10/06/90
20032	TO	10/07/90*
20032	TO	19/11/90
20138	TE	08/01/90
20199	TO	23/02/90*
25912	HO	/10/90
31299	IM	/03/90*
33035	SL	23/01/90
33057	EH	/03/90

Withdrawn

* Subsequently reinstated

08440	SF	03/05/90
08496	CA	14/06/90
08537	IM	25/05/90*
08556	WN	03/07/90
08612	OC	21/09/90
08618	GD	11/11/90
08663	LA	01/05/90*
08704	BY	01/11/90
08729	DR	22/02/90
08747	GD	11/07/90
08796	AF	04/05/90
08797	GD	11/11/90
08808	CL	14/05/90
08820	LO	22/02/90
08838	DY	09/05/90
08841	BS	14/06/90
08843	LO	22/02/90
08851	ML	07/02/90
08871	TI	27/10/90
08930	SF	19/02/90
20004	TO	11/10/90
20006	TO	02/10/90
20020	TO	10/10/90
20026	TO	10/10/90
20030	TO	03/10/90
20031	TO	14/09/90
20032	TO	02/02/90*
20032	TO	10/10/90*
20034	TO	01/10/90
20045	TO	10/10/90
20048	BS	09/11/90
20052	TO	17/11/90
20053	TO	10/10/90
20056	TO	01/10/90
20064	TO	14/09/90
20065	TO	11/12/90
20080	TO	10/07/90
20110	TO	14/09/90
20114	TO	31/01/90
20129	TO	10/10/90
20130	TO	10/10/90
20136	TO	02/10/90
20144	TE	08/01/90
20157	TO	10/10/90
20160	BS	17/12/90
20172	TO	11/10/90
20183	TO	26/01/90
20188	TO	31/01/90
20189	TO	14/09/90
20199	TO	31/01/90*
20199	TO	18/06/90
20224	TO	26/01/90
20227	TO	01/10/90
26023	ED	21/09/90
26039	ED	18/10/90
31124	TE	25/05/90
31170	IM	08/01/90
31198	SF	16/03/90
31208	IM	13/02/90
31231	SF	22/01/90
31240	SF	17/01/90
31257	IM	10/09/90
31260	TE	12/01/90
31292	BS	07/02/90
31293	BS	09/11/90
31299	IM	21/03/90*
31299	IM	10/10/90
31320	TE	28/04/90
33057	SL	13/02/90*
33060	SL	27/10/90
33106	SL	16/11/90
47097	TI	23/04/90
47116	CD	27/07/90
47402	IM	19/12/90
47406	IM	13/08/90
47407	IM	13/08/90
47427	CD	05/02/90
47435	CD	15/03/90
47444	CD	05/11/90
47455	CD	15/03/90
47538	BR	09/11/90
47544	CD	05/02/90
47645	CD	05/02/90
47901	CF	23/03/90
50004	LA	22/06/90
50005	LA	11/12/90
50016	LA	03/08/90
50019	LA	19/09/90
50020	LA	27/07/90
50021	LA	17/04/90
50023	LA	15/10/90
50024	LA	01/02/90
50026	LA	11/12/90
50028	LA	01/02/90
50032	LA	15/10/90
50034	LA	29/06/90
50035	LA	03/08/90
50040	LA	03/08/90
50041	LA	17/04/90
50042	LA	15/10/90
50043	LA	01/02/90
50045	LA	11/12/90
81002	WN	17/10/90
81004	WN	04/04/90
81009	WN	17/02/90
81010	GW	23/05/90
85005	CE	25/05/90
85008	CE	10/09/90
85013	CE	17/10/90
85015	CE	08/09/90
85020	CE	17/10/90
85023	CE	02/04/90
85025	CE	08/01/90
85026	CE	04/05/90
85028	CE	10/01/90
85030	CE	11/09/90
85031	CE	21/05/90
85034	WN	17/10/90
85037	CE	03/09/90
85038	CE	02/01/90
85106	CE	24/10/90
85107	CE	23/05/90

Renumbered

31407 to 31507	24/05/90
31411 to 31511	30/05/90
31412 to 31512	30/10/90
31414 to 31514	/10/90
31416 to 31516	/11/90
31419 to 31519	/06/90
31422 to 31522	21/05/90
31424 to 31524	30/05/90
31426 to 31526	/10/90
31430 to 31530	01/06/90
31431 to 31531	/10/90
31433 to 31533	31/05/90
31437 to 31537	30/05/90
31441 to 31541	/05/90
31444 to 31544	14/05/90
31445 to 31545	/06/90
31446 to 31546	21/05/90
31447 to 31547	/05/90
31448 to 31548	21/05/90
31449 to 31549	/10/90
31451 to 31551	31/05/90
31452 to 31552	/05/90
31453 to 31553	/05/90
31454 to 31554	18/05/90
31455 to 31555	01/06/90
31456 to 31556	/05/90
31458 to 31558	21/05/90
31463 to 31563	/10/90
31465 to 31565	/07/90
31468 to 31568	/05/90
31469 to 31569	/10/90
37355 to 37045	23/05/90
37357 to 37079	/03/90
47531 to 47974	/06/90
47540 to 47975	29/07/90
47546 to 47976	/06/90
47556 to 47844	01/06/90
47570 to 47849	/ /90
47606 to 47842	16/02/90
47614 to 47853	21/02/90
47623 to 47843	16/03/90
47639 to 47851	/01/90
47646 to 47852	07/02/90
47648 to 47850	17/01/90
85003 to 85113	/10/90
85007 to 85112	/03/90
85011 to 85114	/10/90
86403 to 86603	/10/90
86404 to 86604	27/09/90
86405 to 86605	/10/90
86406 to 86606	/10/90
86410 to 86610	/07/90
86411 to 86611	06/09/90
86412 to 86612	/10/90
86414 to 86614	/10/90
86415 to 86615	/10/90
86418 to 86618	11/08/90
86422 to 86622	11/04/90
86423 to 86623	/10/90
86428 to 86628	/10/90
86431 to 86631	/10/90
86434 to 86634	13/04/90
86437 to 86637	/10/90
86438 to 86638	/10/90
86439 to 86639	/10/90

COACHING STOCK

New

10308	BN	15/01/90
10309	BN	02/04/90
10310	BN	02/04/90
10311	BN	02/07/90
10312	BN	26/07/90
10313	BN	15/08/90
10314	BN	06/09/90
10315	BN	21/11/90
10316	BN	02/10/90
10325	BN	19/10/90
10326	BN	21/11/90
10327	BN	20/12/90
10330	BN	02/04/90
10331	BN	20/04/90
10332	BN	17/05/90
10333	BN	11/06/90
11214	BN	15/01/90
11215	BN	15/01/90
11216	BN	24/04/90
11217	BN	24/04/90
11218	BN	02/04/90
11219	BN	02/04/90
11220	BN	13/09/90
11221	BN	02/07/90
11222	BN	26/07/90
11223	BN	26/07/90
11224	BN	15/08/90
11225	BN	15/08/90
11226	BN	06/09/90
11227	BN	06/09/90
11228	BN	02/10/90
11229	BN	02/10/90
11230	BN	15/10/90
11231	BN	19/10/90
11246	BN	13/11/90
11247	BN	13/11/90
11248	BN	18/12/90
11249	BN	20/12/90
11256	BN	02/04/90
11257	BN	02/04/90
11258	BN	20/04/90
11259	BN	20/04/90
11260	BN	14/05/90
11261	BN	14/05/90
11262	BN	07/06/90
11263	BN	07/06/90
12207	BN	15/01/90
12208	BN	02/04/90
12209	BN	02/04/90
12210	BN	03/07/90
12211	BN	26/07/90
12212	BN	16/08/90
12213	BN	07/09/90
12214	BN	02/10/90
12223	BN	25/10/90
12224	BN	21/11/90
12225	BN	20/12/90
12228	BN	02/04/90
12229	BN	23/04/90
12230	BN	14/05/90
12231	BN	11/06/90
12306	BN	15/01/90
12307	BN	24/04/90
12308	BN	02/04/90
12309	BN	02/07/90
12310	BN	26/07/90
12311	BN	15/08/90
12312	BN	06/09/90
12313	BN	21/11/90
12322	BN	19/10/90
12323	BN	13/11/90
12327	BN	02/04/90
12328	BN	20/04/90
12329	BN	14/05/90
12330	BN	11/06/90
12414	BN	15/01/90
12415	BN	15/01/90
12416	BN	15/01/90
12417	BN	24/04/90
12418	BN	24/04/90
12419	BN	24/04/90
12420	BN	02/04/90
12421	BN	02/04/90
12422	BN	02/04/90
12423	BN	02/07/90
12424	BN	02/07/90
12425	BN	02/07/90
12426	BN	26/07/90
12427	BN	26/07/90
12428	BN	26/07/90
12429	BN	15/08/90
12430	BN	16/08/90
12431	BN	15/08/90
12432	BN	06/09/90
12433	BN	07/09/90
12434	BN	07/09/90
12435	BN	02/10/90
12436	BN	02/10/90
12437	BN	02/10/90
12463	BN	02/10/90
12464	BN	24/10/90
12465	BN	25/10/90
12466	BN	25/10/90
12467	BN	20/11/90
12468	BN	15/11/90
12469	BN	14/11/90
12478	BN	02/04/90
12479	BN	02/04/90
12480	BN	02/04/90
12481	BN	20/04/90
12482	BN	23/04/90
12483	BN	20/04/90
12484	BN	14/05/90
12485	BN	14/05/90
12486	BN	17/05/90
12487	BN	11/06/90
12488	BN	11/06/90
12489	BN	11/06/90

Reinstated

5614	HT	08/12/90
18935	NL	08/12/90
18936	NL	08/12/90
18937	NL	08/12/90

Withdrawn

* Subsequently reinstated

1656	CL	07/02/90
1665	CL	10/05/90
1681	NC	07/02/90
1687	CL	07/02/90
1694	MA	05/11/90
1695	MA	05/11/90
1838	OM	09/01/90
1848	OM	06/08/90
1867	OM	16/08/90
1875	OM	06/08/90
1879	OM	16/08/90
1882	OM	16/08/90
1924	ZN	07/02/90
1944	PC	05/11/90
1946	MA	16/10/90
1947	MA	04/12/90
2902	ZN	05/01/90
2911	ZN	05/01/90
3045	BN	14/03/90
3096	CL	10/09/90
3749	DY	11/10/90
3754	NL	16/11/90
3766	BN	13/09/90
3767	BN	16/11/90
3950	NL	16/11/90
3991	DY	11/10/90
3993	CL	01/06/90
4058	DY	11/10/90
4076	CL	01/06/90
4366	HT	10/05/90
4376	CL	01/06/90
4393	DY	11/10/90
4419	BN	16/11/90
4435	BN	01/03/90
4478	LL	26/07/90
4479	LL	26/07/90
4483	PC	19/09/90
4485	LL	17/07/90
4634	FW	24/08/90
4779	LL	18/07/90
4785	HT	10/05/90
4795	LL	26/07/90
4798	LL	26/07/90
4836	NL	26/09/90
4843	NL	20/08/90
4857	LL	24/08/90
4885	NL	20/08/90
4886	LL	24/08/90
4900	BN	16/11/90
4907	NL	20/08/90
4911	BN	16/11/90
4912	BN	16/11/90
4918	LL	24/08/90
4934	LL	24/08/90
4937	LL	14/12/90
4948	LL	02/10/90
4952	LL	24/08/90
4965	LL	24/08/90
4978	LL	24/08/90
4987	BN	24/08/90
4995	LL	24/08/90
5073	LL	16/11/90
5080	LL	16/11/90
5087	LL	16/11/90
5097	NL	16/11/90
5118	LL	16/11/90
5124	IS	16/11/90
5128	NL	16/11/90
5131	NL	16/11/90
5142	MA	13/03/90
5151	IS	26/07/90
5153	EC	26/07/90
5155	IS	19/09/90

Number	Depot	Date
5160	HT	16/11/90
5170	IS	19/09/90
5176	IS	19/09/90
5187	IS	19/09/90
5192	HT	26/06/90
5196	IS	26/07/90
5217	IS	19/09/90
5231	IS	19/09/90
5235	NL	16/11/90
5236	NL	16/11/90
5237	NL	16/11/90
5239	NL	16/11/90
5240	NL	16/11/90
5241	NL	16/11/90
5243	NL	16/11/90
5244	NL	16/11/90
5249	NL	16/11/90
5253	LL	19/09/90
5262	HT	16/11/90
5281	IS	19/09/90
5283	HT	16/11/90
5284	LL	14/12/90
5294	CL	12/12/90
5296	HT	16/11/90
5298	HT	16/11/90
5299	CL	11/10/90
5306	HT	16/11/90
5310	CL	12/12/90
5317	CL	12/12/90
5325	HT	16/11/90
5338	NC	16/10/90
5339	HT	07/08/90
5340	HT	16/11/90
5342	IS	19/09/90
5343	HT	16/11/90
5347	HT	16/11/90
5352	CL	12/12/90
5356	NC	16/11/90
5359	IS	19/09/90
5361	PC	11/05/90
5363	CL	12/12/90
5367	MA	03/10/90
5369	NC	16/11/90
5374	CL	11/10/90
5383	CL	12/12/90
5387	HT	16/11/90
5388	CL	12/12/90
5399	CL	11/10/90
5409	HT	16/11/90
5424	LL	10/09/90
5445	IS	19/09/90
5548	IS	19/09/90
5549	WB	02/10/90
5561	IS	01/06/90
5581	MA	02/10/90
5582	EC	26/07/90
5597	MA	04/12/90
5614	HT	16/11/90*
5677	MA	24/01/90
6331	CA	22/02/90
6337	BN	05/11/90
6400	HT	04/10/90
6405	WB	13/06/90
6406	WB	09/01/90
6505	LA	14/03/90
6506	NC	16/11/90
6512	LA	26/01/90
6515	NL	16/11/90
6520	IS·	29/10/90
6526	LL	28/11/90
7553	IS	28/11/90
7558	IS	14/12/90
7561	IS	19/09/90
9007	FW	16/10/90
9100	IS	19/09/90
9102	NL	16/11/90
9103	CL	11/05/90
9104	CL	11/05/90
9106	CL	01/03/90
9107	CL	26/02/90
9385	NL	16/11/90
9386	NL	16/11/90
9392	NL	16/11/90
9394	NL	16/11/90
9400	IS	13/02/90
9410	NL	16/11/90
9413	OY	01/03/90
9445	IS	05/08/90
9447	HT	16/11/90
9462	HT	16/11/90
9464	MA	17/07/90
13313	CL	20/03/90
13320	CL	10/09/90
13321	CL	10/09/90
13325	CL	16/11/90
13335	OM	17/10/90
13341	OM	17/10/90
13342	BN	16/11/90
13343	OM	02/02/90
13441	OM	17/10/90
13442	OM	26/01/90
13443	OM	17/10/90
13445	LL	14/12/90
13451	LL	14/12/90
13456	IS	19/09/90
13461	IS	19/09/90
13463	HT	16/11/90
13472	LL	14/12/90
13516	LL	14/12/90
13519	LL	14/12/90
13520	LL	14/12/90
13527	LL	14/12/90
13532	LL	14/12/90
13568	DY	04/12/90
13605	NC	16/08/90
17021	FW	16/06/90
17025	BN	14/03/90
17031	OY	09/01/90
17040	LL	14/12/90
17043	LL	14/12/90
17047	LL	14/12/90
17051	LL	14/12/90
17052	LL	14/12/90
17054	LL	14/12/90
17055	OY	09/01/90
17059	IS	26/07/90
17060	LL	14/12/90
17062	LL	14/12/90
17066	LL	14/12/90
17068	LL	14/12/90
17092	LL	14/12/90
17101	LL	14/12/90
17103	LL	14/12/90
17127	IS	19/09/90
17134	MA	16/08/90
18284	IS	11/05/90
18288	IS	19/09/90
18597	LL	11/05/90
18602	OM	17/10/90
18603	NL	16/11/90
18604	LL	14/12/90
18605	OM	17/10/90
18608	NL	16/11/90
18611	NL	16/11/90
18616	OM	17/10/90
18622	NL	16/11/90
18627	NL	16/11/90
18704	OM	17/10/90
18706	LL	14/12/90
18709	NL	16/11/90
18711	OM	17/10/90
18712	LL	14/12/90
18714	NL	16/11/90
18715	OM	17/10/90
18716	LL	14/12/90
18717	OM	17/10/90
18727	LL	14/12/90
18728	OM	17/10/90
18729	NL	16/11/90
18730	OM	17/10/90
18734	LL	19/02/90
18738	LL	19/02/90
18743	OM	04/10/90
18749	NL	16/11/90
18750	LL	18/07/90
18756	LL	13/06/90
18771	OM	17/10/90
18774	NL	16/11/90
18775	LL	26/07/90
18784	NL	16/11/90
18788	LL	14/12/90
18789	LL	14/12/90
18792	LL	14/12/90
18794	OM	17/10/90
18805	NL	16/11/90
18806	LL	18/06/90
18809	LL	14/12/90
18813	NL	16/11/90
18814	OM	17/10/90
18818	OM	17/10/90
18819	OM	11/10/90
18835	LL	01/06/90
18838	NL	16/11/90
18849	LL	14/12/90
18863	OM	17/10/90
18869	OM	17/10/90
18901	OM	11/10/90
18911	CF	10/05/90
18921	LL	14/12/90
18925	LL	14/12/90
18931	LL	14/12/90
18933	NL	16/11/90
18935	NL	16/11/90*
18936	NL	16/11/90*
18937	NL	16/11/90*
18941	LL	14/12/90
18947	LL	19/02/90
18952	NL	16/11/90
18955	NL	16/11/90
18957	LL	19/02/90
18960	LL	14/12/90
18967	NL	16/11/90
18968	LL	26/07/90
18970	LL	26/07/90
18977	OM	11/10/90
18987	LL	19/02/90
18996	NL	16/11/90
18997	NL	16/11/90
19011	OM	11/10/90
19012	LL	18/07/90
19014	OM	07/08/90
19022	OM	17/10/90
19452	LL	14/12/90
19454	EH	10/07/90
19460	OM	09/01/90
19464	EH	10/07/90
19469	WB	09/01/90
19486	LL	01/06/90
19512	WB	09/01/90
19522	LL	14/12/90
19523	LL	14/12/90
19529	LL	14/12/90
19534	EH	09/01/90
19536	LL	14/12/90
19540	WB	07/02/90
19548	LL	14/12/90
19549	LL	14/12/90
19555	LL	14/12/90
19556	LL	14/12/90
25008	FW	03/09/90
26125	FW	16/10/90
34538	LL	26/07/90
35306	LL	26/07/90
35333	LL	14/12/90
35340	LL	26/07/90
35343	LL	26/07/90
35448	OM	17/08/90
35449	OM	30/07/90
35450	OY	19/06/90
35453	LL	26/07/90
35459	LL	18/06/90
35464	NL	14/12/90
35468	CL	26/01/90
35470	LL	26/07/90
35473	LL	26/07/90
35475	LL	26/07/90
35476	OM	16/05/90
35486	BN	07/02/90
35486	BN	11/10/90

Renumbered

From	To
5395	6347
5522	6343
5594	6332
6423	6829
6424	6823
6425	6826
6428	6827
6429	6824
6437	6811
6447	6822
6448	6812
6451	6810
6452	6807
6454	6808
6455	6809
6458	6821
6460	6825
6463	6813
6464	6828
6465	6814
9422	6346
11905	11005
11906	11006
11907	11007
11908	12169
11909	12170
11922	12172
12405	12232
17137	6345
19465	6352
19478	6353
40324	40724
40326	40726
40327	40727
40331	40731
40433	40233
41047	42350
41048	42351
41053	42346
41054	42347
41073	42348
41074	42349

Renumbered from Departmental Stock

ADB 975655 to 6335
ADB 975660 to 6337

Converted from Locomotive

83301 ex 33115 14/02/90

DMUs

New

Number	Depot	Date
52702	HA	14/03/90
52703	HA	27/04/90
52704	HA	12/04/90
52705	HA	13/04/90
52706	HA	13/05/90
52707	HA	17/06/90
52708	HA	04/06/90
52709	HA	03/06/90
52710	HA	03/06/90
52711	HA	04/07/90
52712	HA	03/07/90
52713	HA	06/07/90
52714	HA	08/07/90
52715	HA	03/07/90
52716	HA	21/08/90
52717	HA	21/08/90
52718	HA	21/08/90
52719	HA	21/08/90
52720	HA	22/08/90
52721	HA	22/08/90
52722	HA	23/08/90
52723	HA	23/08/90
52724	HA	25/08/90
52725	HA	24/08/90
52726	HA	25/08/90
52727	HA	25/08/90
52728	HA	25/08/90
52729	HA	25/08/90
52730	HA	03/09/90
52731	HA	11/09/90
52732	HA	29/09/90
52733	HA	29/09/90
52734	HT	03/10/90
52735	HT	19/10/90
52736	HT	04/10/90
52737	HT	02/10/90
52738	HT	05/10/90
52739	CF	05/10/90
52740	CF	05/10/90
52741	CF	05/10/90
52742	HT	20/10/90
52743	CF	05/10/90
52744	HT	18/10/90
52745	HT	30/10/90
52746	HT	07/11/90
52747	HT	09/11/90
52748	CF	15/11/90
52749	CF	23/11/90
52750	CF	08/12/90
52751	CF	08/12/90
52752	CF	10/12/90
52754	CF	14/12/90
52755	CF	11/12/90
52756	CF	10/12/90
52757	CF	15/12/90
52759	CF	19/12/90
57702	HA	14/03/90
57703	HA	27/04/90
57704	HA	12/04/90
57705	HA	13/04/90
57706	HA	13/05/90
57707	HA	17/06/90
57708	HA	04/06/90
57709	HA	03/06/90
57710	HA	03/06/90
57711	HA	04/07/90
57712	HA	03/07/90
57713	HA	06/07/90
57714	HA	08/07/90
57715	HA	03/07/90
57716	HA	21/08/90
57717	HA	21/08/90
57718	HA	21/08/90
57719	HA	21/08/90
57720	HA	22/08/90
57721	HA	22/08/90
57722	HA	23/08/90
57723	HA	23/08/90
57724	HA	25/08/90
57725	HA	24/08/90
57726	HA	25/08/90
57727	HA	25/08/90
57728	HA	25/08/90
57729	HA	25/08/90
57730	HA	03/09/90
57731	HA	11/09/90
57732	HA	29/09/90
57733	HA	29/09/90
57734	HT	03/10/90
57735	HT	19/10/90
57736	HT	04/10/90
57737	HT	02/10/90
57738	HT	05/10/90
57739	CF	05/10/90
57740	CF	05/10/90
57741	CF	05/10/90
57742	HT	20/10/90
57743	HT	05/10/90
57744	HT	18/10/90
57745	HT	30/10/90
57746	HT	07/11/90
57747	HT	09/11/90
57748	CF	15/11/90
57749	CF	23/11/90
57750	CF	08/12/90
57751	CF	08/12/90
57752	CF	10/12/90
57754	CF	14/12/90
57755	CF	11/12/90
57756	CF	10/12/90
57757	CF	15/12/90
57759	CF	19/12/90

Reinstated

* Subsequently withdrawn

Number	Depot	Date
51071	TS	01/90
51101	TS	01/90
51432	RG	01/90
53536	CH	02/90*
54091	NL	03/90
54191	BR	05/90
59082	LO	02/90*

Withdrawn

* Subsequently reinstated

Number	Depot	Date
51062	RG	22/10/90
51131	TS	07/12/90
51174	NL	07/12/90
51181	LA	27/11/90
51182	HA	27/11/90
51194	TS	07/12/90
51212	OO	23/11/90
51223	LA	27/11/90
51241	LA	27/11/90
51312	CF	13/02/90
51327	CF	13/02/90
51337	RG	22/10/90
51418	CH	26/09/90
51436	CF	24/01/90
51455	NL	11/10/90
51495	NL	11/10/90
51513	TS	03/12/90
51524	NL	11/10/90
51569	TS	27/11/90
51662	TS	20/11/90
51799	NL	07/12/90
51800	LO	27/11/90
51813	NL	16/03/90
51817	NL	23/02/90
51823	NL	23/02/90
51829	NL	23/02/90
51830	NL	23/02/90
51834	NL	23/02/90
51840	NL	23/02/90
51842	NL	23/02/90
51843	NL	23/02/90
51847	NL	23/02/90
51868	TS	07/12/90
51898	TS	03/12/90
51902	TS	07/12/90
51905	LO	12/09/90
51941	TS	20/11/90
51991	ED	20/11/90
51996	ED	29/03/90
52019	ED	29/03/90
52035	ED	20/11/90
52043	HA	16/03/90
52064	TS	20/11/90
52066	NL	23/02/90

52069	NL	23/02/90
52071	NL	09/03/90
52072	NL	23/02/90
52075	NL	23/02/90
52077	NL	09/03/90
52080	NL	23/02/90
52082	NL	16/03/90
52085	NL	23/02/90
53020	CA	02/05/90
53027	CA	06/09/90
53030	TS	12/12/90
53046	CA	06/09/90
53056	TS	07/12/90
53082	TS	04/12/90
53086	CF	24/01/90
53128	CF	26/01/90
53169	CF	24/01/90
53176	HA	07/12/90
53194	LO	27/11/90
53212	LA	27/11/90
53215	HA	27/11/90
53224	LO	07/12/90
53239	HA	07/12/90
53244	TS	03/12/90
53247	LA	27/11/90
53260	LA	27/11/90
53431	CH	11/06/90
53442	CH	21/05/90
53444	NH	17/08/90
53451	CH	11/06/90
53493	CH	11/06/90
53494	CH	11/06/90
53512	CH	11/06/90
53516	CH	21/05/90
53517	CH	21/05/90
53529	CH	11/06/90
53534	CH	11/06/90
53536	CH	21/05/90
53639	LA	27/11/90
53844	TS	12/12/90
53880	TS	04/12/90
53893	TS	12/09/90
53932	TS	27/11/90
53952	HT	07/12/90
53962	HT	07/12/90
53965	NL	12/12/90
53966	NL	07/12/90
54008	TS	27/11/90
54011	TS	27/11/90
54028	CA	04/06/90
54041	CA	04/06/90
54070	OO	23/11/90
54075	NH	11/06/90
54191	BR	13/02/90*
54201	CF	27/11/90
54202	BR	13/02/90
54244	HT	07/12/90
54249	NL	07/12/90
54342	NL	12/12/90
54345	HT	10/05/90
54351	NL	11/10/90
54370	HT	10/05/90
54486	CH	11/04/90
55004	LA	04/10/90
55011	LA	04/10/90
55202	DY	22/10/90
55203	DY	22/10/90
55302	DY	22/10/90
55303	DY	22/10/90
55402	DY	22/10/90
55403	DY	22/10/90
55500	NL	23/10/90
55501	NL	23/10/90
55991	CA	05/11/90
59040	HT	10/05/90
59061	HA	07/12/90
59065	LO	11/06/90
59082	LO	/03/90
59086	HA	07/12/90
59090	TS	27/11/90
59104	HA	24/01/90
59107	LA	27/11/90
59124	HA	07/12/90
59130	LA	27/11/90
59163	RG	22/10/90
59206	BY	11/10/90
59246	NL	27/11/90
59249	NL	27/11/90
59302	LO	27/11/90
59304	HA	27/11/90
59381	LE	27/11/90
59385	CF	07/12/90
59389	TS	04/12/90
59421	RG	23/11/90
59424	RG	23/11/90
59444	TS	17/07/90
59448	TS	11/06/90
59525	LA	27/11/90
59542	TS	27/11/90
59561	LA	27/11/90
59571	HA	27/11/90
59593	TS	12/12/90
59596	TS	20/11/90
59606	TS	27/11/90
59610	TS	20/11/90
59612	TS	12/12/90
59613	TS	12/12/90
59616	TS	12/12/90
59621	CP	06/07/90
59622	CP	06/07/90
59627	CP	06/07/90
59631	CP	06/07/90
59653	CP	06/07/90
59694	NL	07/12/90
59715	CP	06/07/90
59716	CP	06/07/90
59717	CP	06/07/90
59719	TS	07/12/90
59722	TS	20/11/90
59723	TS	20/11/90
59725	CP	06/07/90
59744	CP	06/07/90
59760	TS	27/11/90
59789	ED	20/11/90
59809	HA	12/12/90
59817	NL	11/10/90
60125	SU	13/11/90
60139	SU	25/05/90
60152	SU	19/06/90
60153	SU	19/06/90
60522	SU	25/05/90
60523	SU	25/05/90
60610	SU	25/05/90
60671	SU	13/11/90
60825	SU	13/11/90
60910	SU	25/05/90

EMUs

New

319 161	SU	26/09/90
319 162	SU	26/09/90
319 163	SU	29/09/90
319 164	SU	29/09/90
319 165	SU	29/09/90
319 166	SU	29/09/90
319 167	SU	01/11/90
319 168	SU	02/11/90
319 169	SU	07/11/90
319 170	SU	10/11/90
319 171	SU	19/11/90
319 172	SU	23/11/90
319 173	SU	07/12/90
319 174	SU	07/12/90
319 175	SU	11/12/90
319 176	SU	11/12/90
319 177	SU	14/12/90
319 178	SU	18/12/90
319 179	SU	21/12/90
320 001	GW	30/10/90
320 002	GW	31/10/90
320 003	GW	31/10/90
320 004	GW	31/10/90
320 005	GW	31/10/90
320 006	GW	31/10/90
320 007	GW	31/10/90
320 008	GW	31/10/90
320 009	GW	31/10/90
320 010	GW	31/10/90
320 011	GW	31/10/90
320 012	GW	31/10/90
320 013	GW	31/10/90
320 014	GW	31/10/90
320 015	GW	31/10/90
320 016	GW	31/10/90
320 017	GW	31/10/90
320 018	GW	31/10/90
320 019	GW	31/10/90
320 020	GW	31/10/90
320 321	GW	11/12/90
320 322	GW	11/12/90
321 347	IL	29/01/90
321 348	IL	05/02/90
321 349	IL	07/02/90
321 350	IL	08/02/90
321 351	IL	09/02/90
321 352	IL	15/02/90
321 353	IL	20/02/90
321 354	IL	06/02/90
321 355	IL	07/03/90
321 356	IL	08/03/90
321 357	IL	07/03/90
321 358	IL	14/03/90
321 359	IL	15/03/90
321 360	IL	02/04/90
321 361	IL	01/04/90
321 362	IL	04/04/90
321 363	IL	27/04/90
321 364	IL	10/05/90
321 365	IL	21/05/90
321 366	IL	22/05/90
321 444	BY	09/01/90
321 445	BY	12/01/90
321 446	BY	17/01/90
321 447	BY	18/01/90
321 448	BY	23/01/90
322 481	IL	16/07/90
322 482	IL	21/07/90
322 483	IL	24/07/90
322 484	IL	29/07/90
322 485	IL	23/07/90
483 004	RY	01/05/90
483 005	RY	01/05/90
483 006	RY	01/05/90
483 007	RY	01/09/90
483 008	RY	01/09/90

Reinstated

* Subsequently withdrawn

15380	SG
61110	EM*
61111	EM
61208	EM*
61223	EM*
62479	BM*
70086	EM*
70103	EM*
70208	EM*
70214	EM
70223	EM*
70818	BM*
70822	BM
70837	BM
70842	BM*
75224	EM*
75225	EM*
75271	EM
75272	EM*
75280	EM*
75299	EM*
75306	EM*
75340	EM*
75346	EM
75355	EM*

Withdrawn

* Subsequently reinstated

1	RY	10/07/90
3	RY	09/11/90
4	RY	09/11/90
6	RY	30/03/90
8	RY	10/07/90
9	RY	30/03/90
10	RY	10/07/90
11	RY	30/03/90
26	RY	04/12/90
29	RY	09/11/90
32	RY	09/11/90
33	RY	09/11/90
34	RY	10/07/90
92	RY	09/11/90
93	RY	30/03/90
94	RY	30/03/90
95	RY	30/03/90
14031	SG	25/05/90
14032	SG	25/05/90
14089	RE	24/10/90
14090	RE	24/10/90
14091	RE	24/10/90
14092	RE	24/10/90
14209	SG	25/05/90
14210	SG	25/05/90
14213	RE	24/10/90
14214	RE	24/10/90
14237	SG	25/05/90
14238	SG	25/05/90
14295	SG	05/11/90
14296	SG	05/11/90
14323	SG	25/05/90
14324	SG	25/05/90
14325	RE	24/10/90
14326	RE	24/10/90
14331	SG	05/11/90
14332	SG	05/11/90
14335	RE	24/10/90
14341	SG	25/05/90
14342	SG	25/05/90
14345	RE	24/10/90
14346	RE	24/10/90
14347	SG	05/11/90
14348	SG	05/11/90
14377	SG	05/11/90
14378	SG	05/11/90
14381	RE	24/10/90
14382	RE	24/10/90
14393	ZQ	09/11/90
14403	SG	05/11/90
14404	SG	05/11/90
14455	RE	24/10/90
14456	RE	24/10/90
14459	RE	24/10/90
14460	RE	24/10/90
14487	SG	25/05/90
15015	SG	24/10/90
15016	SG	25/05/90
15038	SG	25/05/90
15108	RE	24/10/90
15110	RE	24/10/90
15116	RE	24/10/90
15120	RE	24/10/90
15129	RE	24/10/90
15145	RE	24/10/90
15146	RE	24/10/90
15153	RE	24/10/90
15168	SG	05/11/90
15176	SG	05/11/90
15183	SG	25/05/90
15197	SG	25/05/90
15199	SG	25/05/90
15223	SG	25/05/90
15229	SG	24/10/90
15235	RE	24/10/90
15253	SG	05/11/90
15260	RE	24/10/90
15276	SG	05/11/90
15290	SG	25/05/90
15296	SG	25/05/90
15299	SG	25/05/90
15301	SG	25/05/90
15305	RE	24/10/90
15339	SG	05/11/90
15340	RE	24/10/90
15341	RE	24/10/90
15343	SG	05/11/90
15344	SG	05/11/90
15346	RE	24/10/90
15362	SG	05/11/90
15364	RE	24/10/90
15367	SG	05/11/90
15369	RE	24/10/90
15380	SG	05/11/90*
15415	RE	24/10/90
15416	RE	24/10/90
15418	RE	24/10/90
61066	EM	13/03/90
61082	EM	22/08/90
61098	EM	28/06/90
61110	EM	10/07/90*
61110	EM	11/10/90
61111	EM	24/01/90*
61113	EM	24/01/90
61116	EM	13/03/90
61118	EM	13/03/90
61131	EM	28/06/90
61200	EM	13/03/90
61201	EM	28/06/90
61202	EM	13/03/90
61208	EM	10/07/90*
61208	EM	11/10/90
61214	EM	28/06/90
61216	EM	13/03/90
61217	EM	28/06/90
61219	EM	24/01/90
61221	EM	24/01/90
61223	EM	10/07/90*
61223	EM	11/10/90
61388	SG	25/05/90
61389	SG	25/05/90
61414	EM	13/09/90
61815	GW	12/09/90
61828	GW	23/11/90
61851	GW	03/09/90
62169	GW	20/11/90
62170	GW	20/11/90
62173	GW	20/11/90
62174	GW	20/11/90
62176	GW	20/11/90
62178	GW	20/11/90
62179	GW	20/11/90
62180	GW	20/11/90
62181	GW	24/08/90
62194	BM	10/05/90
62479	BM	17/08/90
68102	EM	13/03/90
69025	BM	09/01/90
69309	BI	17/08/90
70066	EM	13/03/90
70086	EM	24/01/90*
70086	EM	11/10/90
70103	EM	11/10/90*
70103	EM	28/06/90
70108	EM	13/03/90
70110	EM	10/07/90
70111	EM	13/03/90
70116	EM	13/03/90
70117	EM	13/03/90
70123	EM	13/03/90
70125	EM	28/06/90
70190	EM	13/03/90
70197	EM	09/01/90
70200	EM	13/03/90
70208	EM	10/07/90*
70208	EM	11/10/90
70214	EM	24/01/90*
70216	EM	13/03/90
70217	EM	28/06/90
70219	EM	13/03/90
70223	EM	10/07/90*
70223	EM	11/10/90
70302	RE	25/05/90
70315	RE	18/01/90
70807	BN	23/01/90
70818	BM	20/03/90
70832	BM	06/04/90
70842	BM	01/08/90
70864	BM	23/01/90
70871	BM	17/08/90
71000		/ /90
71160	BM	23/01/90
75039	EM	13/03/90
75040	EM	13/03/90
75074	EM	13/03/90
75078	EM	13/03/90
75091	EM	13/03/90
75092	EM	24/01/90
75212	EM	09/01/90
75216	EM	24/01/90
75220	EM	13/03/90
75222	EM	13/03/90
75224	EM	10/07/90*
75224	EM	11/10/90
75225	EM	24/01/90*
75225	EM	11/10/90
75227	EM	24/01/90
75229	EM	31/07/90
75232	EM	31/07/90
75237	EM	09/01/90
75245	EM	28/06/90
75256	EM	31/07/90
75257	EM	10/07/90
75258	EM	10/07/90
75259	EM	10/07/90
75261	EM	09/01/90
75265	EM	28/06/90
75269	EM	31/07/90
75271	EM	28/06/90*
75272	EM	10/07/90*
75272	EM	11/10/90
75273	EM	31/07/90
75274	EM	28/06/90
75276	EM	31/07/90
75279	EM	31/07/90
75280	EM	10/07/90*
75280	EM	11/10/90
75289	EM	10/07/90
75297	EM	31/07/90
75299	EM	10/07/90*
75299	EM	11/10/90
75306	EM	24/01/90*
75306	EM	11/10/90
75309	EM	28/06/90
75310	EM	10/07/90
75312	EM	24/01/90
75322	EM	13/03/90
75326	EM	13/03/90
75329	EM	13/03/90
75332	EM	13/03/90
75336	EM	09/01/90
75337	EM	/ /90
75340	EM	10/07/90*
75340	EM	11/10/90
75344	EM	13/03/90
75346	EM	28/06/90
75348	EM	13/03/90
75353	EM	09/01/90
75355	EM	10/07/90*
75355	EM	11/10/90
75359	EM	28/06/90
75749	GW	03/09/90
75756	GW	23/11/90

75762	GW	21/06/90					
75805	GW	03/09/90					
75818	GW	22/06/90					
76284	BM	23/01/90					
76309	BM	06/04/90					
76310	BM	06/04/90					
76331	BM	04/07/90					
76337	BI	10/05/90					
76409	GW	20/11/90					
76410	GW	20/11/90					
76413	GW	20/11/90					
76414	GW	20/11/90					
76416	GW	20/11/90					
76418	GW	24/08/90					
76419	GW	20/11/90					
76420	GW	20/11/90					
76421	GW	20/11/90					
76428	GW	20/11/90					
76429	GW	20/11/90					
76432	GW	20/11/90					
76433	GW	20/11/90					
76435	GW	20/11/90					
76437	GW	20/11/90					
76438	GW	20/11/90					
76439	GW	20/11/90					
76440	GW	24/08/90					
77106	SU	15/06/90					
77111	SU	15/06/90					

NPCCS

New

82101	OY	04/01/90
82132	WB	04/01/90
82133	WB	04/01/90
82134	WB	04/01/90
82135	WB	04/01/90
82136	WB	04/01/90
82137	WB	04/01/90
82138	WB	09/02/90
82139	WB	09/02/90
82140	WB	09/02/90
82141	WB	09/02/90
82142	WB	09/02/90
82143	WB	09/02/90
82144	WB	09/02/90
82145	WB	15/02/90
82146	MA	03/04/90
82147	WB	07/03/90
82148	MA	03/04/90
82149	OY	08/05/90
82150	OY	08/05/90

82151	OY	23/05/90
82152	OY	13/07/90
82207	BN	15/01/90
82208	BN	02/04/90
82209	BN	02/04/90
82210	BN	02/04/90
82211	BN	17/05/90
82212	BN	24/04/90
82213	BN	11/06/90
82214	BN	03/07/90
82215	BN	26/07/90
82216	BN	16/08/90
82217	BN	07/09/90
82218	BN	02/10/90
82219	BN	26/10/90
82220	BN	13/11/90
82221	BN	07/12/90

Withdrawn

80501	CA	06/08/90
80512	CA	23/04/90
80513	BJ	19/09/90
80514	EN	06/07/90
80582	BJ	18/05/90
80589	BJ	04/10/90
80596	CA	06/07/90
80613	CA	04/12/90
80631	CA	19/09/90
80649	CA	19/09/90
80663	BJ	05/11/90
80674	CA	20/03/90
80682	CA	04/10/90
80695	CA	04/10/90
80699	BJ	04/10/90
80736	HT	06/07/90
80742	HT	15/06/90
80748	BJ	04/10/90
80756	HT	28/03/90
80761	HT	09/03/90
80767	BJ	25/09/90
80769	BJ	04/12/90
80837	CA	04/10/90
80850	BJ	28/03/90
80851	CA	24/01/90
80852	CA	20/03/90
80972	CA	06/07/90
80994	CA	04/10/90
84012	BJ	04/10/90
84024	CA	24/01/90
84036	BJ	05/11/90
84041	BJ	19/09/90

84086	BJ	15/06/90
84108	BJ	24/01/90
84112	BJ	04/10/90
84114	CA	24/01/90
84121	OM	13/09/90
84147	CA	06/08/90
84190	OM	04/12/90
84191	CA	21/06/90
84193	CA	06/09/90
84194	BJ	04/12/90
84242	PC	03/07/90
84279	BJ	30/07/90
84281	BJ	06/08/90
84290	BJ	17/07/90
84318	DY	25/09/90
84331	BJ	04/12/90
84332	BJ	19/02/90
84366	BJ	19/02/90
84373	DY	15/06/90
84402	BJ	25/09/90
84408	BJ	04/12/90
84412	BJ	28/03/90
84415	BJ	13/09/90
84416	BJ	04/12/90
84434	BJ	15/06/90
84543	BJ	11/04/90
84547	BJ	25/09/90
84552	BJ	25/09/90
84554	BJ	04/06/90
84558	OM	25/09/90
92185	BN	19/10/90
92378	CA	29/03/90
93166	BJ	19/02/90
93239	CA	20/03/90
93241	CA	17/07/90
93257	CA	06/08/90
93287	BJ	17/07/90
93300	CA	28/03/90
93301	CA	20/03/90
93304	CA	30/07/90
93306	CA	06/09/90
93307	CA	17/07/90
93321	CA	17/07/90
93325	CA	17/07/90
93329	CA	23/07/90
93338	CA	04/06/90
93339	CA	17/07/90
93343	CA	17/07/90
93359	CA	06/08/90
93374	BJ	30/07/90
93391	CA	16/07/90
93398	CA	04/12/90

93406	CA	13/09/90
93412	CA	25/05/90
93413	CA	17/07/90
93421	BJ	06/08/90
93455	CA	16/07/90
93458	CA	30/07/90
93459	CA	30/07/90
93465	CA	13/09/90
93476	BJ	05/11/90
93482	BJ	19/02/90
93498	CA	11/04/90
93502	CA	06/09/90
93504	CA	28/03/90
93512	CF	06/08/90
93516	CF	06/08/90
93533	CA	16/07/90
93546	CA	26/07/90
93550	CA	13/09/90
93554	BJ	23/07/90
93573	CA	06/08/90
93595	BJ	23/07/90
93601	BJ	06/09/90
93618	CA	13/09/90
93634	CA	05/11/90
93644	CA	23/07/90
93652	CA	17/07/90
93667	CA	06/08/90
93680	CA	05/11/90
93684	CA	26/01/90
93696	CA	05/11/90
93765	BJ	04/06/90
93767	CA	06/08/90
93769	CA	17/07/90
93779	CA	17/07/90
93788	CA	05/11/90
93792	CA	23/07/90
93793	CA	17/07/90
93795	CA	23/07/90
93807	CA	11/04/90
93822	CA	27/02/90
93829	CA	30/07/90
93846	BJ	23/07/90
93851	CA	28/03/90
93853	CA	20/03/90
93863	BJ	07/08/90
93877	BJ	23/07/90
93883	BJ	23/07/90
93888	BJ	23/07/90
93901	BJ	06/08/90
93919	BJ	23/07/90
93925	CA	28/03/90
93933	BJ	20/03/90

99602	SA	30/01/90
99623	CL	13/07/90
99629	SA	03/01/90
99631	CL	13/07/90
99641	CL	13/07/90
99642	CL	13/07/90
99643	SA	26/09/90
99644	SA	03/01/90
99648	SA	16/11/90
99649	SA	03/01/90
99658	SA	03/01/90
99661	CL	13/07/90

Renumbered

80737	to	92301
80790	to	92391
80805	to	92307
80834	to	92390
80843	to	92386
80861	to	92392
80868	to	92388
80893	to	92384
80988	to	92261
84026	to	92389
84104	to	92260
84200	to	92300
84217	to	92306
84240	to	92262
84261	to	92385
84313	to	92259
84339	to	92304
84346	to	92258
84380	to	92387
84427	to	92303
84501	to	92302
84590	to	92305
92185	to	6336
93126	to	95105
93142	to	95101
93353	to	95106
93393	to	95110
93576	to	95107
93600	to	95108
93668	to	95100
93762	to	95102
93942	to	95104
93956	to	95103
95203	to	95400
95213	to	95410
95229	to	95329
95329	to	95229

COACHING STOCK

Deliveries of mark 4 stock to the East Coast Main Line continued throughout the year, with enough available to change the King's Cross–Leeds service to electric haulage. HSTs were released for Western region and Cross-Country services, the latter requiring less first class vehicles. A number of firsts were therefore converted to standards.

The Mark 3s from the Edinburgh–Glasgow push-pull services were transferred to InterCity service on the West Coast Main Line, but not before having been through the works for refurbishment. The 119xx series composites were converted back to firsts.

The result of the above two developments, plus the replacement of loco-hauled services with DMUs and EMUs was a cascade of Mark 2 stock resulting in the withdrawal not only of Mark 1 vehicles, but for the first time significant quantities of Mark 2 air-braked standard class vehicles.

The Mark 2F DBSOs from the Edinburgh–Glasgow push-pull services were rebuilt with new cabs to eliminate the gangway at the cab end, fitted with the new BR standard time-division-multiplex system and transferred to London Liverpool St.–Norwich/Parkeston services.

DIESEL MULTIPLE UNITS

The new Class 158 air-conditioned DMUs eventually went into service, as has been reported earlier. Large numbers of old DMUs were withdrawn, sometimes before replacements were available. These were mainly from Classes 101, 104 and 114, together with all remaining Class 110 'Calder Valley' units. In addition, the two prototype Metro-Cammell Class 151 units were also officially withdrawn. They had been out of service for a long time.

To give the old DMUs an air of respectability, some whack coined the name of 'heritage units' to describe them. Unfortunately the new designation did nothing for their condition.

ELECTRIC MULTIPLE UNITS

A new class (320) and a new sub-class (319/1) were introduced during the year. In addition deliveries of Class 321 continued. Withdrawals were mainly from Classes 302, 303, 311, 415/1, 415/5 and 491.

NPCCS

Deliveries of Mark 3 DVTs were completed, and Mark 4 DVTs were delivered with the Mark 4 passenger stock. These new vehicles plus contraction in the Parcels business resulted in the withdrawal of many BGs and GUVs.

Many BGs were modified for dual braking with old leaf-spring bogies being replaced with surplus Commonwealth or B4 bogies from withdrawn passenger stock.

3R NAMINGS AND DENAMINGS

LOCOMOTIVES NAMED

008	Sheffield Children's Hospital	Tinsley TMD	29/09
009	Three Bridges CED	Three Bridges CED	27/08
233	Philips - Imperial		/03
423	Jerome K Jerome	Bescot TMD	06/05
568	The Enginemen's Fund	Bescot Freight Centre	06/05
194	British International Freight		09/09
	Association	Glasgow Central	09/09
220	Westerleigh	Murco, Westerleigh	12/06
232	The Institution of Railway		/11
	Signal Engineers	BRML Springburn	/11
424	Isle of Mull *	Eastfield TMD	/03
693	St William Arrol	Edinburgh Waverley	23/03
694	The Lass O'Ballochmyle	Ayr	18/10
004	Swan Hunter	Newcastle Central	30/11
010	TSW Today	Laira TMD	17/10
040	City of Discovery	Dundee	27/06
041	Granite City	Aberdeen	27/06
162	Borough of Stevenage *	Brush, Loughborough	/12
209	Herbert Austin	Tinsley TMD	/08
214	Distillers MG	Distillers, Willesden	19/11
218	United Transport Europe	Cowley Rail Freight Term.	05/07
223	British Petroleum	Immingham TMD	/08
298	Pegasus	Stockport	27/07
309	The Halewood Transmission	Halewood, Ford	18/09
330	Amlwch Freighter/Trên		
	Nwyddau Amlwch	Amlwch	12/06
333	Civil Link	York Wagon Works	02/05
375	Tinsley Traction Depot		
	Quality Approved	Tinsley TMD	15/02
458	Country of Cambridgeshire		/12
462	Cambridge Traction &		
	Rolling Stock Depot	Cambridge	29/09
474	Sir Rowland Hill	Kidderminster SVR	01/05
479	Track 29	NRM York	27/07
489	Crewe Diesel Depot	Coalville Mantle Lane	03/06
547	University of Oxford	Oxford	03/10
558	Mayflower *		/03
568	Royal Engineers, Postal		
	Courier Services	Long Marston	20/03
569	The Gloucestershire Regiment	Gloucester Rail Day	01/07
587	Ruskin College Oxford	Oxford	03/10
840	North Star *	Crewe MPD	/12
841	The Institution of Mechanical		
	Engineers *		/03
973	Derby Evening Telegraph	RTC Derby	25/09
077	Thorpe Marsh Power Station	Thorpe Marsh PS	04/09
101	Mutual Improvement	York	28/04
102	Scunthorpe Steel Centenary	British Steel Scunthorpe	19/03
130	Wardley Opencast	Wardley Opencast	06/11
007	Drakelow Power Station	Drakelow Power Station	25/08
008	Moel Fammau	Brush, Loughborough	/01
009	Carnedd Dafydd	Brush, Loughborough	/01
010	Pumlumon/Plynlimon	Brush, Loughborough	/01
012	Glyder Fawr	Brush, Loughborough	03/02
013	Robert Boyle	Brush, Loughborough	10/02
014	Alexander Fleming	Brush, Loughborough	17/02
015	Bow Fell	Brush, Loughborough	/03
016	Langdale Pike	Brush, Loughborough	/03
017	Arenig Fawr	Brush, Loughborough	/03
018	Moel Siabod	Brush, Loughborough	/03
019	Wild Boar Fell	Brush, Loughborough	/03
020	Great Whernside	Brush, Loughborough	/04
021	Pen-Y-Ghent	Brush, Loughborough	/04
022	Ingleborough	Brush, Loughborough	/04
023	The Cheviot	Brush, Loughborough	/04
024	Elizabeth Fry	Brush, Loughborough	/04
025	Joseph Lister	Brush, Loughborough	/06
026	William Caxton	Brush, Loughborough	/05
027	Joseph Banks	Brush, Loughborough	/05
028	John Flamsteed	Brush, Loughborough	/08
029	Ben Nevis	Brush, Loughborough	/07
030	Cir Mhor	Brush, Loughborough	/06
031	Ben Lui	Brush, Loughborough	/06
032	William Booth	Nottingham	23/11
033	Anthony Ashley Cooper	Brush, Loughborough	/07
034	Carnedd Llewelyn	Brush, Loughborough	/11
035	Florence Nightingale	Brush, Loughborough	/11
036	Sgurr Na Ciche	Brush, Loughborough	/08

60037	Helvellyn	Brush, Loughborough	/09
60039	Glastonbury Tor	Brush, Loughborough	/10
60040	Brecon Beacons	Brush, Loughborough	/10
60042	Dunkery Beacon	Brush, Loughborough	/11
60043	Yes Tor	Brush, Loughborough	/11
60044	Alisa Craig	Brush, Loughborough	/12
60045	Josephine Butler	Brush, Loughborough	/12
60046	William Wilberforce	Brush, Loughborough	/12
60047	Robert Owen	Brush, Loughborough	/12
73109	Battle of Britain 50th		
	Anniversary	Folkestone	08/09
73112	University of Kent at Canterbury	Canterbury West	03/04
73133	The Bluebell Railway	Selhurst TMD	/09
86232	Norwich Festival	Norwich station	04/10
86235	Harold MacMillan	Ilford TMD	/10
86419	Post Haste	Stratford	13/07
90008	The Birmingham Royal Ballet	London Euston	29/08
90012	Glasgow 1990 Cultural Capital		
	of Europe	Glasgow Central	28/06
90019	Penny Black	London Euston	01/05
91011	Terence Cuneo	London King's Cross	06/03
91019	Scottish Enterprise	Edinburgh Waverley	12/09

* Name refitted.

EMU NAMED

62945	County of Dorset (2408)	Weymouth	05/10

NAMES REMOVED

20122	Cleveland Potash	/
20165	Henry Pease	/
31296	Amlwch Freighter/Tren Nwyddau Amlwch	/03
31327	Phillips-Imperial	/01
33008	Eastleigh	/11
37411	The Institution of Railway Signal Engineers	/10
43027	Westminster Abbey	/05
43045	The Grammar School Doncaster AD1350	/02
43056	University of Bradford	/03
43060	County of Leicestershire	/04
43078	Shildon County Durham	/04
43097	The Light Infantry	/04
43104	County of Cleveland	/02
43155	BBC Look North	/04
43157	Yorkshire Evening Post	/05
43162	Borough of Stevenage *	/10
47007	Stratford	/11
47016	The Toleman Group	/10
47337	Herbert Austin	/08
47350	British Petroleum	/02
47457	Ben Line	/04
47461	Charles Rennie Mackintosh	/10
47573	The London Standard	/12
47581	Great Eastern	/08
47585	County of Cambridgeshire	/12
47701	Saint Andrew	/10
47703	Saint Mungo	/11
47708	Waverley	/10
47710	Sir Walter Scott	/10
47711	Greyfriars Bobby	/12
47717	Tayside Region	/12
47842	Odin	/06
47973	Midland Counties Railway 150 1839–1989	/03
73004	The Bluebell Railway	/08
73138	Post Haste	/07
86232	Harold Macmillan	/09
86235	Novelty	/09

* Later refitted.

◄**CLASS EXTINCT.** The remaining Cla
110 'Calder Valley DMUs were all wit
drawn during 1990. Originally built as 3-c
sets, they had a very high power/weig
ratio, each power car having two 180 h.
Rolls-Royce engines. They were origina
built for the Calder Valley route, and we
also the original units used on the Sheffiec
Manchester express service via the Hop
Valley route which replaced the elect
loco-hauled service via the Woodhea
route. Needless to say this slower and le
comfortable service was not regarded as a
improvement by regular passengers!

A 2-car Class 110 set on 1st May 1989 wi
52086 leading with the 11.20 Sleaford–Do
caster at Gainsborough Trent Bridge
Geoffrey Hu

◄1990 saw the last use of Class 101s
Scotland. Most were withdrawn or transfe
red away in May, but a number includir
most of those in Strathclyde PTE livery we
retained until early October. In this view c
27th July, set 101 304 stops at Bishopbrig
with the 16.26 Falkirk–Glasgow at Bisho
briggs.   *Maxwell Fowl*

▼Mark 2F DBSO 9712 as modified and r
furbished leads the 10.30 London Liverpo
Street–Norwich on the approach to Cc
chester on 6th October. this particular exan
ple has had its centre window blanked off.
David Brow

Politics & Competition

THE DEPARTMENT OF TRANSPORT (DTp)

The staff of 2 Marsham Street busied itself with supporting the DVLA's launch of an expanded 'Select Registrations' scheme. After parting with between £280 and £2580 "you can create your own personal 'H' registration mark using any number in the exclusive 1–20 range together with three letters of your choice." One civil servant explained that: "The numbers 21 to 100 are not being issued. You would be rather cross if you paid for H20 PAT and then saw someone else driving around with H21 PAT, which had cost nothing."

It also emerged during the year that 2,300 DTp staff deal with roads, 135 with railways, 20 with other public transport and 40 part-time with cycling matters!

FERRIES & PORTS

On 14th August, Hoverspeed's first high-speed 'SeaCat' Catamaran ferry left Portsmouth on her inaugural crossing to Cherbourg. The 'Great Britain', able to carry 383 passengers and 80 cars (but no HGVs), can cruise at 35 knots, some 15 knots faster than a cross-channel ferry. Newer 'SeaCats' should be able to accommodate up to 450 passengers. Although slower than their ancient and expensive-to-run hovercraft predecessors, they should not be disrupted by bad weather as much; the two narrow hulls are designed to pierce waves instead of riding over them.

A total of 11 catamarans are being delivered, for use on Portsmouth–Cherbourg, Dover–Calais/Boulogne, and some new routes. They can halve journey times and all should be in service by the time the Channel Tunnel opens in June 1993. Between Dover and Boulogne a SeaCat will be able to match the projected 35 minute crossing time for shuttle trains. On entering service, stories soon appeared of passengers feeling ill, in true APT-style! Reliability proved poor too.

Sealink and P & O continued to invest in larger ferries with P & O also announcing plans to order new catamarans twice as big as Hoverspeed's – each holding up to 1,000 passengers and 300 cars. The new ships were hyped as being more luxurious than ever before and reflected the general attempt to move 'up-market'.

For all this competition in the run-up to the opening of the Tunnel, the Channel – and particularly the ever-busier Straits of Dover crossings – remained one of the most expensive ferry journeys in the world in terms of cost per mile.

The ferry companies complained that they would not be able to compete with the Tunnel unless the road on the last seven miles of the M2/A2 into Dover were turned into dual carriageway. In 1993, ferries will still have to sail through fog and on rough seas, and watch their assets depreciate and deteriorate a lot faster than the railways' and Eurotunnel's! At the year's end, Dover's prospects for the future looked reasonable, as did Ramsgate's. Folkestone's future looked less assured.

AIR TRAVEL

1990 was a year of rapid change, reduction in the growth of demand and ensuing 'retrenchment' and failures. Worst hit were airlines dealing to varying degrees with charter traffic. The economic recession, the doubling of aviation fuel prices, high overheads, previous ambitious expansion plans (many airlines has borrowed up to the hilt) all served to depress the industry.

However, facilities and capacity at airports continued to grow, most notably at Heathrow (terminals 1, 3 and 4), Gatwick, Manchester (Europe's fastest-growing airport), Stansted (for 1991), Glasgow, Cardiff and Newcastle. Two airports went to the market in 1990: British Aerospace bought a 76% stake in Liverpool (Speke) Airport, and is studying a £1.2 billion

development to handle 40 million passengers by 2005. Luton council invited offers for its airport. Punctuality remained a problem although the first stage of major CAA investment in new computers (and other equipment) was completed at the main West Drayton air traffic control centre; the entire £750 million investment will be complete by 1996.

With work progressing well on the Stansted rail-air link, the biggest anomaly remained Heathrow, it having relied on its hopelessly inadequate Underground link since 1977. The Heathrow Express will not be ready until 1993. In contrast, Gatwick has been linked by rail to London since 1930 with a dedicated high-speed link to London Victoria since 1984.

BIRMINGHAM INTERNATIONAL AIRPORT is Britain's fifth busiest, and fastest-growing 'regional' airport, although at only 77 minutes' journey time from London Euston, it could almost be regarded as another south eastern airport. Handling almost 3½ million passengers a year it is already served by 42 airlines taking people to 82 destinations. In 1990 work was well-advanced on the new £60 million Euro-Hub terminal, a short, covered, walk from the existing MAGLEV-served terminal 1. It is being specifically designed for efficient 'hub and spoke' operations for both international and domestic flight transfers – mainly for British Airways but also for expanding Birmingham European Airways and Brymon Airways. The consortium paying for Euro-Hub expect it to open in June 1991 and to have a capacity of 2.5 million passengers per year.

With the abolition in 1990 of 'gateway' status to London, Manchester and Prestwick, Birmingham is keen to attract trans-Atlantic scheduled services in this new 'open skies' environment. With around 6% of Birmingham International's passengers using BR to get to and from the airport – and rail's share probably increasing when the Midland Metro Link 2 is built – both parties in the two-way rail-air partnership are likely to benefit.

In July, a £3.3 billion offshore international airport sited in the Thames Estuary was proposed. Designed to limit congestion at Heathrow (40 million passengers per year), Gatwick (21.4 million) and Stansted (1.3 million), 'London Marinair' would cover a 12 square wide site and provide 4 x 4.5 km runways. Capable of handling 45 million passengers a year, it could be linked to its terminal and baggage-handling buildings at Tilbury by a 200 mph magnetic levitation train, similar to the Japanese-designed train sold early in July to Moscow Sheremetyevo Airport.

All over Europe the battle intensified for status as a hub airport, Paris CDG, Palma, Brussels, Berlin, Munich, Stuttgart, Hamburg, Dusseldorf, Nice, Marseille, Amsterdam, Birmingham and Manchester trying hardest.

By October, it emerged that the government was drawing up plans to force councils to put their regional airports on the market. The reasons: to raise over £600 million for the exchequer, reduce public spending, to hopefully serve more destinations by becoming 'more commercial' and ease air and terminal congestion in the South East.

Other clouds on the horizon for the industry concerned continued air congestion and growing concerns about air transport's extravagant use of energy and high pollution: British Airways' fleet of aircraft emits some 12 million tonnes of carbon dioxide alone. Aircraft engines can also emit carcinogens, nitrogen oxides, carbon monoxide and other pollutants. Major advances in fuel efficiency have been made in the last ten years but there is a long way to go.

ROAD HAULAGE

It was revealed in 1990 that no less than 20% of HGVs stopped

Hoverspeed introduced its 'Seacat' catamaran ferry in an attempt to prevent some passengers switching to Channel Tunnel train services from 1993. Pictured here undergoing trials, the Seacat was later withdrawn from service for modifications to be effected.   *Hoverspeed*

Roger Freeman replaced Michael Portillo a Minister for public transport on 4th May.
Department of Transpo

and checked in the previous year were overloaded. As seems the case with most cars and coaches, HGV drivers frequently exceed their speed limits by an average of 10 mph; HGVs travelling at 70 mph on motorways have become the norm. With only a few companies chosing to fit speed governers to their vehicles and the recent vast increases in engine power outputs, speeding became easier.

Manufacturers did make a greater effort to streamline lorries, sometimes encouraged by some major customers such as the Post Office and BRS. Their bodykits, added to standard vehicles, should be able to offer fuel savings of up to 25% due to reduced wind resistance. 'Active aerodynamics', as found in primitive form on VW's new Corrado car, (and which are aimed at altering the vehicle's body angles to reduce drag and increase stability at different speeds), are a further way off for commercial vehicles.

COMPANY CARS

The car magazines remained full of advertisements for police radar-detectors, aimed mainly at company 'executives'. When armed with these snooper devices, they are practically free to speed to their heart's content, deigning to observe speed limits only when there are speed traps around.

In his Budget the Chancellor announced some tightening of tax concessions to company car owners for private motoring. At the moment, an average of two-thirds of mileage is private at a cost to the Treasury of £1 billion per year. The tax on Britain's 3 million company cars (14% of the total) is still a fraction of the true value of the perk. Personal tax is presently based on the size of a car's engine. As the tax burden is fixed, most employees opt for the biggest, most potent and gadget-laden model at a given engine capacity that they are allowed. Hence, unlike in the rest of Europe, we see legions of powerful Sierras and Cavaliers pounding our motorways.

'The Economist' said of company cars: 'The present crude banding system on cars is a distortion ... The taxman ought to require companies to reveal at the end of the each tax year how much each company car insured for private use has cost them in depreciation, insurance, servicing and fuel. It should then tax all of that as personal income, less the proportion of the car's annual mileage demonstrably clocked up on company business – commuting excluded.'

Finally, a Gallup survey for General Accident at the end of the year found that almost half of company car drivers thought

it acceptable to drive at 90 mph on motorways, compared wit a quarter of drivers of privately-owned cars.

RIVER TRANSPORT

One of the world's most under-utilised rivers, The Thames would become the backbone of a new hover-catamaran servic in plans announced in September. This follows the limite success of the existing relatively infrequent Riverbus service The £50 million scheme would link new termini at Tilbury i Essex, Gravesend and Dartford in Kent (each incorporatin huge car parks) with termini at Docklands and London Bridge An air cushion would raise the vessels to increase speed to maximum of 60 mph and reduce wash. Passengers would b guaranteed seats and served food, drinks and newspapers b stewardessess. The service is planned to start in 1991.

BUSES/COACHES

Following the success of trials of minibuses, three of the coun try's biggest bus operators joined forces to design a purpose built vehicle for the future. South Yorkshire Transport, Ulste Bus and London Transport Buses have discovered that passen gers prefer smaller, more frequent buses. Mini and 'midi' buses offer rapid acceleration and greater security from vio lence and vandalism. One-person-operated double deck buse are correspondingly unpopular with passengers and are bein slowly phased out.

In all major cities, buses had to fight through traffic jams These were caused by cars, often occupied by the drivers only The limited number of bus lanes did not help; for example, i London there are 40 miles of bus lanes compared with 12 miles in Paris (where they are also rigidly enforced).

On a general note, total bus mileage continued to grow an bus passenger miles to fall. In short, buses became emptier Fares continued to increase in real terms.

CARS

On the surface, the car companies continued much as before with their so-called 'green wave' advertising masking reality Some manufactures believed that the inclusion of certain ke words would boost sales: 'life' and 'world' were two favourites Volkswagen (VW) showed its new Passat acting as a guardia angel, swooping into a New York neighbourhood and pluckin a defenceless Shirley Temple-type girl from the mean streets The intimation is that buying one could save you, and you

new age' family, of course, from what is actually the product of its own use. At the end of the year VW launched its new Polo with catalytic converters fitted as standard across the range, possibly a mixed blessing.

The car companies' marketing agencies continued to see the environment as a whimsical sales 'pitch'. Miles per hour rather than miles per gallon (mpg) remained the main selling point. Vauxhall launched its 176 mph, 3.6 litre, Lotus Carlton to 'liven up' what it regarded as its rather staid image. Some 380 'firm inquiries' for the £48,000 car were received by Vauxhall in the first two months. Others condemned the new car's launch.

Advertisements often showed empty mountain roads, often little blurred to give an impression of speed. In one Alfa Romeo advertisement the word blood appears four times, heart twice and bones and skin once each, all key words designed to emphasise thrills. In other adverts, Vauxhall talked about some of its Astras as 'heart stopping', BMW one of its models as 'a ... dark horse', Peugeot its 205 GTi as 'a sheep in wolf's clothing'.

In September the mood at the normally-glitzy Birmingham International Motor Show was more subdued than usual. Producers were glum due to disappointing sales, in turn due to economic recession. The initial post-Kuwait invasion petrol price rises did not help matters.

The Motor Show exhibited (or could lead a buyer to) 70 models capable of twice the legal speed limit or more. BMW, Mercedes and Audi have recently limited their top cars to 155 mph, a thoughtful move.

On a more positive note, 1990 was the year that the huge motoring organisations turned greener. The AA and RAC urged motorists to drive more gently and slowly to conserve fuel. The AA also called for: cheap, efficient and comfortable public transport (using trains and buses is estimated to be the equivalent of 130–200 miles per gallon per passenger); higher petrol taxes instead of vehicle excise duties (increasing the marginal cost of journeys and so discouraging those less necessary); more car sharing. They might also have mentioned better signposting and more urgent research on in-car navigation systems (one out of every ten miles is superfluous due to faulty navigation). Changed land-use planning policies – so that new developments do not assume universal car ownership – could also conserve fuel.

On a similar subject, some motorists are still not aware that their cars are guzzling fuel far more quickly when their engines have not warmed up. The average car journey is about eight miles by which time most engines have still not reached optimum operating temperature. Cold-start fuel consumption of 10 mpg is not uncommon.

The motoring organisations reflected the trend amongst private car buyers and many other companies by ensuring that a greater proportion of the vehicles in their roadside assistance fleets were diesel-powered. The AA chose a large fleet of Peugeot 309 GLDs for its inspectors. Along with Citreon, these cars share a highly-acclaimed range of diesel engines.

One criticism levelled against the more environment-friendly diesel engine has been its laggardness. This is no longer true, especially when large diesel engines are matched to small car bodies. The recently-released 1.8 litre Peugeot 205 turbo-diesel has very brisk performance as well as the usual good fuel economy and reliability. Depreciation should be slower than with petrol-driven counterparts.

Pressure mounted on the Chancellor to reduce the tax on Derv to increase the price difference with petrol. The present tax difference in Britain is 0.2%; in Germany, for example, it is 13%, in Italy 36% and Spain 25%.

In the past, diesel engines have produced much soot but work is now progressing well on virtually eliminating particulate emissions. Diesel fuel is still, however, relatively sulphurous.

Behind the scenes the motor industry was spending large amounts on research and development into improved and alternative technology and fuel sources:

- 'Lean burn' technology. Rover's K-series engine approved in its Rover 200/400 and Metro models. As with the more advanced piston design on Ford's High Compression Swirl (HCS) and Compression Valve Hemi (CVH) during the 1980s, Rover's new engine incoporates several new features aimed at increasing both economy and performance.
- Reduced wind resistance. This is made up of frontal area multiplied by the drag coefficient, Cd. These values have fallen over the years and Cd figures of around 0.30 are the norm. Cds of 0.20–0.25 are not far away.
- Weight reduction, as demonstrated to a degree by the Citroen AX range. There is great scope for the use of stronger, lighter materials in car construction. Hopefully, the sandalous craze of increasing car weights in the late 1980's has now come to an end.
- Better maintenance and tuning.
- Forced induction, or the turbo, (properly tuned to provide a wide torque spread) on an engine can offer increased performance and economy compared with a non-turbo engine of the same capacity. Improved combustion can reduce pollution too.
- Catalytic converters. These devices are 'bolt-on' partial cures rather than a preventative measure. Pre-heating 'cats' make them more efficient when the engine is started (and

Cecil Parkinson resigned from the post of secretary of state of transport on 26th November after an undistinguished tenure. On his appointment in 1989 he had said: "When all the fuss dies down I must get myself on a bus or train. I haven't been either for years." Mr Parkinson is pictured talking to the press at London Marylebone Station a week before his resignation. *David Carter*

Malcolm Rifkind became the new secretary of state for transport on 28th November, replacing Cecil Parkinson. He was still secretary of state for Scotland when pictured here at Inverness performing various ceremonies and publicity stunts for the re-opening of the Ness Viaduct. The date is 9th May. *David Carter*

therefore still cold). Three-way converters are better than two-way ones. The EC states that all new cars should have one fitted by 1992.

• Improved engine management. Some top Vauxhall Carltons and Senators cars switch off three out of the six cylinders when the engine is on 'part-load', for example when driving gently round town or when idling in traffic jams.

• Diesel-electric hybrid cars show great potential, with Volkswagen leading the field. VW's 'Eco-Golf' prototype can use its diesel engine for more rapid acceleration or above a certain speed and use electric power in town; in traffic jams no power is used at all, of course. It is capable of achieving 113 mpg and a reduction of 50% in the emission of nitrogen oxides and carbon dioxide is claimed.

• Petrol-electric hybrids could run on similar principles, perhaps using the new generation of cleaner two-stroke engines being developed. Such engines could alternatively act as a generator, which in turn feeds electric motors, as on diesel-electric locomotives.

• Electric cars. General Motors (GM) leads this field. The problems of range, weight, cost, performance and battery life are gradually being overcome. Regenerative braking – as used on some electric locomotives – could boost battery life. There is, of course, a need to monitor emissions from the power stations that generate the electricity! GM's 'Impact', officially launched in January can reach 60 mph from a standstill in 8 seconds. Its tyres have about as much rolling resistance as conventional tyres.

• Alternative fuels. Liquified hydrogen, methanol, natural gas and liquid petroleum gas all produce fewer pollutants than petrol when burned but can produce problems of cost and practically to varying degrees. As a general rule, the greater the hydrogen to carbon ratio, the cleaner is the fuel. There is considerable scope for the development of 'Flexible Fuel Vehicles', or FFVs.

Cars are far more fuel-efficient now than ever before. Technology, spurred on by legislation in the USA (from 1966) and Europe (from 1971), has made huge strides. However, the Department of Energy has forecasted a maximum 28% improvement in car fuel efficiency between 1990 and 2010; the Department of Transport's lowest forecast for car traffic growth for the same period is 41%.

In December, Ford exhibited a plastic/aluminium alloy engine after three years' working alongside European institutions and companies. The experimental 1.0-litre power unit spends much less spends much less time warming up, with a potential 20% reduction in hydrocarbons during this period.

In the same month the Tokyo Electric Power Co. (TEPCO) launched its rival to GM's 'Impact' electric car. The unnamed plastic prototype can reach 112 mph and run for up to 311 miles between charges.

Throughout the year the various car magazines featured the occasional articles about transport politics with particular emphasis given to measures to reduce congestion and pollution. In December 'Autocar & Motor' managed a major article on the TGV Atlantique, 'Fast Lane' an article on the government's uneven treatment of Railfreight compared with road haulage. Times must be changing.

The Gulf crisis served to remind motorists of the 1974 and 1979 fuel shortages, albeit briefly. Most carried on driving fast and furiously, at least as far as the next traffic jam. Consumption of petrol remained at 24 million tonnes per year and what Mrs Thatcher referred to as "our great car economy" must have remained so.

ROADS

The problem of congestion grew more acute all over Europe. In Paris, 1.4 million cars were travelling daily into a city where there are officially only 700,000 parking spaces. The city saw the introduction of a strategic network of 'axes rouges' where parking and stopping is forbidden, and unloading severely restricted.

Instant removal of illegally-parked cars and heavy fines e[n]forced by an army of police and traffic wardens ensured so[me] success and traffic flow improved. French drivers, who are s[o] to cherish their 'right' to park anywhere they like, were n[ot] all happy about the new routes. The French government al[so] announced plans for a new orbital motorway, the Sup[er] Périphérique.

At the Conservative conference in October, Cecil Parkins[on] did finally launch an 'anti-parking blitz' on 300 miles of priori[ty] 'red routes'. Fierce penalties as a deterrent would be "goo[d] news for all who depend on the roads – not least bus users[." Their introduction would start early in the New Year.

The Department of Transport released provisional estimat[es] for recent growth in road traffic. Traffic (vehicle-km) was i[n]creasing at 6% a year. Even though the 'Roads for Prosperit[y'] programme predicted an 83–142% increase by the year 202[5] an annual 6% increase, if maintained, would top the high[er] forecast by 2004! When the figure is broken up, car-km showe[d] a 7% increase, each car, incidentally, carrying an average 1[.5] people!

In December, the Department of Transport published i[ts] 'Action for the M25' following recommendations by consul[tants. Although some key stretches of the motorway were a[l]ready being extended to four lanes as part of a £1 billion co[n]struction programme, the plan made it clear that, in the shor[t] term, better use would have to be made of existing carriagewa[y] widths. This would include reduced-width lanes and possibl[y] replacing the hard shoulder with 'lay-bys at frequent interva[ls] to allow for breakdowns'. A fifth lane on some sections of th[e] 117-mile motorway might also follow, probably initially be[t]ween the M3 and M4 interchanges. The Department's consul[tants would also investigate the provision of collector-di[s]tributor roads along the motorway to siphon off more loc[al] traffic, where appropriate.

In the longer term, the Department would proceed with th[e] studies of four orbital corridors outside the M25 – effectivel[y] a second motorway around London. Earlier in the year, how[ever, transport secretary Cecil Parkinson scrapped all the roa[d] schemes proposed by the London Assessment Study consul[tants. Although a major retreat, the government pledged t[o] continue other road building in the capital at a cost of £1 billio[n] including widening of the North Circular and new roads in th[e] Docklands area.

Work continued on the (now) £16.75 billion roads prog[ramme. The Department of Transport claims that 37 Sites o[f] Special Scientific Interest (SSSI) are affected, but this i[s] thought to apply to those schemes with firm routes. One con[servation group has estimated that 150 SSSIs may be affected.

Traffic forecasts used to justify each scheme in the hug[e] roads programme predict a 30–50% increase in traffic betwee[n] 1990 and 2005. With the government's Cost-Benefit Analys[is] (CoBA), the more traffic forecasted to congest the existin[g] network, the greater the benefits (mostly time saved) tha[t] CoBA shows in building new roads. Chose your forecast!

The year ended as it began, the roads full of motorists yearn[ing for a Britain without cars and roads, except the one the[y] are in and on. Robert Atkins, a few months earlier ministe[r] for roads and traffic, had maintained that "increased traffi[c] demand is mainly a function of economic growth rather tha[n] road building."

Finally, the Prometheus programme (see 'Today's Railway[s' Review of the Year' volume 3, p.7) has produced, amongs[t] other things, 'automatic intelligent cruise control' which per[mits vehicles to travel at a continual 120 km with just 50 c[m] between them. 'The Economist' explains how the system, de[veloped by Volkswagen, works: 'Once the car has been steere[d] onto a special track on a highway, acceleration, braking an[d] steering are all taken care of by an on-board computer. A[s] the car nears its pre-programmed destination, the ... syste[m] automatically shuts off and the car 'undocks' from the convo[y], reverting to driver control.' Whether we see such a system o[n] the M25 remains to be seen!

A Railway Diary for 1990

JANUARY

1. PRESERVATION. Manor No. 7828 ODNEY MANOR is first steam locomotive through Berwyn tunnel on Deeside extension.

7. SIGNALLING. Installation is completed of simplified bi-directional signalling (SIMBIDS) in the Severn Tunnel.

8. PRESERVATION. Bo'ness & Kinneil Railway linked to main line.

9. SCOTRAIL. Haymarket depot receives its first Class 158 DMU No. 158 701 for staff training purposes.

11. CHANNEL TUNNEL. A £400 million package to fund the Channel Tunnel project for the next three months is announced by Eurotunnel after talks with contractors Transmanche-Link.

12. CHANNEL TUNNEL. Eurotunnel announce that over one third of all tunnelling has been completed.

20. NEW HALT. The new Rams Line Halt serving Derby County Football Club's ground is used for the first time. Class 150 No. 150 143 is the first train.

21. ETHIOPIA. A passenger train and a freight train collide head on in Djibouti, killing 13 people, following a point-switching error.

21. MIDDLESBROUGH. The last train calls at Cargo Fleet station on the line to Saltburn.

22. ACCIDENT. Class 415/4 EMU No. 5408 collides with the buffer stops at Beckenham Junction when arriving with the 07.45 from London Bridge. The leading bogie is derailed.

24. BEST STATION. York station is awarded top place in the Transport 2000 award for customer care.

25. GALES. High winds cause havoc to rail services throughout the country.

26. LAST TRAIN. Class 415/416 EPB units Nos. 5614 and 6241 form the 19.28 Holburn Viaduct to Orpington service, the last public trains to use the service. Construction starts immediately on the new sub-surface St. Pauls Thameslink station on the upgraded cross-London Thameslink line, originally opened in May 1988.

26. SOUTH AFRICA. Management and unions settle a 12-week rail strike over wages, which resulted in 27 killings and 23 000 sackings.

26. UNDERGROUND. In its first full travel pattern survey for almost a decade, LUL starts a 10-week programme to find out when and where its sample of 1½ million people go.

27. PRESERVATION. Danish Class E 4–8–4 arrives in UK bound for Peterborough.

28. DISRUPTION. Vandals drop rubber tubing on to OHLE near Lea Hall station between Birmingham and Coventry. It gets caught in a Class 86's pantograph causing severe damage. Train services are disrupted for 24 hours.

29. MERSEYSIDE. Work starts on the new £420,000 station at Whiston, situated on the Liverpool–Manchester Victoria line between Hyton and Rainhill.

31. NETWORK SOUTHEAST. The Great Northern Line wins the annual Minister of Transport's Cup. High standards of train service punctuality, reliability and cleanliness were attained during 1989.

31. NETWORK SOUTHEAST. The £500,000 refurbishment of the concourse at King's Cross is marked.

31. NEW NAME. West Midlands PTE adopts the marketing name 'Centro', the new name to create public awareness that it is an independent organisation.

31. PRESERVATION. BR grants licence for GWR group to occupy former Southall shed.

31. STRIKE. A quarter of services operating to and from Waterloo station in London are cancelled because of an unofficial 24-hour strike by around 200 drivers protesting at the sacking of a colleague.

FEBRUARY

01. PRESERVATION. KING EDWARD I test run from Tyseley to Banbury.

01. REPAIRED. After three days of diversions via Beighton Jn, services between Chesterfield and Sheffield are restored. A landslip had blocked the down line near Bradway Tunnel on 28th January.

02. DOCKLANDS. Tunnel boring for the extension of London's Docklands Light Railway from Tower Gateway to Bank is completed.

02. VISITOR. The mothballed Stoke–Oakamoor freight branch sees its first rail traffic in 12 months, a BR Research test train.

03. PRESERVATION. Severe flooding on Swanage Railway.

04. DEVELOPMENT PROPOSALS. Rosehaugh Stanhope Developments submits a detailed planning application for a £400 million offices, shops and restaurant scheme on the site of London's Holburn Viaduct station, closed by BR the week before. Rosehaugh is also involved with the Broadgate Development next to Liverpool Street station and the King's Cross redevelopment plan.

04. FARE INCREASES. British Rail and London Underground fares are increased between 9 and 15%, well ahead of inflation.

04. FLOODING. Heavy rain causes extensive flooding around Kingussie and closure of the Perth–Inverness main line. The West Highland lines are similarly affected.

05. ACCIDENT. A two year old boy dies in Leeds after being hit by the 09.57 Liverpool–Scarborough train; the boy had crawled up the embankment after getting through a hole in the garden fence damaged in recent gales.

05. MIDLINE. Construction of Tame Bridge station, situated between Bescot and Hamstead, starts today. Centro is funding the new £600,000 station.

05. TICKETING. The last Edmondson card tickets from a British Rail station are issued at Pembrey and Burry Port station between Llanelli and Carmarthen.

06. NEW STATION. Only a week after the decision was made to build a 'temporary' platform at Over, two miles south of Gloucester, the first train is allowed to call. Whenever the River Severn floods, as now, passengers will use buses between Over and Gloucester stations to by-pass flooded sections of line.

06. REFURBISHMENT. A £400,000 package of improvements is completed at Beverley station.

07. ELECTRIFICATION. Cecil Parkinson, secretary of state for transport, approves the £36 million electrification of the 32-mile West Midlands Cross-City line which links Lichfield Trent Valley with Redditch. Cynics point to the forthcoming Mid-Staffordshire by-election. New Class 323 EMUs will operate services.

08. REVENUE PROTECTION. BR announces that on-the-spot fines will be introduced in an effort to recoup some of the £50 million lost annually through fare dodging. Passengers caught without tickets on the selected lines will have to pay a £10 fine.

09. BRAZIL. Three people die and 40 are injured when two commuter trains collide at Oswaldo Cruz, north of Rio de Janeiro.

10. WELSH VALLEYS. Services return to normal after three days' severe disruption due to flooding.

12. SOVIET UNION. Four people are killed when four coupled locomotives pass a red light and hit a stationery passenger train near the Armenian city of Kirovakon.

13. COMMITMENT. John Prescott, Opposition transport spokesman commits a future Labour government to repealing the law which prevents taxpayers' money being used to build a fast Channel Tunnel rail link.

14. ACCIDENT. The rear coach No. 75898 of a 12-car Class 305/308 formation is derailed whilst on ECS working out of East Ham sheds. Commuter services are disrupted.

14. BREL. The 100th Class 321 EMU built at BREL Ltd's York works is delivered to Network SouthEast. Since October 1988 York has averaged almost six Class 321 vehicles every week.

14. DAMAGE. A boat strikes the Southern Region's Chelsea Bridge causing damage. Single-line working is introduced on the Kensington Olympia–Clapham Junction line.

14. DISRUPTION. A 12 car ECS train becomes derailed near East Ham depot causing damage to track and OHLE. Services into London Fenchurch Street are severely disrupted.

14. VANDALISM. Levenshulme station, between Manchester Piccadilly and Stockport is severely damaged by fire caused by arsonists.

15. ACCIDENT. Rail services between Sheffield and Leeds are severly disrupted after a train ploughs into a herd of cattle on the line at Wombwell near Barnsley.

15. FINANCE. Michael Portillo, transport minister, announces a £220 million increase in BR's external finance limit, therefore raising total funds available to £635 million.

16. SIGNALLING. BR awards contracts worth £10 million to develop and supply two pilot automatic train protection (ATP) systems. GEC/GS will supply the SELCAB system for installation on the Chiltern Lines; ACEC Transport will develop and supply the TBL Track Beacon system for use on the London Paddington–Bristol line.

17. NEW LIVERY. The privately-owned rake of Mark 1 coaches run by Traintours runs in its new livery. Pilkington, glass manufacturers, have sponsored their repaint and internal refurbishment.

18. DIVERSIONS. The discovery of buried wartime bombs in Southampton's (Eastleigh) Airport – which runs parallel to the main line to London – leads to some diversions via Laverstock Junction, Salisbury.

18. SCOTRAIL. Rail services on the Perth–Inverness line are restored, two weeks after the River Tay burst its banks and washed away 300 metres of railway embankment at Dalguise, north of Dunkeld.

19. DOCKLANDS. Cecil Parkinson, transport secretary, officially inaugurates work on the £240 million extension of the Docklands Light Railway to Beckton. Mowlem-Taylor Woodrow and Balfour Beatty are contractors.

22. PRESERVATION. 60009 test run from Derby to Sheffield.

22. SUPERTRAM. Michael Portillo, minister for transport, announces that the Sheffield Supertram project meets Department of Transport criteria but that funding will be delayed.

23. ANGLIA REGION. The £300,000 modernisation of Clacton station is marked in a ceremony.

26. STORM DAMAGE. The Chester–Holyhead line is breached by the sea at Towyn, between Rhyl and Abergele. The town is flooded. Elsewhere in the country, high winds bring down OHLE in many areas and diesel haulage substituted.

27. INTERCITY. A new marketing scheme to reward loyal customers "in a tangible way" is launched. The 'InterCity Frequent Traveller' scheme offers 'points' for tickets bought with 're-

wards' when the points are traded in. A similar 'Air Miles' scheme offered by, amongst others, the petrol companies has not been very successful.

28. ACCIDENT. The 20.19 West Croydon–London Victoria strikes a fallen tree at Gipsey Hill and is derailed. The Class 455/8 unit No. 5820 then hits 5802 on the 20.06 London Victoria–West Croydon. No-one is seriously hurt.

28. PRIME MINISTER. During a visit to Yorkshire, Mrs Thatcher is caught up in heavy snow and is unable to return to London by road or air. She is forced to join a crowded Blackpool–York DMU between Bradford and Leeds before boarding the 18.10 HST to London King's Cross. She travels in the back cab of a 'pacer', no doubt reinforcing her dislike of rail travel. The InterCity train is held up for six minutes so she can make her connection.

28. RAILFREIGHT. RFS Engineering unveils three new designs of steel-carrying wagons, the first to meet the operating requirements of the Channel Tunnel. The protoypes have TOPS codes BGA, BHA and BJA.

28. WEST YORKSHIRE. The WYPTA announces that it has secured six ex-Network South-East Class 307 EMUs for use on Doncaster–Leeds services. It is admitted that the units are 'not in their first flush of youth' but say that they will be more reliable than Class 142/144 Pacers.

MARCH

01. ACCIDENT. The 14.46 shuttle from Stourbridge Junction to Stourbridge Town crashed through the buffer stops at the latter.

01. CHANNEL TUNNEL. The first train to enter the terminal site at the Dollands Moor sidings, near Cheriton runs today with a load of concrete tunnel linings.

01. CRITICISM. The Consumers' Association criticises BRs 'hit and miss' policy of compensating passengers whose trains are late, delayed or withdrawn. It calls for a scheme of statutory compensation.

01. NORTHERN IRELAND. The 20.35 Belfast Central–Londonderry hits a car at an open level crossing south of Ballymena killing two people in the car and one train passenger. This is the first fatality on Northern Ireland Railways since 1979.

01. PRESERVATION. Opening of the Great Railway Show in Peter Allen building of National Railway Museum York.

03. SAFETY IMPROVEMENTS. Following several accidents over the years, including the one on 1st March, AWS equipment is installed on the Stourbridge Junction–Stourbridge Town branch. The layout at Town station is also altered.

04. ACCIDENT. The HST forming the 19.30 London Paddington–Bristol ploughs into debris

left on the line by vandals just west of Bath. The train is severely damaged.

04. ANNIVERSARY. The Forth rail bridge celebrates its centenary.

04. LINE REOPENS. After seven days' operation of buses between Colwyn Bay and Chester in place of trains due to storm damage to the track at Towyn, the line is re-opened.

04. PRESERVATION. 60009 works the Forth Bridge Centenary Special.

08. CHANNEL TUNNEL PROGRESS. The Mitsubishi tunnel boring machine (which completed the 3.2 km landward south running tunnel from Sangatte to the Coquelles terminal in December 1989) starts its return journey to Sangatte in the north running tunnel.

10. SCOTRAIL. Heavy rain causes severe flooding of the West Highland line near Fort William. Services are cancelled.

12. NETWORK SOUTHEAST. Testing of the electrical supply for the Fareham–Botley electrification project is completed.

12. TICKETING. BR extends the open-station concept to all North Wales Coast Line Stations.

12. UNDERGROUND. A collision is narrowly avoided at King's Cross when a Piccadilly Line train travelling the wrong way after setting down passengers. It continues on a collision course with a packed train travelling in the opposite direction. Disaster is averted by the quick reactions of the driver of the packed train who pulls together two low voltage wires from his cab window to short the train's electricity supply.

14. PRESERVATION. 71000 'DUKE OF GLOUCESTER' works test run from Derby to Sheffield.

18. BANGLADESH. Six die when part of a train becomes uncoupled and falls into a canal at Gologhat.

19. SOUTH YORKSHIRE. Engineers bring the Swinton curve into use.

25. FRANCE. Paris (Gare de Lyon)–Clermont Ferrand services are operated by electric traction throughout from today.

26. NETWORK SOUTHEAST. It is announced that driver-only trains on the London Euston–Northampton line is being delayed while modifications are carried out to the monitoring equipment on platforms. This follows the introduction of Class 321 trains on the route.

27. NETWORK SOUTHEAST. The first electric trains operate over the newly-energised stretch of line between Fareham and Botley.

29. PRESERVATION. 46229 'DUCHESS OF HAMILTON' works test run from Derby to Sheffield.

29. RESIGNATION. Following the previous day's Board meeting, Dr. Tony Ridley resigns as

a director of Eurotunnel plc and his directorsh of the group companies.

30. CRIME. Vandals place a sleeper across t track at Pinhoe, on the eastern side of Exete 50016 'Barham' is damaged whilst hauling t 05.56 Exeter–London Waterloo.

APRIL

01. PRESERVATION. New station opened Birmingham Railway Museum.

01. PROVINCIAL. Work starts on the ne down platform at Bromsgrove, in readiness fo the summer timetable.

01. RETIREMENT. Sir Robert Reid, BR chai man, retires after 43 years of working for the rai ways. He became chairman in September 1983

02. RED STAR. The road collection and deli ery part of the £70 million a year business is re-o ganised. From today, 80 contractors running 5C vehicles will handle distribution by road.

02. UNDERGROUND. Designers DCA unve their mock-up of the Underground's new Centr Line stock; 85 trains, each of 8 cars, have alread been ordered at a cost of £300 million.

03. NETWORK SOUTHEAST. The £270,0C modernisation of Knebworth on the Great Nort ern Line is marked.

05. METROLINK. Trackbed construction is ir augurated on Manchester's Metrolink light ra system.

07. PRESERVATION. Return to main line re venue earning service of DUKE OF GLOUCES TER.

08. CATERING. BR cancels its contract wit Ginsters of Cornwall for the supply of cornish pa ties, the new contract going to Pork Farms of No tingham.

09. CONTRACT. RFS Engineering of Donca ter win a contract, worth £1.5 million, to desig and build 90-tonne hopper wagons for RMC In dustrial Minerals Ltd. of Buxton. This follows £20 million contract for the re-bodying, overhau and repair of BR's coal hopper wagon fleet.

09. NEW ORGANISATION. The Environmen tal Transport Association is launched with the backing of the World Wide Fund for Nature and Transport 2000. It aims to offer a 'green' alterna tive to the AA and RAC – a good breakdown service combined with environmental transpor campaigning.

09. STRATHCLYDE. It is announced that the five new stations opened in Strathclyde in 1989 are proving highly successful. The stations are 'earning' £250,000 a year over their first-year cap ital costs.

10. PRESERVATION. National Railway Museum on tour opens at Swindon in No. 19 Shop.

PROJECT EXCHANGE. The bridge carrying the Stafford–Birmingham line over the Birmingham–Derby line was replaced in a five-day possession at Easter 1990.

◀At 16.00 on 13th April the old bridge has been demolished and the cross-sections and rubble are on the Derby line.
Chris Milner

▼The following day with the new bridge girders being lifted into place.
Fastline Promotions

Project Exchange
Bridge Rebuilding Birmingham
EASTER 1990
Delays here. Please ask for details.

▶Traffic was diverted via the Lifford Curve at King's Norton and the Camp Hill line. Tyseley 4-car suburban set T 413 rounds the Lifford Curve with the 14.48 Birmingham New Street–Lincoln. *Chris Milner*

◀The new Swinton curve in South Yorkshire was opened on 19th March. The new double-track curve lies on the same route as an earlier curve closed in the '60s. Incidentally, the original curve was closed illegally and a special bus service had to be provided for a time after the intervention of the then secretary of the National Council on Inland Transport who lived at Swinton! Here 156 483 is pictured using the curve on 27th March with the 16.07 Sheffield–Cleethorpes. *Peter Hill*

PLATFORM 5 at Sheffield Midland station has been temporarily dismantled at its south end for renewal of the supports which carry it over the River Sheaf. In this view teaken on 14th April is seen the River Sheaf (which runs from left to right) and the Porter Brook (which joins it at this point). An HST simmers in Platform 2 as work proceeds.   *M.A. King*

11. BREL. BREL Ltd. and the Czechoslovakian engineering company CKD Tatra sign a co-operation agreement.

12. BRIDGE REPLACEMENT. In a five-day possession, Bridge 373A, east of Birmingham's New Street station is replaced. Services affected are diverted. The old bridge had carried traffic on the Coventry–Birmingham line over the Birmingham–Derby line since 1893.

12. LONDON PADDINGTON. Services are severely disrupted when contractors working at Old Oak Common accidentally sever the main signalling cable.

13. CENTENARY. The Lynton–Lynmouth cliff railway celebrates its centenary.

13. COMPENSATION. BR announces its intention to spend more than £5,000 restoring gardens ruined by weedkiller which was carried by the wind when the railway line was sprayed at Salisbury. Several people complained that everything in their gardens had turned bright yellow.

13. NETWORK SOUTHEAST. Just over a year after the last major shutdown, Liverpool Street station is closed for four days from today for major track alterations.

13. PRESERVATION. Return of 46229 to the Settle & Carlisle line.

14. SIGNALLING. Northallerton's signal box is abolished, with control of its section of line going to York and Darlington.

15. SHEFFIELD. Work on the repair of supports and the replacement of a trackbed around and under Platform 5 of Sheffield Midland station (from which this company takes its name) is completed. The River Sheaf flows below the platforms.

16. PRESERVATION. Last steamings at Dinting Railway Centre.

23. CHANNEL TUNNEL. The total tunnelling distance in all three tunnels reaches 75.7 km, 50% of the total.

23. CHILTERN LINES. Automatic signalling on the 22 km section of line between Amersham and Aylesbury is commissioned. When complete, the whole line will be controlled from Marylebone's integrated electronic control centre and ten traditional signal boxes closed.

25. STRIKE. More than 200 BR drivers at London Waterloo walk out in an unofficial stoppage in a protest over new working arrangements. The Waterloo & City Line is worst affected with no services operating.

26. UNIONS. British Rail's 'no strings' offer of 9.3% on basic rates to all staff covered by the Railway Staffs National Council (effective from 7th May) is accepted by the three rail unions.

30. ENERGISATION. The current to OHLE between the east end of Leeds station and Neville Hill maintenance depot is switched on marking the completion of the £1.8 million project.

30. INCREASED CAPACITY. Cecil Parkinson, secretary of state for transport, approves in principle the lengthening of platforms at 63 stations on London (Charing Cross/Cannon Street/ Victoria)–Dartford/Sevenoaks/Hayes routes. Twelve-coach Networker trains will then be able to be accommodated.

30. UNDERGROUND. LUL places contracts worth £81 million for the complete refurbishment of over 140 trains on the Circle, Hammersmith, Victoria, Bakerloo and Northern Liner.

MAY

01. PAY. The National Union of Railwaymen accepts BR's 9.3% pay offer. ASLEF also accepts.

02. CIVIL LINK. Today marks the formal launch of a network of dedicated train services to transport civil engineering materials between suppliers, depots and worksites. Departmental Class 47 No. 47333 is named 'Civil Link'.

02. PRESERVATION. No. 4472 'FLYING SCOTSMAN' returns to main line duty.

02. STRATHCLYDE. The first of the £29.5 million fleet of new Class 320 units, No. 320 301 arrives in Scotland.

03. NETWORK SOUTHEAST. Rainham's station is officially opened, re-built at a cost of £672,000.

04. GOVERNMENT RESHUFFLE. Mr Roger Freeman, junior health minister, becomes transport minister following Mr Michael Portillo's move to the post of local government minister.

04. PRESERVATION. Steam Heritage Award of £3,000 presented to KING EDWARD I preservation Group.

05. PRESERVATION. S160 2–8–0 'FRANKLIN D ROOSEVELT' enters services on the Watercress Line.

07. AUSTRALIA. Six people are killed when a commuter train runs into the back of a steam-hauled charter train at Brooklyn in Sydney's northern outskirts.

07. REFURBISHMENT. Repairs costing £180,000 to the viaduct carrying the Twyford–Henley line over the Thames between Wargrave and Shiplake are completed.

09. ELECTRIFICATION COMPLETE. Sec-

retary of state for transport Cecil Parkinson opens the £22 million Solent Link which links Portsmouth and Fareham with Eastleigh and Southampton. He also opens Hedge End station. His train fails en route to the ceremony.

09. SAFETY. London Underground publishes 'Your ticket to safety', a widely-distributed booklet outlining the safety programme and measures passengers can take to avoid accidents.

09. SCOTRAIL. The new Ness bridge is opened to traffic, built at a cost of £2.5 million. Secretary of state for Scotland Malcolm Rifkind takes over the controls of 156458 over part of the bridge.

11. NETWORK SOUTHEAST. Class 86/4 No. 86401 operates the last southbound loco-hauled 'Northampton Cobbler', the 07.37 Northampton–London Euston service. Class 321s reign supreme from today.

13. SHEFFIELD. An oil painting that has hung in a graffiti-daubed waiting room at Sheffield station is valued at £17,000. It will be exhibited at the Royal Academy.

14. DEPARTMENT OF TRANSPORT. The new minister of state for public transport, Roger Freeman is given his new responsibilities. As Cecil Parkinson's second in command, he will be responsible for railways, buses, taxis, London Regional Transport, transport in Docklands, the Channel Tunnel link and encouraging private sector involvement in transport projects. Robert Atkins remains minister for roads and traffic, Patrick McLoughlin stays minister for aviation and shipping.

14. SLEEPER SERVICES. InterCity withdraws the sleeper service between Stranraer and London Euston. Air competition is blamed for declining traffic over the years.

14. SOUTH YORKSHIRE. Swinton station is opened to the public and is served by Sheffield–Doncaster and Sheffield–Leeds/York trains. The new station has cost £650,000 to build, funded by the South Yorkshire PTA with a 33% grant from the European Regional Development Fund. The associated Swinton curve has cost £3.4 million, funded by InterCity and the Transport Authority with a 50% grant from the ERDF.

14. UNDERGROUND. The East London Line becomes orange on the journey planner (i.e. Underground map).

14. WEST YORKSHIRE. Steeton and Silsden station opens to the public. The West Yorkshire PTA paid £270,000 for its construction.

15. ELECTRIFICATION. Completion of the Doncaster–Leeds stage of the ECML electrification project is officially marked in Leeds, transport minister Roger Freeman attending the event.

15. PRESERVATION. 46201 'PRINCESS MARGARET ROSE' test run from Derby to Sheffield.

16. ACCIDENT. Four permanent way staff are killed by a runaway wagon on the Metropolitan Line near Chorleywood station.

16. BELGIUM. The SNCB's previous 206 km/h speed record achieved in 1969 is beaten by 12 km/h during a special test run between Courtrai and Deinze as part of a programme to prepare the Belgian network for higher speeds.

16. PAY. The NUR becomes the last union to accept LUL,s 9.3% pay offer.

17. REFURBISHMENT. Hinckley station's £235,000 modernisation is officially marked.

18. AIR COMPETITION. The Sheffield Development Corporation signs a deal with the construction group Budge for a £100 million international airport complex to open in 1993. It will be operated by the BAA subsidiary, Airports UK.

18. NEW RECORD. A TGV Atlantique shortened and modified set No. 325 reaches 515.3 km/h (320.2 mph), a new world record. The speed is reached south of Vendôme's new station.

18. RAILFREIGHT. Roger Freeman, minister of state for transport, announces that Railfreight Distribution is to invest £40 million in 700 new freight wagons for more deepsea container business.

19. CHANNEL TUNNEL PROJECTS. The government approves increased spending on Channel Tunnel projects from £350 million to £600 million. Included is the expansion of Waterloo station, the North Pole maintenance depot, Tonbridge–Redhill electrification and the purchase of 20 Class 92 locomotives for Railfreight.

19. PRESERVATION. Kent & East Sussex Railway. First public passenger train in Northiam from Wittersham Road.

20. REHEARSAL. BR staff and the emergency services practice dealing with an accident at Reading station. Exercises such as this are held several times a year in different parts of the country to test contingency plans and liaison.

21. CONFERENCE. Speaking at a conference in London on European transport, Cecil Parkinson proclaims that Britain is leading the fight to convince other EEC members "that railways should not be subsidised against airlines, road transport and ferries."

21. FIRE. Passengers are evacuated from the 06.30 Manchester Victoria–Huddersfield after the Class 142 unit caught fire in Standedge Tunnel.

24. LAST DELIVERY. The final Class 321 EMU (No. 321366) to be delivered from BREL's York Works to Network SouthEast is handed over. Since 1988, 114 Class 321s have been built at a cost of £100 million.

24. NETWORK SOUTHEAST. Work on the construction of a £4 million DMU maintenance shed at Aylesbury starts. Elsewhere on the Chiltern Lines, plaques are unveiled at Wendover, Great Missenden and Stoke Mandeville to mark their refurbishment at a total cost of £1 million.

24. RECORD. Jonathan Carter from Leeds wins BR's 'Young Supertraveller of the Year' prize. Regaining his title last held in 1985, Jonathan managed to clock up 125,386 miles by train in 1989.

25. ENVIRONMENT. Mrs Thatcher commits Britain to only stabilising 'greenhouse' gas emissions at current levels by 2005.

26. PRESERVATION. Contents of Wolferton museum auctioned.

27. ACCIDENT. Class 08 No. 08819 collides with Class 155 Super Sprinter No. 155 323 (vehicle 52323) causing severe damage to both. The incident occurs at Bristol Bath Road Depot.

27. PRESERVATION. First day of operations along Gloucestershire and Warwickshire Railway extension to Gretton Meadows.

29. NETWORK SOUTHEAST. The new Thameslink alignment between Blackfriars and Farringdon in central London is opened, as is the partially complete St. Paul's Thameslink station. The new station replaces Holburn Viaduct which closed in January.

30. CRIME. The 16.30 London Paddington–Cardiff HST is attacked as it passes through St. Anne's, Bristol. One passenger receives a direct blow to the head from a brick thrown through the window. By all accounts, he narrowly avoids death.

30. FRANCE. The French government allocates £40 million to GEC-Alsthom for research into high speed train travel.

JUNE

04. PRESERVATION. Duke of Gloucester re-opens Northiam station on the Kent % East Sussex Railway.

04. SERVICES WITHDRAWN. Following the withdrawal of the subsidy from Corby District Council, passenger services are withdrawn on the Kettering–Corby line. Ironically, the new public transport minister's constituency is Kettering.

08. AIRPORT LINK. A ceremony is held to mark the start of the Tyne & Wear Metro extension to Newcastle International Airport. The £12 million project comprises 3.5 km of route with an expansion of Bank Foot station and a brand new airport station. The airport is contributing £2.36 million to the scheme's funding.

08. OPINION. A MORI opinion poll reveals 55% of the British to be in favour of building the high speed line to the Channel Tunnel.

08. POLICING. British Transport Police publishes its annual report. Sex crimes, are up by 61% on BR and 46% on the Underground. Crimes of violence and offences of endangering passenger safety, such as placing obstructions on the line, are both also up. Detection rates are down.

09. TRACK IMPROVEMENTS. The West Coast Main Line is closed to allow tracks to be realigned at Weedon, near Rugby. Services are diverted via Northampton.

11. NETWORK SOUTHEAST. NSE director Chris Green officially applies the finishing touches to the last three modern sliding doorsunits to be painted in NSE livery.

11. NETWORK SOUTHEAST. Transport Minister Roger Freeman officially opens the refurbished concourse at Cannon St. station. The refurbishment has cost £700,000 and marks completion of the first phase of development. In addition, a new £90 million office development is being built above the station platforms.

16. EXCURSION. The first through train to Minehead for 19 years runs when the 'Quantock Explorer' travels direct from Manchester via the Taunton Cider connection at Norton Fitzwarren. 47457 travels as far as the connection where steam takes over.

16. PRESERVATION. West Somerset Railway: first through train from BR to Minehead for 19 years.

17. PRESERVATION. Inaugural passenger train on Bodmin & Wenford Railway hauled by Class 08 No. D 3559 and Bagnall 0–4–0ST No. 19.

19. PRESERVATION. 42,000 sq. ft. museum opened at Butterley by chairman of East Midlands Tourist Board.

20. ACCIDENT. A woman, her son (4) and a neighbour's daughter (7) are killed when hit by the 17.33 London King's Cross–Hull at Bessacarr crossing, south of Doncaster.

23. CHANNEL TUNNEL SERVICES. British Rail appoints the John Brown engineering division of Trafalgar House to supply project management services for £1.1 billion of work to provide Channel Tunnel international rail services. It includes construction of the international terminal at Waterloo, work at Willesden and at the North Pole servicing depot.

23. PRESERVATION. First public open day of Scottish Industrial Railway Centre at Minnevey, Ayrshire.

25. ELECTRIFICATION. Overhead wires between Skelton Bridge Junction (7 km north of York) and a point 2 km north of Northallerton station are energised.

25. LINE RE-OPENS. After two weeks' work at Weedon, the WCML is re-opened to traffic. A new maximum speed of 100 mph applies to the two-mile stretch giving a one-minute cut in journey times.

25. UNDERGROUND. Edgware Road on the Bakerloo line closes for 12 months for a £3 million lift replacement to take place. The station is to be refurbished with particular attention paid to passenger security, safety and communications.

27. NEW TRAINS. BR awards a contract to Hunslet Transportation Projects Ltd. for 37 three car Class 323 EMUs to operate in the Midlands and in the Network NorthWest area. Services operated by the new trains will include the Birmingham Cross City Line and the new Manchester Airport service.

27. PRESERVATION. Dean Forest Railway. Norchard to Lydney Lakeside officially opened by Sir William McAlpine.

29. RACE RELATIONS. BR is accused of racial discrimination in rejecting all 19 black Asian guards who applied for promotion at London Paddington. All four white applications were accepted.

30. LAST TRAIN. Network SouthEast operates the last Class 307 train from Southend Victoria to London Liverpool Street.

JULY

01. PRESERVATION. First North Wales Coast Express hauled by No. 71000 'DUKE OF GLOUCESTER'.

02. CUTBACKS. British Rail advises the West Yorkshire PTA that it intends to withdraw its share of support for the Wakefield–Huddersfield service from May 1991. BR blame reductions in the Public Service Obligation Grant from central government.

02. NETWORK SOUTHEAST. Driver-only operation begins on the London Liverpool Street–Gidea Park–Shenfield and Southend route using Class 315 EMUs. On the south west lines out of London Waterloo the introduction of DOO is postponed.

03. CRUSH. Despite a fire alert on the Waterloo and City line and a signal failure on the Bakerloo, thousands of rush-hour commuters are allowed to continue pouring onto the Underground platforms at Waterloo. A dangerous crush develops, between 08.15 and 09.00 with, apparently, little communication between BR and LUL.

03. WEST YORKSHIRE. After its move from Network SouthEast, the first Class 307 EMU, adorned in Metro livery, is officially launched.

05. DIVERSION. Because of a derailment at St. Helens, Liverpool–Preston services are diverted via St. Helens Jn. and Golborne Jn.

09. CONTRACT. British Rail Research wins a £500,000 contract from LUL to investigate ways of reducing track noise and vibration.

09. WEST YORKSHIRE. Metro and the West Yorkshire PTA present a letter of confirmation to BREL Limited for three Class 321 EMUs.

10. KING'S CROSS. BR welcomes the parliamentary select committee's approval to let the King's Cross Railways Bill proceed further.

10. PRESERVATION. Bure Valley narrow gauge 15" railway opens for business by Pleasureworld Limited.

11. ADVERTISING. BR is told to take more care with its advertisements after complaints about crowded trains and poor catering facilities. The Advertising Standards Authority warns against misleading the public.

11. POLLUTION. Cecil Parkinson opens a new car-hire HQ in Hertfordshire and uses the occasion to preach the virtues of cutting car engine sizes to reduce pollution levels. He points out that each 100 cc reduction cuts emissions by 3%. He had arrived in a 3.6-litre Daimler Sovereign.

16. ACCIDENT. EMUs Nos. 317 330 and 317 334 collide at Hornsey carriage slidings, injuring one of the drivers and causing extensive damage to vehicles 77043 and 77077.

17. BRITISH RAILWAYS BOARD. Approval is sought to close the unstaffed stations at Greatham and Grangetown in County Cleveland due to lack of demand.

18. PRESERVATION. Alan Hay killed on North Wales Coast express.

19. AIRPORTS. BAA buys most of Southampton Airport for a price between £15 million and £20 million. Airport UK, a subsidiary of BAA, has operated the airport since 1984. BAA now owns or manages two-thirds of Britain's airports.

19. REFURBISHMENT. The £500,000 refurbishment of Chippenham station is marked in an official ceremony. Car parking space has been expanded to accommodate up to 650 cars.

20. NETWORK SOUTHEAST. The first of five Class 322 EMUs for Stansted Airport services is delivered from BREL Limited. The Stansted units feature public telephones, and a trolley refreshment service. Around one third of the airports potential 8 million passengers a year are expected to use the Stansted Express.

21. SCOTRAIL. The rear coach of the 19.00 Glasgow Central–Ayr, formed of Class 318 unit No. 318 255 is derailed as it starts its journey. Seventeen passengers are injured.

23. NORFOLK. Thetford Station is severely damaged by fire.

24. NEW MARKET. British Rail announces that it will establish a new subsidiary company to exploit its telecommunications assets. A new company, BR Telecommunications Limited (BRT) will sell spare capacity on its internal network. BRT would take responsibility for a network totalling over 17,000 route kilometres, this including over 2,500 route kilometres of optical fibre cable.

25. FREIGHT INITIATIVE. Transport minister Roger Freeman launches Charterail, a joint BR/GKN venture. It will exploit intermodal technology.

25. UNDERGROUND. Plans for work totalling £120 million to expand capacity at Tottenham Court Road, Holborn and London Bridge stations are unveiled to the public.

26. ANNOUNCEMENT. Cecil Parkinson revises BR's External Financing Limit (EFL) to £700 million for 1990/91, an increase of just over £100 million.

26. CONTRACT. The British Railways Board announces that its preferred tenderer for the contract to convert 35 two car Class 155 DMUs into 70 single car Class 153 vehicles is Hunslet Barclay of Kilmarnock.

26. MINISTERIAL CHANGES. Lord Brabazon becomes minister for aviation and shipping and all Department of Transport business in the

◀ Whinhill station on the Wemyss Bay Branch was opened on 14th May. On 20th August, 318 252 is pictured passing with a Wemyss Bay-bound service. *Tom Noble*

▼ Unusual power for the 17.07 Liverpool Lime Street–Preston on 5th July in the form of 20010 + 20082. because of a derailment at St. Helens, the train was diverted via St. Helens Jn. rejoining the West Coast Main Line at Golborne Jn. They are pictured at Springs Branch, Wigan. *Paul Senior*

House of Lords. Christopher Chope becomes new minister for roads and traffic. Patrick McLoughlin will support Roger Freeman, the minister for public transport.

7. STRATHCLYDE. Five new stations are opened on the 10 km Paisley Canal Line: Dumbreck, Corkerhill, Mosspark, Crookston and Paisley Canal. Strathclyde Regional Council, with assistance from the European Regional Development Fund and the Scottish Office, has invested over £3 million in the line's re-opening. Dumbreck has two platforms, the rest single platforms.

8. SERVICE WITHDRAWN. After months of vandalism and disturbances, West Yorkshire PTA and BR agree to withdraw the 22.51 Leeds–Doncaster service.

8. WYE VALLEY. Government funding for feasibility studies into a £37 million electrified rail system centreing on the Wye Valley between Chepstow and Hereford is approved.

30. CHANNEL TUNNEL ACCIDENT. A seventh worker dies whilst working on the British side of the Channel Tunnel. Two have died on the French side since work began.

30. PARCELS. Track 29 is launched, a new nationwide, overnight door-to-door freight service. The rail-based service guarantees delivery to any place on the UK mainland before 1700 the next day.

31. NETWORK SOUTHEAST. The £400,000 refurbishment of the up platform buildings at Newbury station is completed.

AUGUST

01. ACCIDENT. The 07.02 Tonbridge–Reading DMU collides with the eight-coach 09.24 Reading–London Waterloo, about to leave platform 4b. The driver of the Tonbridge train is trapped.

01. HEADQUARTERS DECISION. Eurotunnel decides to locate its main operational HQ at Calais, adjacent to the shuttle terminal and TGV station. It will open in 1992.

03. ACCIDENT. The 22.18 Manchester–Penzance is hit from the rear end at Stafford by a Class 310 EMU No. 310 102 forming the 22.36 Stoke–Soho carriage sidings ECS. The driver of the EMU is killed.

03. HEATWAVE. High temperatures cause delays to services as BR imposes speed reductions on parts of the network.

06. CHANNEL TUNNEL PROGRESS. The service tunnel is 90% bored and lined this week with the British and French service TBMs only 5.16 km apart. Both running tunnels are now over 50% bored. Another landmark is reached: a total of 100 km of tunnelling is completed.

07. PRESERVATION. 30th anniversary of opening of Bluebell Railway.

08. PRESERVATION. North York Moors Railway public shares issue launched to raise £500,000.

11. DECADE. The Tyne & Wear Metro celebrates its 10th anniversary.

11. RESIGNALLING. Work starts on a major part of the £2.2 million scheme to resignal lines in the Stourbridge area.

18. FRANCE. Large demonstrations are held in Provence against the SNCF's plans to extend its TGV line south of Valence to Avignon, Marseille, Fréjus and also south-west to Montpellier and the Spanish border. Opponents point to 'environmental damage' and the more urgent need to improve rural rail services.

18. PRESERVATION. The former Garsdale turntable on the Keighley & Worth Valley Railway is used for first time by P3 No. 2392.

20. POLAND. At least 11 people are killed and 22 injured when an express crashes into a train stopped at a red signal near Warsaw.

20. SCOTRAIL. Newton Street tunnel (between Greenock West and Fort Matilda) is re-opened after its eight weeks' enforced closure due to structural damage.

20. UNDERGROUND. Mornington Crescent station loses its lift service. LUL says that the 83-year-old lifts are beyond economic repair. Passengers should descend or ascend the 86 steps between platforms and ground level. The escalators at Aldwych, Angel, Edgware Road and Hamstead are also on their last legs.

22. ACCIDENT. The 09.36 Manchester Piccadilly–Sheffield DMU, formed of cars 51418/ 59688/53977 collides with the 09.33 Rose Hill (Marple)– Manchester Piccadilly DMU (51913/ 54497) at Hyde Junction. Twenty-five people are injured.

24. UNDERGROUND. The new transport minister Roger Freeman criticises London newspapers for their "constant sniping." He insists that "the reality is that millions of passengers are carried quickly and safely to their destinations each year and our Underground system is the envy of the world."

25. PRESERVATION. 75th anniversary of Ravenglass and Eskdale Railway.

26. CZECHOSLOVAKIA. Eleven die when a passenger train hits a freight train near Spalov, 100 km north east of Prague.

27. CHANNEL TUNNEL LANDMARK. The British north running tunnel boring machine breaks through into the newly-constructed crossover cavern 7.8 km out from Shakespeare Cliff. The cavern is 163 m long, 21 m wide and 15 m high and will enable trains to switch between the two running tunnels for maintenance and in emergencies.

29. DERAILMENT. Class 421 (4 Cig) No. 1221 becomes derailed at Ash Vale Junction whilst operating the 18.55 Guildford–Ascot.

31. WEST YORKSHIRE. Following previous fines of £57,750 and £43,312, West Yorkshire PTA fines BR £86,613 for services not provided.

SEPTEMBER

03. DERAILMENT. Class 37s Nos. 37679/683, hauling the 00.36 Tunstead–Oakleigh become derailed at Northwich.

03. LINE SIDE CLEARANCE. BR reveals that nearly 65,000 tonnes of surplus materials and rubbish have been picked up from line sides over the past 14 months. 'Operation Cleansweep' was launched in June 1989 in an attempt to reduce vandalism and improve the environment.

04. FRANCE. The Barcelona–Genève 'Catalan Talgo' collides head-on with a St. Gervais–Marseille express on the Valence–Grenoble line. The driver of the Marseille train is killed.

05. SHEFFIELD. The first trains serve the new station at Meadowhall Interchange, part of a £7.5 million rail/bus interchange next to the new £400 million shopping complex.

08. PRESERVATION. '257 SQUADRON' at Folkestone Central for Battle of Britain celebrations.

10. UNIONS. The National Union of Railwaymen merges with the National Union of Seamen to form the National Union of Rail, Maritime and Transport Workers following a 3:1 vote in favour of the move. The RMT will have nine sponsored MPs in Parliament, including John Prescott, shadow transport secretary. Jimmy Knapp will be general secretary, Sam McCluskie his deputy.

10. WEST YORKSHIRE. Walsden station, near Todmorden, reopens after a gap of 29 years. West Yorkshire PTA paid £240,000 to reopen it.

11. CHANNEL TUNNEL PROGRESS. A fourth tunnel boring machine (TBM) reaches the end of its task when it breaks through at Holywell. The Howden TBM had bored 8.2 km from Shakespeare Cliff. As the 1.1 km section of cut-and-cover tunnel between the Cheriton terminal and Holywell is already complete, this means that the entire UK landward section of the running tunnel north is complete and ready for fitting out. After decommissioning, the TBM will be displayed at the Eurotunnel Exhibition Centre.

11. PROVINCIAL. After months of delays the Class 158 is launched at BREL Derby Carriage Works. The total order is for 447 vehicles at a cost of £200 million.

12. CEREMONY. Malcom Rifkind, secretary of state for Scotland 'switches on' the power at Edinburgh for overhead wires as far south of Belford.

12. FIFE. Work starts on Kirkcaldy's new £590,000 station.

13. UNIONS. The RMT says that over £1 billion must be spent on BR safety improvements following the inquest verdict on the victims of the Clapham railway accident; improved technology – such as Automatic Train Protection – and better staff training and pay are called for.

15. PRESERVATION. The first class 9F to leave Barry, No. 92240 enters traffic on Bluebell

▶ the first Class 91 into Edinburgh Waverley – 91019 is propelled into the station prior to its naming ceremony on 12th September.
Tom Noble

Railway.

17. CELEBRATION. A plaque is unvieled at Bromsgrove station to mark the opening of the new platform and conecting footbridge, and the 150th anniversary of the Lickey incline.

18. CEREMONY. Chris Green, director of NSE, places 'the final golden bolt' to mark the completion of London Liverpool Street's £6.5 million roof, the new 'Victorian' steelwork having been tastefully designed. This is an important stage in the station's £155 million redevelopment.

18. IMPROVEMENTS. Twyford station's £520,000 refurbishment is marked in a ceremony.

18. PRESERVATION. First of 14 Finnish steam locomotives arrive for preservation.

20. NEW STATION. Worle station, Weston-super-Mare, is officially opened. The £700,000 station has been jointly funded by BR and Avon County Council. The car park can hold up to 200 cars.

20. PRIVATISATION. Liberal Democrat leader Paddy Ashdown suggests that private train operators should be allowed to run over tracks maintained by a state-owned track authority.

21. PRIME MINISTER. Mrs Thatcher is forced to use Swiss Railways near Zürich when bad weather grounds her helicopter during a tour of Switzerland. The weather does not stop the train.

21. UNDERGROUND. Despite having possession of the Victoria Line at Seven Sisters, a 20-man permanent way gang is forced to run for their lives when a train bears down on them at about 05.00. This is the fourth such incident in recent months. Fortunately, no-one is injured.

22. CHANNEL TUNNEL ACCIDENT. The tunnels are evacuated following a leak of toxic gases in one of them. Several workers inhaled the fumes and are taken to hospital.

22. CHILTERN LINES. Marylebone station is closed as part of the £14 million Chiltern Line resignalling. Trackwork is also rationalised. The £70 million total route modernisation of the line is scheduled for completion in 1991.

23. PRESERVATION. Debut of 'DUKE OF GLOUCESTER' on the Settle & Carlisle line.

23. TELEVISION. As part of Channel 4's 11-day 'Going Loco' season of over 50 documentaries, shorts and feature films, Equinox: 'Trouble on the Line' produced by Paul Fabricius is screened. The documentary criticises Department of Transport attitudes towards BR and its unfair treatment compared with roads in Britain and railway systems abroad. This Sunday evening programme attracts 1.43 million viewers.

24. ADVERTISING. InterCity screens 'Relax More' for the first time. The new ad. uses characters from the original 'Relax' ad. unsuccessfully attempting to do the same things they did on the train – playing chess, reading, etc. – whilst travelling by car in heavy traffic.

24. CONSERVATIVES. The agenda for the following month's Bournemouth conference is released. More than half the (record) 93 resolutions on transport call for more investment in road and rail. Calls for privatisation of BR are thin on the ground.

25. CONSERVATION. The Railway Heritage Trust publishes its annual report for 1989/90. Financial support of £1.23 million has been given to 47 projects throughout the BR system. As in previous years, the major share of expenditure on all projects was met by BR.

25. ENVIRONMENT. The government releases its environment white paper 'This Common Inheritance'. Opposition environment spokesman Bryan Gould criticises it as "long on waffle and short on policy."

26. ANNIVERSARY. The Eurotunnel Exhibition Centre in Folkestone announces that, two years after its opening, no less than 600,000 visitors have passed through their doors.

26. CHANNEL TUNNEL. Cecil Parkinson decides to appoint a security inspector, with wide-reaching powers, to oversee measures being taken to counter the threat of a terrorist attack on the Tunnel.

26. NETWORK SOUTHEAST. Work starts on a £400,000 scheme to modernise Bacons Yard rail bridge between South Bermondsey and London Bridge.

27. ENVIRONMENT. Cecil Parkinson, transport secretary, and John Wakeham, energy secretary head a new group of ministers from today, all appointed to take forward the initiatives outlined in the government's environment white paper. They will have to preside over the compilation of annual state-of-the-environment reports on their department's activities and responsibilities.

◄On 17th September Birmingham–Cardiff express services were rerouted via bromsgrove instead of via Kidderminster. 156 419 is seen at Bromsgrove at the new Platform 2 with the 12.00 Birmingham–Cardiff. *Stephen Widdowson*

▼A general view of the new station at Worle. *Colin Marsden*

28. MIDLINE. Centro and BR announces a delay of six months for completion of the Cross-City electrification project in Birmingham.

28. OFFICIAL LAUNCH. The Class 158 is launched by Cyril Bleasdale, director ScotRail at Blair Atholl.

29. RENAMING. The old Stansted station officially becomes Stansted Mountfitchet. The station has not carried the word Mountfitchet since 1845.

30. FRANCE. The SNCF completes its TGV Atlantique network with the introduction of services from Paris to Tours and on to Bordeaux and Biarritz. Journey times are slashed.

30. WATERLOO. The London station is closed for the day whilst signalling equipment is moved in preparation for its role as terminal for Channel Tunnel services.

OCTOBER

01. BRITISH RAILWAYS BOARD. After several months of working in a non-executive role, Sir Bob Reid officially becomes BR chairman.

01. NETWORK SOUTHEAST. All West Anglia services operated by Class 321 and 322 EMUs (plus Class 315) go over to driver only operation.

01. PROVINCIAL. Class 156s take over Leeds–Carlisle services.

01. REVENUE PROTECTION. BR announces a crackdown on fare evasion on the London Fenchurch Street–Southend line, said to be costing £5 million a year. A team of ticket inspectors will carry out random checks on trains and will have the power to levy a fine of £10 or the cost of the ticket, whichever is the greater. At stations there will be red and green channels, as with Customs. Spot checks will be made on people passing through the green channel. The scheme will start on 29th October.

01. STUDY. BR commissions an independent inquiry into the working methods and equipment (such as platform TV monitors) on some Southern Region services out of Waterloo following ASLEF's refusal to co-operate with the introduction of driver-only trains. The union says it is worried about safety.

02. APPROVAL. Delegates at the Labour Party conference make a special point of applauding Neil Kinnock's commitment to a joint public-private high-speed rail network connecting with the Channel Tunnel.

02. INDUSTRIAL ACTION. 350 electrical maintenance staff vote in favour of strike action in protest at BR's decision to close three of the ten OHLE maintenance depots on the London Midland Region – at Manchester (Longsight), Stafford and Bedford. The RMT union argues that response times to emergencies will be slower and that pressure on staff will increase "which flies in the face of the principle established by the Hidden Report after Clapham."

03. ACCIDENT. A German freighter hits the piers of Goole swing bridge. The bridge's main structure is not damaged but trains are slowed until checks are made. Strong currents and a lack of river pilots are blamed for the latest in a series of collisions by boats.

03. FERRIES. Sealink sheds jobs in a plan that also involves major investment and changed working practices. Sealink, taken over by Stena Line earlier in the year, is investing £75 million on its Dover–Calais and Folkestone–Boulogne operations and cutting the workforce on these routes by 320. Two new ships for the Harwich–Hook route and better port facilities will cost £81 million. A new Southampton–Cherbourg service is announced for July 1991.

03. LABOUR PARTY CONFERENCE. Defending his criticism of the government's record on investment in safety on the railways, John Prescott says: "Cecil Parkinson recently called me a 'vulture' and a 'rotweiler'. Sensitive guys like me get upset when these sorts of comparisons are made."

03. OXFORD. The new £3.5 million station is officially opened. The building is larger than the one it replaces. Eleven ticket office windows and four self-service ticket machines are incorporated in the concourse. During the ceremony, 47587 is named 'Ruskin College, Oxford' and 47547 'University of Oxford'.

03. RAIL FARES. Jimmy Knapp, RMT general secretary, accuses BR of "deceit" after hearing that Provincial's fares had risen this week by an average of about 10% in addition to the May increases "BR is quietly putting up fares in different parts of the country through individual networks to avoid a national outcry." A leaked BR internal report shows the need to account is separate from the 'operating' account.

04. FARE PLANS. A 9.6% average increase in InterCity and NSE fares from 6th January 1991 will mask wide variations. Long-distance commuters and passengers benefitting from investment in new trains will pay more. Saver/SuperSaver and APEX fares will increase less in price. Most Provincial fares will be unchanged.

04. PLEA. The National Trust says it is disappointed by the failure of the environment white paper to tackle damage to the countryside caused by unnecessary or badly thought-out road schemes. Citing several examples, the Trust calls for ministers to investigate alternatives to a road-based transport policy, including the £15 billion road-building programme.

04. SUBSIDY. Within hours of InterCity and NSE announcng their proposed fare rises, transport minister Roger Freeman announces a 20% increase in BR's Public Service Obligation – the first increase for 8 years. The increase ceiling is for NSE and Provincial to install new safety equipment. The April 1990–March 1991 grant will be £600 million, compared with £504 million the year before. The new ceiling represents the limit on PSO grant within the EFL revised on 26th July. Corporate plan targets are unaffected.

04. UNIONS. ASLEF general secretary attacks the planned BR fare rises as "disgusting." However, he pledges that this union would quickly submit a pay claim "to make sure we get our share."

05. CHANNEL TUNNEL MILESTONE. The two service tunnel TBMs begin boring the last mile. A total of 110 km has now been bored in the three tunnels.

05. COACH TRANSPORT. Cecil Parkinson announces that, from April 1991, speed limiters will be compulsory on all coaches built since 1974.

05. INTERCITY. Following their introduction in Scotland, APEX tickets become available today between Liverpool Lime Street, Runcorn and London.

06. PRESERVATION. Debut of Schools No. 30926 'REPTON' and Class Q7 0–8–0 No. 63470 on NYMR.

06. PRESERVATION. Peter Willis killed on Watercress Line.

06. WILLESDEN. Major track and signalling work is started to enable construction of the new North Pole train maintenance depot to be used for Channel Tunnel international trains. Services into London Euston are disrupted for one week.

07. ELECTRIFICATION. Main civil engineering work on the Birmingham cross-city line electrification project is started.

07. PRESERVATION. Centenary of opening of Forth Bridge.

07. SCOTRAIL. Prince Edward switches on the floodlights illuminating the Forth rail bridge which is in its centenary year. The ceremony is followed by a firework display.

09. CROSSRAIL. Cecil Parkinson approves the construction of the £1.5 billion East-West Crossrail project in London. He also authorises BR to spend £80 million more on improving the London–Folkestone line. Throughout his speech at the Conservative Party conference, delegates offer the transport secretary noticeably muted applause.

10. CEREMONY. The £200,000 refurbishment of Caerphilly station is officially marked.

11. REVENUE PROTECTION. An extra £150,000 is collected from 8,000 passengers during a purge on fare-dodging on the London Underground system.

12. CORNWALL. The Department of Transport approves the proposed diversion of services to Newquay via Parkandillack. Goonbarrow to St. Dennis Jn by the existing route will be closed.

15. CHANNEL TUNNEL PROGRESS. Another landmark is reached: the two service tunnel TBMs are less than 1 km apart, or 988 metres to be precise.

15. ROYAL TRAIN. New figures detailing the Queen's expenses show that, in 1990, the cost of official travel by train including maintenance of the Royal Train will come to £1.43 million. This year, the Royal Train renewal programme will amount to £0.85 million.

16. UNDERGROUND. A Brixton–Walthamstow Victoria Line train nearly runs over its own driver when he leaves his cab to report a signal stuck on red. He had not switched his controls from automatic to manual, securing the train. The train stops at the next station, Seven Sisters, and no-one is hurt.

24. RAID. British Transport Police make early-morning raids on the CRCC at Derby, and homes in the surrounding area, concerning apparent irregularities in recent competitive tendering procedures.

25. CHANNEL TUNNEL FINANCES. Most of the 210 banks backing Eurotunnel agree to provide it with an extra £21 billion.

25. SOUTHERN REGION. The 75th anniversary of the introduction of third-rail electric trains south of the Thames is officially celebrated with the launch of an exhibition at London Waterloo station.

26. CHANNEL TUNNEL FINANCE. Two hundred banks finally agree to fund an extra £1.8 billion, or most of the cost overruns which have forced construction costs to £7.2 billion.

26. COURTS. The Railway Inspectorate announces its intention to prosecute BRB over an alleged offence relating to the overturning of a rail crane during track work at Faversham, Kent, on 10th March 1990. The crane operator escaped with minor injuries.

27. STRIKE. French Channel Tunnel workers strike for a day demanding higher pay. About 40% of the workforce is absent.

29. PRESERVATION. Duke of Gloucester formally opens Severn Valley Railway boiler shop.

30. CONTACT! The British and French service tunnel TBMs establish contact by means of a 110-metre long probe. The meeting point is 22 km from Shakespeare Cliff and 16 km from Sangatte.

NOVEMBER

01. DOCUMENT. The Department of Transport publishes 'Transport Statistics for London'. Amongst the findings: commuting into London fell 15,000 in 1989 compared with 1988. However, compared with 1982, it is up 38% on the Underground, 21% on NSE, but there were falls of 26% on the buses and 18% by car.

01. FIRE. A fire fills part of the Channel Tunnel and causes its evacuation. The Health and Safety Executive will investigate.

02. RELEASE. Robert Morgan, the Purley accident train driver, is released from prison after the original sentence was quashed.

03. WATERLOO. Demolition of Waterloo's 1936 signalbox to make way for the new International Station begins.

05. CHANNEL TUNNEL RAIL LINK. BR appoints W.S. Atkins to carry out an independent review of options for the route between the North Downs and central London. Included among options being studied by the BR project team are those from Ove Arup and Rail Europe.

06. CANCELLATIONS. Barton-on-Humber–Cleethorpes services are replaced by buses between Barton-on-Humber and Habrough due to a shortage of DMUs.

07. ROAD CRASHES. Six die in a multiple pile-

up on the M42 near Birmingham, the worst accident to occur on the motorway to date. Traffic jams of up to 20 miles build up after the accident. Meanwhile in southern Holland, at least eight die in a similar accident.

08. RAILFREIGHT. The thousandth Channel Tunnel lining segment train hauled by 33051 and 33051 'Shakespeare Cliff' runs from the Isle of Grain construction site to Shakespeare Cliff, Dover. So far, 35,000 segments have been moved with another 150,000 to go before the Tunnel is completed.

12. EUROTUNNEL SHARE OFFER. Dealing opens in subscription rights to the new £532 million rights issue. Special incentives, from reduced-rate travel to lower-cost ways of buying and selling the stock, are offered for even small purchases. Almost 78% of the 560,000 private shareholders in Eurotunnel live in France.

12. NEW BRIDGE. Engineers complete the replacement of the wrought-iron rail bridge at Par Harbour. The 1882-built bridge is replaced by a concrete one. Over the weekend no passenger trains ran between Par and St. Austell.

12. PRESERVATION. A1 Steam Locomotive Trust launched to build a new Peppercorn Class A1 pacific locomotive. Its number will be 60162.

12. PRESERVATION. First test steaming of 42968 on Severn Valley Railway.

14. CHANNEL TUNNEL PROGRESS. The first mechanical and electrical milestone of tunnel installation work is reached, 5 km of power cable placed in the UK land running tunnel north. Meeting the deadline earns TML a bonus of £2 million.

15. CARDIFF. A plaque is unveiled to mark the completion of a £600,000 project to improve track and modernise signalling at Cardiff Queen Street.

16. PRESERVATION. Great Central Railway extension to Leicester North (formerly Belgrave & Birstall) opened.

17. BROMSGROVE. Lickey banking locomotive No. 37197 is derailed on catch points when the 01.00 Gloucester–Bescot Speedlink service comes to a stand on the incline and then slips back.

18. RECORD. In the week ending today, the four marine running tunnel TBMs bore a total of 1178 metres beneath the Channel. Progress is particularly rapid in the UK running tunnel north.

19. ACCIDENT. A track worker dies during a trackside scrub-cropping operation at Pelaw on the Newcastle upon Tyne–Sunderland Line.

19. CORNWALL. The Liskeard–Looe line reopens to passenger traffic after a two-week closure. Engineers reconstructed the East Looe River's embankment to protect the line from flooding.

19. NETWORK SOUTHEAST. The government approves a new fleet of 69 Class 159 vehicles for London Waterloo–Exeter services, at a cost of £34.5 million. These DMUs are adapted Class 158s mostly originally ordered by Provincial.

19. NEW ORGANISATION. The BRB announces the formation of European Passenger Services Limited, a wholly-owned subsidory. EPS Ltd will be responsible for the provision and marketing of international passenger services when the Channel Tunnel opens.

20. CHANNEL TUNNEL PROGRESS. The UK landward running tunnel south TBM breaks through at Holywell, the last of the three to be completed.

20. ROADS. Cambridgeshire county council approves Britain's first experiment in road pricing for Cambridge. Every car will be fitted with a congestion meter, which will automatically shut off the petrol tank if the bill is not paid. The scheme is unlikely to start for another five years.

20. UNDERGROUND. Cecil Parkinson decides that a Bill to extend the East London Line to Dulwich in the south and to Dalston and Highbury in the north will not be submitted this year because London Transport has more pressing priorities.

21. DERAILMENT. Train Services to and from London Liverpool Street are severely disrupted following the derailment of part of the 22.34 Trafford Park–Felixtowe freightliner train at Channelsea Curve, Stratford.

22. DISRUPTION. The 04.40 staff train from Royston to London King's Cross, formed of Class 313s No 313 047/030 brings down almost 2 km of OHLE near Stevenage. Services are severly disrupted.

22. POLICING. A £1.4 million British Transport Police Station is opened at Wembley Park Underground Station.

22. RESIGNATION. Mrs Thatcher decides to stand down as prime minister after over 11 years in office. The average tenure of her transport secretaries since 1979 has been 17 months, roughly half the average longevity of other cabinet position tenures.

23. STRATHCLYDE. The last of 22 new Class 320 EMUs, commissioned by Strathclyde Regional Council (via the PTE) at a total cost of £30 million, is handed over.

25. ELECTRIFICATION. Work starts on the £1.3 million Drem–North Berwick electrification project. Capital costs are being shared between ScotRail and Lothian Regional Council.

26. RESIGNATION. Cecil Parkinson resigns from his position as secretary of state for transport. He will retire from Parliament at the next General Election. 'Private Eye' magazine suggests that it is the first time Mr. Parkinson has withdrawn at the right moment.

28. NEW PM. John Major, MP, is appointed Britain's new prime minister.

28. NEW APPOINTMENTS. The Rt. Hon. Malcolm Rifkind, QC MP, is appointed secretary of state for transport in prime minister John Major's new Cabinet. He inherits a heavy burden of legislation in this most troubled of new departments of state. Michael Heseltine, MP, becomes the new secretary of state for the environment, a post he last held in 1983.

29. CHANNEL TUNNEL PROGRESS. The French underland running tunnel TBM ends its journey back where it started at the access shaft at Sangatte. 'Pascaline' is the only TBM to have completed two of the 12 tunnel drives and last saw the light of day on 8th March. All Channel Tunnel underland drives are now complete.

DECEMBER

01. BREAKTHROUGH. At 11.13, British and French workers shake hands under the English Channel. Using a bewildering technology of lasers, computers and satellites, the British meet the French only 60 mm out of alignment vertically, and 100 mm laterally. 'Percement 1990', as the French call it, is achieved by Graham Fagg and Philippe Cozette. The Financial Times comes up with the headline: 'Continent of Europe no longer isolated'.

01. SAFETY. The Railway Inspectorate is transferred from the Department of Transport to the Health and Safety Executive.

02. RAID. A BR clerk is bound and gagged at gunpoint in a booking office raid which nets £1000. The incident is at Mottingham station, Bromley, south London.

03. EUROTUNNEL SHARE OFFER. Despite difficult trading conditions, the share offer closes and is deemed a success.

03. FRANCE. A Marseille–Lyon freight train carrying lead-free petrol becomes derailed near Vienne in the Rhone Valley. Nine of the 22 wagons catch fire.

03. NEW NAME. BR's Provincial sector becomes Regional Railways.

04. REWARD. Fast work on digging the Channel Tunnel has earned the TML consortium a £7 million bonus it is disclosed. Six new project tunnelling records were set the week before.

05. DELAY. Malcolm Rifkind, transport secretary, states in a Commons written answer that BR will not be able to run through passenger trains from the North to the Continent until at least 1994. He blames the delay on problems with the

design and supply of the seven 'regional' high speed trains.

06. SUGGESTIONS. British Rail makes its Staff Suggestions Scheme awards. The scheme was re launched in 1988 and the current staff participation rate of 5.2% continues to rise. The annual savings to BR for adopted suggestions is running at £5.6 million.

07. CLOSURE. BREL announces that Derby Locomotives Works will close in 1992.

07. RAILFREIGHT. BR announces that Normanton, West Yorkshire, will be the first site for its regional Channel Tunnel freight terminals. The £22 million depot will be a joint venture between BR and Amec, an engineering redevelopment company.

08. WEATHER. The rail network is thrown into chaos following heavy snow.

10. NETWORK SOUTHEAST. The unveiling of a commemorative plaque marks the completio of the £500,000 refurbishment of Bicester North station.

11. LIGHT RAIL. Roger Freeman announces government funding for Sheffield's 'supertram' network. Three lines will radiate from the city centre to Meadowhall, Mosborough and Middlewood, and the total cost will be in the region of £230 million.

11. NETWORK SOUTHEAST. The refurbishment of Horsham station's booking hall, at a cost of £320,000, is officially marked.

11. WATERLOO. Roger Freeman officially inaugurates work on the £100 million London terminal for Channel Tunnel trains. Up to 1200 people will work at the construction site from today.

12. REPORT. The National Economic Development Council argues that London Heathrow needs to be integrated into both the UK and European rail networks. Apart from the Heathrow-Paddington rail link, awaiting parliamentary approval, there needs to be a westward extension to the main line nearer Reading. A southern extension to BR's Staines–Feltham line and direct passenger and freight services from Heathrow to continental Europe are also urged.

17. REPORT. The Railway Inspectorate's report into the Purley Accident on 4 March 1989 is published. Recommendations include development and installation without delay of a suitable ATP system for BR.

20. COURT ACTION. Commuters on the 07.05 Norwich–London Liverpool Street obtain a High Court writ requiring BR to provide a better service.

20. ELECTRIFICATION. Approval for the £10 million third-rail electrification of train services from Hooton to Chester and Ellesmere Port is announced by Roger Freeman.

20. NETWORK SOUTHEAST. The rearmost vehicle of the 05.56 Clacton–London Liverpool Street, formed by Class 312/7 EMU No. 312 714, becomes derailed.

21. INDUSTRIAL RELATIONS. BR conceded to RMT union that Longsight and Stafford OHL depots will stay open after all. Bradford depot would be closed.

28. NEW YORK. One passenger dies and 145 are injured when an electrical fire spreads smoke through one of the subway tunnels below the East River between Manhattan and Brooklyn. The accident, it is alleged, was caused by inadequate maintenance and symbolic of the city's crumbling infrastructure.

31. CABINET PAPERS. Documents released to the press today under the '30-year rule' show that ministers in the Macmillan government felt that the promotors of the Channel Tunnel project at the time were seeking 'financial support from the government ... quite inappropriate to a private venture'.

31. QUEEN'S NEW YEAR'S HONOURS. Alastair Morton, co-chairman of Eurotunnel receives a knighthood and becomes a 'Sir'. His French counterpart, M. André Bénard receives an honorary knighthood (KBE).